MY FRIENDS CALL ME BOB

EXTENDED FAMILY EDITION OF UNBELIEVABLE BUT TRUE

ROBERT WYNGAERT

CONTENTS

Foreword — ix
The Early Years — xi

1. 1938-1950 — 1
2. 1950-1953 — 13
3. 1953-1956 — 18
4. 1956-1957 — 25
5. 1958 — 34
6. 1958-1961 — 40
7. 1961-1965 — 46
8. 1965-1969 — 57

Bar-B-Delight — 75

9. 1970s — 76
10. 1970s — 91
11. 1970s — 94
12. 1970s — 98
13. 1974 — 103
14. 1975 — 106

Camping Alouette Inc. — 115

15. 1976 — 116
16. 1977 — 120
17. 1978 — 124
18. 1979 — 127
19. 1980 — 134

20. 1981	138
21. 1982	143
22. 1983	147
23. 1984	152
24. 1985	159
25. 1986	164
26. 1987	174
27. 1988	183
28. 1989	189
29. 1990	198
30. 1991	205
31. 1992	213
32. 1993	217
Full-Time Campground Owner	229
33. 1994	230
34. 1995	237
35. 1996	252
36. 1997	268
37. 1998	275
38. 1999	280
39. 2000	289
40. 2001 and 2002	295
41. 2003	306
42. 2004	313
43. 2005	325
44. 2006	335
45. 2007	343
Retirement	359
46. 2008	360

47. 2009	382
48. 2010	390
49. 2011	399
50. 2012	415
51. 2013	426
52. 2014	435
53. 2015	447
54. 2016	457
55. 2017	467
56. 2018	476
57. 2019	487
58. 2020	503
59. 2021	517
Epilogue	522
Wyngaert Wealth Essentials	523
Amanda Lynn Petrin	525
Johanne Wyngaert	527
Acknowledgments	529
About the Author	531

To Barbara; my soulmate and the love of my life.
To my children: Linda, Danny, and Sandra.
To my Grandchildren: Chelsea, Amanda, Rikki, Steve, Paul, and Eric.
To my Great-Grandchildren: Harry and Nathan.

JP, Sandra, Paul, Amanda, me, Chelsea, Steve, Rikki, Barbara, Rudy, Linda, and Danny.

FOREWORD

I decided to write my autobiography on March 11th, 2013, with the assumption that at seventy-five years old, my biggest adventures were behind me. However, even as I wrote about all the lessons I learned during my many years on earth, I kept experiencing new miracles and discoveries.

When I thought I was done writing and started editing my story, the world was devastated by the coronavirus pandemic, and I was caught in a backyard explosion. I'll share more on that later, but it just goes to show that your life story doesn't end until your time comes. And even then, the hope is that you've touched enough people, and left enough of a legacy that your story continues years after you're gone.

I wrote this autobiography to share the principles

FOREWORD

and values that guided my life. I am eighty-three years old, and not only do they still stand, but I am constantly reminded how important they are.

I was never an expert or a professional in all of my life's creations and accomplishments, but I always did the best I could with what I had and where I was. Challenging myself to do things that others wouldn't, or said I couldn't.

With little or no official education, I always had to rely on others to guide and inspire me. Now, I hope my legacy will inspire others to fulfill their dreams and wishes.

We all have a purpose in life, to make the world a better place, and we only have one lifetime to do it in.

My name is Robert Wyngaert, and this is my story.

THE EARLY YEARS

ONE
1938-1950

"A journey of a thousand miles begins with a single step."
-Chinese Proverb

My parents, Joseph Wyngaert and Suzanne Van Uytfanck, were both born in Belgium, but moved to Canada when they were children, as refugees from World War One. Both of their families arrived with nothing but their suitcases, and were given small farmhouses by the government, which were more like sheds, in Montreal, Quebec. They were very grateful to be accepted in Canada.

ROBERT WYNGAERT

Joseph Wyngaert and Suzanne Van Uytfanck on their wedding day.

It was in one such farmhouse on Notre-Dame Street that I was born on March 30th, 1938, across from a large industrial factory that manufactured military equipment. I had three older siblings; Irene (born in 1929), Roger (1932), and Georges (1935).

My mother wanted another girl, and I had a head full of thick, curly hair, so she would put me in dresses. Luckily, this didn't last very long, as Palmyre, the baby of the family, was born in 1942. My mother gave birth to all five of her children in that tiny house, never seeing the inside of a hospital. I had trouble pronouncing Palmyre's name at the time, but my father would sometimes call her 'fille', the French word for 'girl'. I misunderstood him and called her 'Fay', but the name stuck. To this day, that is what everyone except the government calls her.

Palmyre (Fay), Georges, Roger, and me.

My mother's mother lived in the house with us, while my father's parents lived in a farmhouse similar to ours, across the street. One night when I was very little, my grandparents' house caught fire. My grandmother managed to make it out, but my grandfather died trying to climb out of the window. I still have an old picture of the two of them together, but I don't really remember him.

MY FRIENDS CALL ME BOB

My Grandparents.

One thing I do remember from those years, is my parents' vegetable farm. They would go to the Bonsecours market every week with a horse and wagon to sell their produce. We were allowed to eat whatever the customers didn't want, so nothing went to waste. This might be where I got my reputation for eating whatever everyone else wouldn't. I do not like throwing food away. I think I get this from my mother, who never made herself her own plate at meals – she just ate what was left on everyone else's plate after they finished.

You see, back then, we had no money. We didn't have indoor plumbing, except a hand pump for water. I would go with my grandmother and a little four-wheel wagon to pick up the coal that fell from box cars along the railway track, so we could use them for heating. Still, there were many days where we went without, so any liquids left out on the counter in the winter would be frozen solid by morning.

ON ONE OF those really cold winter days, my brothers and I were playing by a large creek behind our house when we spotted a wooden board on the ice in the middle of it. Roger didn't think the ice was thick enough for us to get to it, but Georges was confident he could make it, and set off to do just that. He was almost at the board when the ice cracked beneath him, and he fell through.

I froze, looking on in horror as Roger sprang into action, quickly and carefully making his way to the hole Georges had disappeared into. I loved both of my brothers, but Roger was six years older and had his own friends, while Georges, who was only three years older, was my best friend. We did everything together.

Roger brought the wooden board over to the edge of the opening, so he could distribute his weight across it more evenly and put his arms into the freezing water to fish our brother out. Later, Georges would tell me he could see the branches under the ice, but couldn't hold onto any of them. Luckily, Roger was able to grab Georges' hat. It was the kind you tied around your neck, so Roger pulled on the hat, and Georges came with it. We rushed him inside and warmed him up, but I will never forget how terrified I was at the thought of losing Georges, or how much I looked up to Roger for saving his life.

OUR LITTLE FARMHOUSE was getting to be very cramped with my parents, five children, and both of my grandmothers, so we moved to Mackayville – now known as Longueuil – on the South Shore of Montreal. There was a little barn and a garage in the back of the house, so we converted the garage into a tiny apartment for one of my grandmothers to live in.

My parents enrolled me in the local public school, St-Jean-Eudes, which was run by nuns. It consisted of approximately twelve classrooms; eight for French students and four for English students. Although we spoke French at home, with the occasional Flemish swear words, my parents put me in the English classroom, so I would have better employment opportunities later on.

It was a smart decision in the long run, but at the time, it made my life very difficult. I did not speak English, I was a foreigner, and I was small and weak; the perfect target for bullies. I would take a longer road home from school to avoid the French kids who wanted to beat me up. My brothers both had their own classrooms, and were therefore unable to protect me. It was a very scary part of my childhood, that might be responsible for my later interest in martial arts, to ensure no one could ever make me feel that way again.

Me and Georges fishing.

At least once a year, my father would take us boys fishing in the Laurentians. He insisted that we leave the fishing cabin at five in the morning, so we could get to his 'secret' fishing spots without being followed. I would have said he was being paranoid, but we always came home with more fish than any of the other fishermen. We would often take friends with us—such as Ronnie, Bobby, and my father-in-law later on – and meet up with cousins when we got there.

I hated waking up that early, so one year I tried to sleep in by pretending I couldn't hear my dad. I thought I was clever, but my dad sent my cousin Pierre – who was six-foot-two and two-hundred pounds – to sit on me until I got up. I never made that mistake again.

Most years I brought my friend, Albert Ferris, who always hung around with Georges and I, like the three musketeers. He didn't really like waking up early either, and he didn't have a cousin to force him, so one year we ended up leaving without him. He had to wait around the fishing cabin all day for us to get back, which was in the late afternoon.

My dad had bought a nice ham for our supper, but once we got back to the cabin, my dad went straight to the ice box and discovered that the entire ham – that he thought would feed the family – was gone. The only thing left was the bone. Albert, who we called Berdie, had eaten it all while he waited for us. For years, Berdie would randomly bring up, "Remember that ham?", but no one else found it funny.

Dave, Georges, me, and Berdie.

After about three years at St-Jean-Eudes, the school board transferred the English students to an old abandoned house on Holmes street, to make more room for French students. This suited me fine, as the new school was much closer to our house. I was fluent in English by then, and I knew how to look after myself. I was still small, but I was wiry and fearless, which quickly garnered me a reputation as someone you did not want to mess with. As you can imagine, this got me into a lot of trouble.

In the middle of my fifth year of elementary school, at twelve years old, I was expelled for fighting – although I would call it defending myself. My parents told me I had two choices: I could find another school, or I could go to work.

I chose the latter.

TWO
1950-1953

"I am not a product of my circumstances. I am a product of my decisions."
-Stephen Covey

My first paying job was delivering 'Le Courrier du Sud', the local newspaper, and other advertising materials. My route began on Grande Allée Street, not far from our house, but it covered the main towns of the South Shore: Ville Jacques Cartier, St-Lambert, Mackayville, and Greenfield Park. Thankfully, it was only three days a week.

    My father felt this meant my remaining four days could be spent working for him. He had recently decided it was time to upgrade the family to a more modern house, so he bought land on Grande Allée to build a duplex. This kept me very busy.

Before my father would leave to work as a foreman of maintenance at Canada Packers, he would give me a list of things to do, expecting them to all be done by the time he got home. I had no idea how to frame a wall or install Gyproc, but boy did I learn fast! If something wasn't done properly, or to his satisfaction, I would have to take it down and do it all over again the next day. I hated it at the time, but I learnt some valuable skills that I still use, seventy years later. I have taken on countless major renovations and construction projects throughout my life, seeing them through from conception to completion, stemming from those days with my father.

ABOUT A MONTH after my family moved into the duplex I helped build, our old house caught fire due to faulty electrical wiring. We all rushed over and tried to put it out, but the house was made of wood, and we hardly had any water, so all we could do was watch it burn. Thank God no one was inside!

A demolition at my father's work gave him access to some free lumber, so we rebuilt the old house after the fire. Though I was available to him, and knew a lot more about construction this time around, it was still no easy task. Between my job and the construction, I would spend my days off digging holes four feet deep for concrete pillars to support the house, then wake up at 6 a.m. the next day to deliver newspapers. I was spread very thin.

My favorite part was the time I spent with my father's mother, who I fondly called Mémère. Since we were only using secondhand wood for the house, she taught me how to salvage the large wooden planks that were caked with dirt, as well as the long nails inside them. I had to clean each board and pull out all of the nails, then straighten them and segregate by size. It was physically exhausting, but my Mémère was a strong old lady who made it look easy.

IN APRIL 1952, after building two houses and delivering countless newspapers in extreme weather conditions, I was ready for something less physically challenging. Georges was working for a customs broker on St. James Street in Montreal, so I asked him if he had any ideas. It just so happened that there was an opening as an Office Clerk for another custom broker on McGill Street. I was fourteen and had just gotten a permit to work, so I went to Daniel Kiely Inc., and met with the owner, Mr. Jack Boyne. I could barely see over the counter where Mr. Boyne, a powerful and physically imposing man, stood.

I wasn't qualified for office work, with my education lacking and all of my experience stemming from construction projects. However, they must have been pretty desperate, because I was hired on the spot.

They offered me 18$ a week, which was less than I was making delivering newspapers, but in a much better environment, with great potential for advancement. I accepted without hesitation.

Since we lived on the South Shore and my new job was in Montreal, I travelled back and forth on the Montreal Southern County Railroad. It was about an hour commute, that I usually spent catching up with friends. In the winter, they would have a pot-bellied coal burner stove in the carriages to keep us warm.

Everything about my new job was difficult for me. As a Custom Long Room Man, my responsibilities were delivering and picking up documents from various customers (like a human fax machine), typing up and then mailing documents, as well as processing parcels and packages through customs. I had never considered school to be that important, until I found myself having to read, write and type day in and day out at the office. At the time, there were ads everywhere to get your high school equivalency through correspondence, so I signed up with the American School and completed their courses over the next three years.

I would always try to time my document deliveries so that I was on the road around lunchtime. I didn't always have enough money to make myself a lunch, or to buy one, so I relied on family members. If I was near Woolworths, I could count on my sister Irene, or Denise Laurendeau, the lovely young lady

Irene had set Georges up with, to buy me lunch and a slice of apple pie whenever I stopped in. If I was around Bleury Street, my godmother Yvonne would make sure I was well-fed. She was soft and gentle, like my mother, and always made me feel at home.

MY FAMILY WAS LIVING COMFORTABLY in the second house my father and I built, renting out the duplex, so on my days off, I was able to relax and hang out with my brother, Roger, who had a horse, a goat and a few other animals. He didn't always have money to feed these animals, so he would bring Georges and I to pick up hay along Taschereau Boulevard. It wasn't really hay, but the city maintenance crews would cut all the tall grass and leave it on the side of the road. Once we had a full load, Georges and I would sit on the pile of hay to hold it down, picking apples from the trees as Roger drove us home. Little did we know, those apples were on private property, and one day, the owner sent the police after us. Luckily, the cop was a friend of my dad's, so he let me off with a warning, but I never went near that tree again.

THREE
1953-1956

"If you love someone, set them free. If they come back, they're yours; if they don't they never were."
-Richard Bach

Now that I was fifteen years old, with a steady job, I was able to catch the attention of some of the girls my age. There were two best friends, Patricia Weldrick and Mary Melinski, who were both interested in me. I didn't mean to hurt Mary's feelings, but when Patsy asked me out, I had no choice but to say yes. I think Mary was upset with me at the time, but she got the last laugh, as Patsy and I broke up within a year. We lost touch, but I ran into Mary over the years, especially once our daughters became best friends. But I'm getting ahead of myself.

I started playing football for the Chambly County Flyers, a new team conceived by our coach, Rudy Presner. We would have games against the St. Lambert Combines, the Rosemont Bombers, and the St-Hubert Air Force Base, but we very rarely won. The other teams were better, more experienced, and better equipped than our old helmets, shoulder pads and cleats. It would have been nice to win sometimes, but it was still a lot of fun, and we had some very pretty cheerleaders.

IN 1953, Jack Boyne held a year-end celebration at the Ritz Carlton Hotel, and all of the employees were invited. I was single at the time, so I thought I might ask one of our cheerleaders. Instead, my immediate supervisor, Melvin Hedge, offered to set me up on a blind date with a terrific young girl he thought I would really like. Her name was Barbara Thompson, and she was his younger cousin – fifteen years old, just like me.

I can't remember what dress she wore, but I remember it was very nice, and with her hair all done up she looked like a million bucks. She was some beauty – she still is – and I couldn't believe my luck. My fondest memory of the evening was during the meal, when Barbara was trying to cut her steak. At one point, her knife slid, and she sent peas flying right into my boss' lap at this very fancy dinner. It was embarrassing at the time, and I was foolishly worried I would lose my job over it. We managed to have an excellent time anyway, and laugh about the incident to this day.

Barbara, Bobby, and Joan.

From there, Barbara and I hit it off very quickly. She worked at Northern Electric and lived in Rosemount with her parents, two brothers, and five sisters, ranging from four to eighteen years old. Her father, Robert Thompson, worked at Northern Electric, while her mother, Ina, was a stay-at-home mom who loved to write jingles for Hallmark. Joan was the oldest, and closest in age to Barb. They were best friends, like Georges and I. After Barb there was Doreen, then Carol, Bobby, and Ronnie. Finally, there was Marilyne and Donna, the babies of the family.

I still lived on the South Shore, so I had to ride the train and a couple of buses to get to her house. I loved to take her to Habib's for supper on Saturdays, walks on Mount Royal, or town hall dances with her sister, Joan, and her boyfriend, Bob Smith. As Barbara already had a brother named Bobby, and Joan's boyfriend was Bob, Barbara's little sisters called me 'Wyng-hart'. Considering they had trouble with 'Barbara' and called her 'Wawa', I thought it would have been easier for them to start calling the other Bob 'Smith', but I also found it cute that they gave me a nickname.

AFTER FALLING asleep and missing my stop on the train more than a few times, I helped Roger buy a car, so that he could drive me to Barbara's. At the time, he had a license but no car, while I had money and no license. It seemed like the perfect arrangement.

There was a jeweler, Harry Stein, who worked in the office right next to mine, so for Barbara's sixteenth birthday, I got her a compact for her makeup. It became a tradition over the years, for me to go to him whenever I needed to get her a present.

MY FAMILY WAS CATHOLIC. Not that we went to church every Sunday, but we did honor the rule that you can't eat meat on Fridays. One week, wanting to impress her, I brought Barbara to a fancy restaurant. It was a Friday night, so I scoured the menu for something without meat and settled on 'filet mignon'. I wasn't sure what kind of fish it was, but it sounded delicious. Imagine my surprise when the waiter showed up with a fancy, expensive...steak. I couldn't send it back, and I didn't want to let Barb know how silly I had been, so I ate what would later become her favorite cut of meat, feeling guilty the whole time. Thankfully it wasn't a mortal sin!

WHILE BARB WOULD GET ready for our dates, I would sit on the balcony and talk to her father, also a Robert. Our conversations were always interesting, and would often run long, so even after Barbara was ready for me, I would stay there talking to him. Barbara did not appreciate me spending so much of our precious time together talking to her father instead of paying attention to her. Eventually, the combination of those talks, the long distance between our houses, and my determination to play football instead of going dancing with her, became too much, and she ended things with me. She started going out with a man named Axel Swenley, who took her to shows and did the things she wanted me to do.

I was devastated, but I tried my best to move on. I started dating Mary Meany, a cheerleader who didn't mind spending her time watching my football games. I brought her as my date to our Fundraising Dance at the Royal George School, in Greenfield Park. At the end of the meal, when they announced the winner of the Most Valuable Player of the Year Award, I was shocked to hear my name. I truly appreciated the honor, but I didn't feel like I deserved it as much as most of the other players. When I asked, 'Why me?', they told me it was because they could always rely on me; their offensive and defensive guard. "You block them all, no matter the odds."

A FEW MONTHS LATER, I got a call from Joan, to see if I would be interested in going on a date with Barbara. Apparently, Axel wasn't the guy for her, and I was more than happy to take his place. I had to break up with Mary first, but it worked out well, since she ended up marrying my friend, Pat House.

. . .

WHEN I TURNED EIGHTEEN, our football team went bar hopping in Montreal. I wasn't used to drinking – only at a few social events – so the alcohol hit me a little hard. After a few bars, we came across a tattoo parlor. Most of the guys were too scared, or maybe weren't drunk enough yet, but Rudy got a tattoo on his arm. He chose 'Betty', the name of the girl he was in love with.

He suggested I get one as well, for Barbara. I don't know if it was because I was so happy I got her back, or because of the many beers I drank that night, but I eventually gave in and got a heart with 'Barbara' in it on my right forearm.

This was a terrible decision, as I got an infection from the unsanitary equipment at the parlor. My arm swelled up to double its size, and I needed to take antibiotics to get rid of it.

Things didn't work out so well for Rudy either, as Betty ditched him shortly after we got the tattoos. It turned out that choosing Barbara's name was the only part of the tattoo I didn't regret. As my career advanced, I had to wear long-sleeved shirts to hide it, even in the summer. Not to mention that when you get older, tattoos becomes faded and illegible. Overall, I do not recommend them.

FOUR
1956-1957

"Life is a near-death experience."
-George Carlin

In the spring of 1956, Barbara and I were faced with a dilemma. My brother, Georges, was marrying Denise Laurendeau on May 12th. That same day, Barbara's sister, Joan, was marrying Bob Smith. I wasn't going to miss my brother's wedding, and Barb was her sister's maid of honor, so we were in quite the pickle. I was starting to question whether Barb would forgive me if we each went to separate weddings, but religion saved the day. As my family was Catholic, Georges' wedding was in the morning, at 10 a.m., while Joan, who was Protestant, was getting married in the afternoon. As long as nothing unexpected happened, we should be able to make it to both.

It was a very stressful morning for me, but everything ran on time and we made it to both weddings. I considered the day a success, but something shifted in the way people treated Barbara and I. Now that we were both eighteen and going to weddings together, people started asking us when our wedding would be. When Lilianne, who lived in Barb's building, saw us coming home one day, she asked, "So, when's the wedding?"

My plan was to smile and ignore the question, but Barb said, "Ask him."

I knew I wanted to spend the rest of my life with her, but now I could see I had to do something about it. I went to see Mr. Stein, and the next time someone asked about the wedding, I went along with it. It was only years later that I found out how much it annoyed Barb to hear me talking like our engagement was a given, before I'd even asked her.

ON JUNE 20TH, I woke up feeling funny, but I still made my way to work, figuring it was just something I ate, and that it would pass. As the day went on, the pain in my stomach got worse, and I'm pretty sure I spiked a fever. I tried to soldier on, but when the pain got so bad that I threw up, I requested permission to leave work early. Seeing the state of me, my supervisor said yes without hesitation.

I set off for Canada Packers, hoping my dad

could drive me home. As I was walking there, the pain got so intense that I knew there was no way I would make it. I used the first phone booth I saw to tell my father I was very sick and needed him to pick me up on Mill Street. By the time he got there, I had collapsed on the sidewalk from the pain.

I was vaguely aware of him carrying me to his car so he could drive us to the hospital. Unfortunately, it was voting day, so the roads were jammed, and we got stuck in heavy traffic. My dad took one look at me and knew I needed medical attention as soon as possible, so he used the sidewalk to pass cars and get me to the closest hospital he could find, which happened to be a maternity one on Sherbrooke Street. My dad left his car in the middle of the sidewalk and carried me in.

It didn't take long for them to diagnose me with Peritonitis, which meant my appendix had burst, slowly spreading bacteria throughout my body. I needed immediate surgery to remove my appendix, and a course of very strong antibiotics to hopefully kill the bacteria. Ideally, you want to get to the hospital before the appendix bursts, because once it does, your chances of survival diminish significantly. My father's fast thinking – and disregard for the rules of the road – and the doctors saved my life that day. It was the first time I almost died, but it would not be the last.

. . .

I DON'T REMEMBER how long I was in the hospital, or much of my recovery, but it was a long time. Every day, without fail, Barbara would come and visit me with homemade lemonade. I don't know what I did to deserve someone like her, but I am so grateful for it.

Barbara and I.

In September, Barbara convinced me to talk to her father about getting a job at Northern Electric, where he was a supervisor. By then, I was making more than double what I started out with at Daniel Kiely, with $42 a week, but Barb was making $80 as an engraver, with a monthly piecework bonus.

I had taken an evening course at the Automobile School of Montreal, thinking I might try being a mechanic, but although I did well in the course – passing with 88% – I did not enjoy the work. Luckily, it wasn't wasted, because it gave me the freedom to take care of my own cars, without having to rely on garages and mechanics.

Her dad spoke to Mr. Brooks in the personnel department, and to my surprise, I was hired to work on relays. I received 1.27$ an hour, plus a monthly piecework bonus. Everything was perfect, with Barb and I both making good money. I bought my first car, a 1952 Monarch, for 700$.

My first car.

That Christmas, Barb came to my parents' house to open presents. She liked staying over because we now had hot running water, and I liked having her close, even if we had to stay in separate bedrooms. That night, I asked Barbara to marry me. I had already asked her parents, who were thrilled. I used the ring I bought from Mr. Stein, and although I knew we were meant to be together, my heart still burst with joy when she said yes.

IN THE SUMMER OF 1957, we spent two weeks of our vacation time at Barbara's Aunt's cottage in Lac des Plages, just North of Montreal. On our way there, the weather was far from ideal for an inexperienced driver like me. There was a torrential downpour, where I could hardly see anything in front of me. I drove slow, just to be on the safe side, but even that wasn't enough to save us from sliding off the gravel road when we got to a very steep curve. I managed to maneuver the car so it hit a large tree from the back side, instead of head on. Barb and I were both okay, but my new car was scrapped. We took our bags and walked to a nearby hotel so we could call someone to pick us up.

While we were walking to the hotel, Barb's family got worried about us not being there yet, so her father came looking for us. I never imagined that he would slip on the exact same part of road I did, at a much faster speed, so his car ploughed right into mine. At the speed he was going, if my car hadn't been there to cushion his impact into the tree, I am sure he would have died, or at least been seriously injured. As it was, he met up with us at the hotel, and we took a taxi to the cottage together.

· · ·

LATER ON IN THE TRIP, I asked Barb to go out on a rowboat with me. She agreed, but warned that I was not allowed to 'rock the boat', as she could not swim. When her brother, Bobby was little, he'd almost drowned, so all of her siblings were afraid of the water, and none of them learned how to swim.

Having grown up with the creek behind our first house, and going on many fishing trips with my dad, I thought she was being silly. Still, I told her I would be good.

Once we were in the middle of the lake, I wanted to show off a bit for my fiancée, so I was careful to keep the boat as balanced as possible before I stood up and dove in. I could hear Barbara scream as my head hit the water. I hurried up to the surface so I could smile and reassure her I was okay – maybe do a few breaststrokes – but she was furious. I tried to swim over so I could get back in the boat, but she grabbed on to the oars and started rowing back to shore. I couldn't believe she was that terrified of the water that she was going to leave me in the middle of the lake, so far from the shore. Or that she could row that quickly!

I apologized and asked if she would please let me back on the boat. She categorically refused, terrified the boat would tip if I tried to climb back in. I couldn't promise that wouldn't happen, so I swam beside the boat for as long as I could.

"Please Barb, can I just hang on to the back of the

boat? I'm exhausted," I begged between shallow breaths.

"No," she said, and I could tell she meant business.

"Barb, I will drown if you don't let me hold on," I warned.

She looked at me, the fear ever-present in her eyes, weighing the likelihood of the boat tipping from me hanging on to the back of it. "Fine," she agreed, but she was not happy.

I was so relieved once we got back on dry land, but I learnt a very valuable lesson that day. In the future, **always listen to Barb.**

FIVE
1958

"You shouldn't marry the person you can see yourself having a good life with. You should marry the person you know you wouldn't have a life without."
-Unknown

I don't remember much from the months leading up to our wedding, on June 7th, 1958. I assume there was some kind of planning, maybe a bridal shower, but I don't think I had a bachelor party. Georges was going to be my best man, with Joan as Barb's maid of honor, and my tux was rented. All I had to do was wait until the day and say, 'I do'.

MY FRIENDS CALL ME BOB

Barbara and I on our wedding day.

That was my plan, but my stress-free world was turned upside down when I was laid off from

Northern Electric the day before my wedding. It came completely out of the blue, and all I could do was hope that it wouldn't be long until they called me back. And try not to ruin the wedding over it.

Since I'm Catholic and Barb was raised Protestant, we weren't allowed to get married inside the church, so the ceremony took place behind it. Barb even had to take courses and promise the priest that we would raise our children Catholic when the time came.

When I saw her walking towards me in that dress, I completely forgot about my unexpected layoff and our unconventional ceremony. It was the happiest moment of my life.

AFTER THE CEREMONY, we had a selection of chicken salads and cold cuts for our seventy-five guests. We had a few friends and work colleagues, as well as both of our families. Roger came with his wife, Kay, Georges was at the head table with Denise, Irene came with her husband Rolland, and Fay brought Bruce, a friend of mine from football. While I was the second youngest in my family, Barb was the second oldest in hers, so Joan was the only one of her siblings who came with her husband, Bob Smith.

MY FRIENDS CALL ME BOB

Near the end of the meal, the catering team came up to me, asking how we were going to pay. I was shocked, having been under the impression that the bride's family pays for the wedding. I found out that rather than paying for the food, Barb's father bought us a really nice fridge for our new place. It was very generous of him, but I had not come prepared to pay any caterers. I gave them what I had, then went around asking my brothers if any of them could lend me some money. It was something ridiculous like 100$ to feed 75 people, but in that time, it was a lot, and I did not have it on me.

Luckily, Berdie – the one who ate my dad's ham – was able to lend me the money, assuring me I could pay him back after the honeymoon. While Georges was the brother who was like a best friend to me, Berdie was the friend who was like a brother to both Georges and I. He saved the day.

WE LEFT for our Honeymoon in a red, 1954 Pontiac Sedan I got for 800$ with the insurance money from our crash. We went to Atlantic City, but stopped on the way in Lake George, and splurged on a meal at Roberto's. It was so fancy that they had men there to open the doors for us when we walked up. Barb was impressed that they had delicious shrimp the size of her hand, while I was amazed that this beautiful woman was now my wife.

In Atlantic City, we stayed at a Bed and Breakfast, and bought a little stove so we could cook our own meals and not have to spend too much money in restaurants. We spent our days walking along the Boardwalk, too broke to actually do anything that cost money.

The entire trip was 125$, which was all the money I had for it. Luckily gas was only 25 cents a gallon at the time, because I don't think I would have had enough to get us home otherwise.

Me and Barbara on our honeymoon in Atlantic City.

Once we were back in Quebec, Barb and I settled into the bottom floor of my parents' duplex, with Georges and Denise as our upstairs neighbors. We couldn't afford to have our own phone line, so we shared theirs. Whenever there was a call for us, they would bang on the pipes to let us know. Money was tight, but family was never far away, especially with our backyard being linked to my parents'. One thing is for sure, Georges, Denise, Barbara and I became very close!

SIX
1958-1961

"Failure will never overtake me if my determination to succeed is strong enough."
-Og Mandino

That summer, the city was putting in water and sewer lines, so I was able to keep busy by helping my neighbors get hooked up. Backhoes were hard to find in those days, and expensive, but with all of my experience digging for my father's buildings, I was able to perform this very physical work. Those skills also allowed me to help my neighbor build his garage. It was nowhere near what I was making at Northern Electric, but every bit helped.

This was around the time I joined the YMCA's judo club with my good friend Kevin Jones, where I became the secretary-treasurer. It was nice to have a more recreational way to keep in shape, and Harold Tokai, our instructor, taught me so much about strength, the responsibilities of power, and discipline.

FINALLY, in August, my father helped me get a job at Canada Packers, doing freezer work. I had to bring large boxes of pork trimmings in and out of freezers, then place the frozen product into a large machine that would mince it so it could be turned into bologna and sausages.

I stayed there until March of 1959, when they laid me off due to lack of work, just as Northern Electric recalled me to be a Mechanical and Electrical Relay Technician. I was very grateful to Canada Packers for getting me out of a tough spot, but it was also nice to not have to lug around frozen meat anymore.

A FEW MONTHS LATER, I woke up in the middle of the night to something that sounded like an explosion. Growing up during the war, I had become used to the blackouts, so I figured all of the preparation had been for this, and we were being attacked. I assumed the steam came from a bomb, so I woke the entire building and brought them outside to safety. It was then, once my brain got over the immediate fear, that I realized it was just a defective thermostat that burst the pipes and blew up our hot water tank. Boy did I feel silly!

We took it as a sign to do some renovations. Barb and I were both making good money at the Northern again, so we could afford it. We also made some new purchases, like a television, a sofa, curtains, drapes, etc. I had just been laid off when we moved in, but we were now able to make our little house a home.

Denise and Georges.

I also splurged on a 1960 Pontiac Parisienne. It

was 4700$, the most expensive car I had purchased by far – in cash no less – but it was brand-new. I had quickly developed a taste for good-looking, expensive, luxury cars, an affliction that still plagues me to this day.

I would drive Barb and I home after work, where my mother would have a wonderful, hot meal waiting for us. My mother was the nicest, sweetest woman you could meet, who always went out of her way to do nice things for other people. Barb is very much like that as well, so on the days she wasn't working, she would go over to my mother's and help her with cleaning and other chores.

Once the work was done, weekends were filled with activities, such as visiting friends and family. It seemed like we were always with Georges and Denise, since they lived so close, but my best friends at the time were Pat House, who you may remember married my ex-girlfriend Mary, and Kevin Jones, who married her sister, Alice. Kevin and I were very involved in our judo training, even competing against other Judo schools, where I would sometimes face Bob Smith. It was a time where we were young, happy, and carefree.

I was perhaps a little too carefree and cocky, so my friends encouraged me to join the Knights of Columbus, a Catholic Fraternal Organization. The night I was sworn in was quite an experience that I will never forget. I would tell you all about it, but then I would have to kill you. Well, not really, but I did swear to not tell anyone what happened. What I can say is that through a series of exercises, they showed me that united we are stronger, while divided we fall.

IN JANUARY OF 1961, I was asked to transfer to Northern Electric's branch in Belleville, Ontario. I enjoyed my job and could see this was a great opportunity, but Barbara's job, as well as both of our families, were in Montreal. I told them it wasn't possible for me to move to Ontario, but they weren't able to keep me on in my current position, so they laid me off. Again.

Luckily, I had learnt my lesson the first time Northern Electric let me go. In April 1960, when my father told me Canada Packers was looking for part-time workers to do maintenance on weekends, I immediately jumped at the opportunity. Even with my full-time job at the Northern. Extra income never hurts, and I knew it meant I would be in a better position if I got laid off again, which just so happened to be the case.

IT TOOK four months before I was hired at United Aircraft of Canada. As luck would have it, that was the same week Northern Electric asked me to come back to work in another department. Although I liked working at the same place as Barbara, and they were offering almost double what I would make at United Aircraft, I refused their offer. The pay bump with United Aircraft was negligible, but I was excited to be able to work closer to home on the South Shore. Plus, United Aircraft had a much bigger potential for advancement, without me needing to move far away.

After my job at Daniel Kiely taught me the importance of an education, I made it a goal to always be learning, saying yes to every opportunity. I successfully completed training on basic IBM machines from the Data Processing Institute, so I was hired at United Aircraft as a foreman clerk until they got an opening in the computer department.

A foreman's clerk was the lowest paying job they had, making even less than the janitors. The computer department remained out of my reach, but thanks to my supervisor, Ken Bloxham, I was quickly promoted to a general foreman's clerk. From there, it took less than nine months for me to become assistant foreman on first shift. Before long, I was head foreman on second shift. It meant working evenings, which was inconvenient, but I was also the one in charge.

SEVEN
1961-1965

"Family is not an important thing. It's everything."
-Michael J. Fox

By the end of 1961, Barb was pregnant with our first child, as was Kevin's wife, Alice. One day, they called me at work to say Alice had gone into labor and no one could reach Kevin. Back then, we didn't have things like cell phones, so unless you knew exactly where someone was, you had no way of reaching them. I offered to go find him, but Alice asked me to bring her to the hospital instead. When I arrived, the nurses asked who I was, saying it was immediate family only beyond that point. Alice looked at me like she did not want to be alone, so I told them I was her husband. They let me stay with Alice until Kevin arrived, after Nancy's birth, much to the nurse's confusion.

Linda.

February 13th 1962 became one of the best days of my life when my beautiful daughter, Linda Susan Wyngaert, was born. Her birth changed my entire outlook on life – I suddenly had big responsibilities. I had to make sure she would always be safe and happy, with a roof over her head and food in her belly. She is the spark that lit the flame inside my heart and made me the man I am today.

When Linda was just a few months old, Barb had to go to the hospital for surgery on her gallbladder. She'd been having issues since the beginning of her pregnancy, but the doctors had to wait for Linda to be born before they could do anything about it. Back then, fathers weren't nearly as hands-on as they are now, and we couldn't afford to have me take the time off work to take care of Linda while Barb was gone. So, we brought Linda to stay with Barb's mom, Ina.

Before she went to the hospital, Barb gave her mother a list of rules and things that Linda would need, all based on 'The Common Sense Book of Baby and Child Care' by Doctor Spock. Ina, who had already raised eight children, promptly threw the list in the garbage and trusted her own instincts as soon as Barb was out the door.

MY FRIENDS CALL ME BOB

Our house on Laurier Street.

In early 1963, Fay's boyfriend, Bruce, was helping his aunt sell her three-bedroom house at 1551 Laurier Street. Barb was pregnant with our second child, so the duplex would soon be cramped, and I really wanted to own my house, rather than paying my dad rent. It was quite the fixer-upper, so I was able to buy it for only 3000$, thus becoming a homeowner. The house wasn't livable, so Barb insisted that I do some major renovations before she would even consider moving in. I managed to make the ground floor acceptable to Barbara just before our son, Daniel Robert Wyngaert, was born on April 4th.

ROBERT WYNGAERT

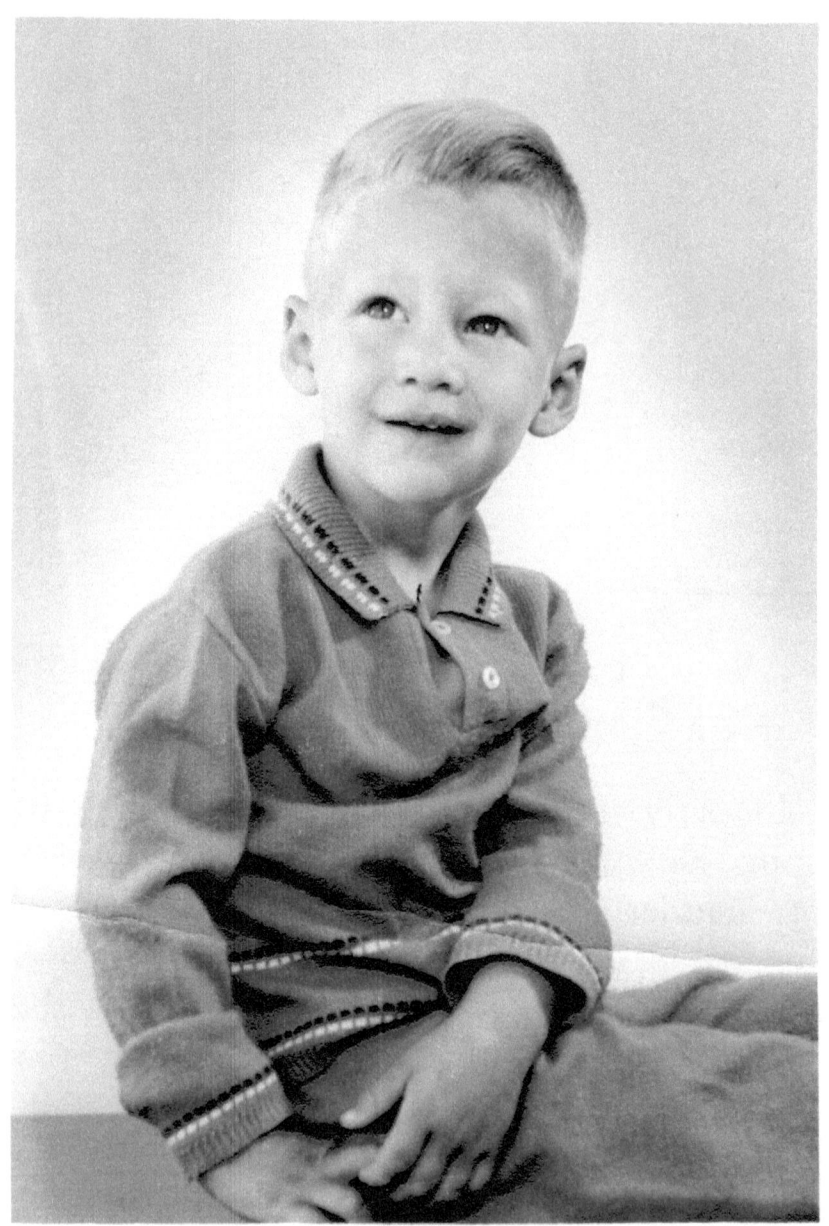

Danny

While Linda was my beautiful baby girl, Danny was the son I always wanted, who I could teach things to, and would eventually take after me. Only his name wasn't meant to be Danny.

On the day of our son's baptism, Barbara was still recovering, so she didn't come to the church with us. We had decided we would name him Steven, but once I got inside, with the priest looking down at me, I got nervous and couldn't remember the name anymore. When the priest asked me, I froze, and my mother said, "Daniel," which then became his name. Barb was definitely not happy with me.

IN 1964, Canada Packers was looking for a foreman to watch over their weekend employees. When they discovered that my day job was as a foreman at United Aircraft, they put me in charge of the twenty-two part-time, week-end employees. Our main responsibilities were to clean the plant facilities in depth, which they couldn't do while the plant was in operation. We had to steam wash all of the department floors and equipment, the receiving and shipping docks, the rendering department, the underground tunnel the animals came from, the stockyards across the street, and the smokehouses. Not to mention all the laundry and snow removal. I implemented a system to keep track of how much time each employee spent doing each task, understanding that efficiency was of the essence.

I was able to hire men that I knew to be good workers, like my friend Regis Lemieux, as well as my brother Georges. Roger tried it out for a little while, but he didn't appreciate working under his baby brother's supervision. My dad was already a supervisor, which led some people to think I got the job thanks to him. I quickly proved myself, but my mother asked me to take it easy on Georges, who had a heart condition, so I lightened his load and helped him out when I could. My family connection, as well as how I showed Georges preferential treatment, led to us being called the Brown Brothers. As in brown-nosers.

It was a big blow at first, but as everyone got to see my work ethic and realized that I deserved the position, I stopped seeing it as a taunt and began to own it. My brothers and I from then on referred to ourselves as the Brown Brothers, with pride.

The 'Brown Brothers': Georges, Roger, Fay, me, and my father.

We sometimes got special assignments, such as painting the facility. One day, we were painting the exterior metal fire escape on the tallest building – approximately fifty feet high. None of my men were willing to paint the top portion that led to the roof. I don't believe in asking people to do things I wouldn't be willing to do myself, so I said I would do it.

I am not afraid of heights, but I don't really like them either. As I approached the top, the steel supports broke loose from the roof, leaving me hanging from the ladder in midair. I tried not to panic, hoping the lower supports would hold until I shimmied down. It was clear to everyone there that if the supports gave out, no matter what my men did, I would be a dead man. The silence was deafening, so all I could hear was the rather loud pounding of my own heart, until I finally got to safety. I am not sure what would have happened if someone else had been in my place, but I guess that once more, it just wasn't my time to go.

IN ADDITION to my full-time job at United Aircraft and my part-time one at Canada Packers, I spent all of my free time renovating our house from top to bottom, interior and exterior. I added a new roof, bricks, changed the windows...I even put in a fence with cartoon character stickers to make the kids smile. Whatever I didn't know how to do, I found people to do it, or to teach me. It was a lot of work.

Sandra and I.

Barb, in addition to looking after the children, got a job working at the new Dunkin' Donuts with Denise. She stayed there until a few months before January 5th, 1965, when Sandra Ann Wyngaert completed our little family. Just as beautiful as her big sister, Sandra filled us both with joy.

Having three kids was a really big responsibility, and I had to make sure I could provide for them. In the sixties, we didn't have things like Medicare and maternity leave, so in the span of three years, we lost half of our family's income, and a huge chunk of my salary went to paying the doctors for three deliveries, and Barb's gallbladder surgery.

Linda, Danny, and Sandra.

EIGHT
1965-1969

"Believe in yourself. Have faith in your abilities. Without humble but reasonable confidence in your own powers, you cannot be successful or happy."
-Norman Vincent Peale

I was working at Canada Packers on October 9th, 1965, while the rest of my family was going to Joan's for her son's birthday party. It wasn't long into my shift that the security guard came and found me, out of breath, like he'd had to look all over for me. All he could tell me was that I had to get to the Notre-Dame Hospital as soon as possible.

I don't know how I managed to drive there, knowing someone I loved was badly injured, or worse, and I didn't even know who. When I got there, they told me that Barb's mother, Ina, had been in a car accident. Barbara's father had been on his way to pick Barb and the kids up with Ina, Bobby, and Ronnie in the car. Luckily, Barb's father and brothers were okay, except for Bobby's concussion, but Ina did not make it.

The Thompsons had a superstition about putting new shoes on tables, believing that it brought death. That morning, Glenn had received a new pair of shoes, and someone who wasn't aware of the superstition had put them on the kitchen table. I never saw it as more than a silly superstition, but from that day forward, no one dared put shoes on any table anywhere near a Thompson.

I still had both of my parents, but my mother-in-law's death devastated me, so I couldn't even imagine what it would do to Barbara. I was the one who had to go home and tell her what happened. I can't remember the words I used, or her reaction in that moment, but it was the hardest thing I've ever had to do in my entire life.

Barbara, as you can imagine, was absolutely destroyed. Everyone was. Ina's death left Mr. Thompson with a house full of young children who had just lost their mother. Joan moved in for a few months to help him out, while Barb and I offered to adopt the two youngest; Marilyne and Donna. Barb's father categorically refused to split up his family, insisting that he would take care of his own children.

THE FOLLOWING YEAR, Joan and Bob Smith were having trouble getting a mortgage for a house. I had a good job and no mortgage of my own, so I made a deal with my brother-in-law. I found a house close to ours, gave the down payment and secured a mortgage, all under my name. I even put in 500$ to renovate it for them. All Bob had to do was make the monthly payments for me, and once the house was paid off, it would be his. The small catch was that Bob would also have to stay sober. His drinking had definitely hindered their getting a mortgage on their own, and he'd had a tendency to start fights when he was drinking. He'd had a difficult life, attending Shawbridge (a Youth Detention Center) as a boy, but he had recently stopped drinking so he could be the man Joan and his children needed him to be. Instead of dwelling on the mistakes of his youth, Bob used them as a cautionary tale to inspire others to turn their own lives around. He had joined Alcoholics Anonymous to overcome his addiction, then proceeded to sponsor countless others battling their demons. Many of them were strangers who simply needed a hand, but he helped family members too. One of my nieces had a very difficult time when she was younger, and he was instrumental in her recovery. He also introduced one of his sponsees to the person that would become the love of his life for over forty years, helping him to never touch another drop. Bob turned his career around as well, becoming a CN Police Officer to keep people safe.

By early 1973, Bob Smith was still sober, and done paying off the house. Boy did he surprise me by selling it for nearly five times what I paid for it. I co-signed with him for a beautiful new house on Montgomery Street. Bob Smith had completely turned his life around for his family.

Now that Sandra, our youngest, was a year old, Barb went back to work at Northern Electric, and we hired Mrs. Drummond to watch the kids while we were gone. She had already raised three children of her own and was an absolute godsend.

Barb was doing shiftwork, which meant one week she would work days, the next nights, then evenings... it was all over the place. Mrs. Drummond would pick the kids up before Barb left for work, then would bring them back in the evenings to give them their baths, put them to bed, and wait for me to get home from Vic Tanny's, where I exercised after work. Mrs. Drummond loved our children and went above and beyond what a babysitter should do, like crocheting the kids clothes and teaching Barbara how to drive. All of this for 28$ a week, which we considered a bargain.

. . .

IT WAS at Northern Electric that Barb met a woman named Janet, whose father had recently passed away. They got to talking about their shared experience of losing a parent, eventually deciding to introduce Janet's mother, Liz, to Mr. Thompson. Although Barb would have nightmares of her mother coming back to life and being heartbroken over it, we were all happy to see her father not be so sad and lonely anymore. Liz brought her own four children into the marriage – Janet, Blondie, Cecil and George – but she also helped Robert raise his girls, and was kind to our kids.

IN 1967, my supervisor, Ken Bloxham, left United Aircraft. The city was offering grants to build accommodations for visitors to Expo67, so he took them up and built a campground on an airstrip with his friend, Dan Hayes. They made a killing that Summer, so Ken decided to sell all of the apartment buildings he owned, so he could run the campground in the summer and spend his winters in Florida. Ken was known at work as the Gentle Giant, due to his imposing frame and kind demeanor. When he proposed that I buy one of his apartment buildings for 35000$, I told him he was crazy if he thought I could afford something like that. Not only did he explain to me that the rents would cover the mortgage, he co-signed it for me. Ken was a good guy, and I trusted him, so I went for it and bought his apartment building.

One of my first renters was Barb's sister, Doreen. She was moving to the South Shore from Montreal, and having trouble finding a place big enough for her family of five. I was glad to be able to help them out, but slightly apprehensive about the investment as a whole.

AS IT TURNED OUT, Ken was right about the rents covering the mortgage, but they didn't cover the repairs that come along, or big-ticket items, like replacing hot water tanks. You also have to be on-call 24/7, in case something ever happens. I got a friend, René-Paul Paquin, to help me take care of any emergencies if I wasn't available. Mostly if it involved plumbing, which was his specialty.

One winter night, I got a call at two o'clock in the morning, saying that water was leaking into the bedroom of one of the upstairs apartments. I called and left a message with Paquin's wife, since water leaks tended to be his domain, and headed to the apartment to shovel the roof. The ladder I had was shorter than I would have liked, so it rested against the building, and I had to hoist myself onto the actual roof. I went around and shoveled off all of the snow, then resigned myself to climb back down the ladder, knowing I would have a considerable drop. I looked around in the dark, but try as I might, I could not find the ladder. As it was resting against the wall instead of sticking up over the roof, I had to stick my head over the ledge to find it. Even then, it was nowhere to be found. Suddenly, the drop from the roof to the ladder was much preferable to the drop from the roof to the ground. At this point, I was either going to have to jump, or freeze to death on the rooftop.

I was contemplating which was better when I heard Paquin shouting my name from below. You cannot imagine the relief I felt at hearing his voice. He found the ladder and guided me to it, then climbed up so he could place my feet on the top rung of the ladder when I hung over the roof's ledge. It was quite the adventure, that I never want to repeat.

IN 1968, my father offered me a piece of land beside his house on Holmes Street, as a thank you for all of the construction work I had done with him years before. Instead of just building a new house for my family, I decided I would build an apartment building, so we would have somewhere to live, but also earn money from it. I went to the city with plans for what I wanted to build, armed with knowledge from my recently purchased property, but they told me I wasn't able to have windows on one side unless I bought the land beside it. The notary looked up the owner, and I was able to buy the second plot of land for something close to 600$ – where we would one day put in a pool. I didn't have the money to build the apartment, and I had just finished renovating our own house, so I wasn't rolling in credit either. Luckily, my father gave me 15 000$ for my house on Laurier, that I would sell once we moved into the apartment. He charged me 10% interest on the loan, but I wouldn't have been able to do any of it without him. In those days, you couldn't get a mortgage unless the building was already built.

I have had great successes in my life, but none of them would have been possible without the support of my family, and the people who believed in me. Working at United Aircraft introduced me to a multitude of contractors and suppliers who helped me out and gave me a chance. Jean-Guy Brosseau did the excavation so we could put in the foundation. My brother-in-law, Robin Graham, did the plastering. Perico, a company in Longueuil, financed all of the material when I couldn't afford to pay for it. Ralph Marrion helped with labor, as did Regis Lemieux.

When I was working at Northern Electric, Regis worked in the stall next to mine, and quickly became one of my best friends. His help was instrumental in constructing the apartments, coming to work during any spare time he had. Even my mother helped out, coming over every day after the workers had left to clean the place up. Not that we had a lot of workers. Usually it was just me, putting a few hours whenever

I wasn't working at United Aircraft or Canada Packers. I sacrificed a lot to build what I believed would be a better future for my family. I was not often present for them during these times, but I always provided for them. None of it was easy.

This was around the time I was training to obtain my black belt status from the Canadian Kodokan Black Belt Association. As you get to the higher belts, you don't just need to demonstrate your knowledge, you need to win competitions in order to advance.

One such fight was against Terry Farnsworth. It wasn't necessarily spectacular at the time, I just eliminated him with a strangulation technique and won the match. What made the fight memorable is that years later, Terry won Canada's first Olympic Gold Medal in Judo. I was very fortunate to have had the opportunity to compete with him, and when you think of it, I literally beat the world champion in Judo!

The fight for my own black belt happened at the Maurice Richard Arena in 1968. My opponent was Charles Maingon. I watched a few of his previous matches during the competition, so I knew he was going to try to get me with a sieo nage – a shoulder throw. As soon as he attempted to throw me, I jumped over his shoulder and took him down with a strangulation technique – my favorite. When the official yelled "Hipo", I nearly had tears in my eyes.

I was shocked beyond words when they gave the fight to Maingon. I felt ashamed and heartbroken. Even the officials realized it was a bad call, but they could not reverse it.

For seven years, I had been pouring my heart and soul into judo, training whenever I could, and prioritizing it in my already overwhelmingly busy life. After this supposed defeat, I just couldn't do it anymore. The officials eventually realized they'd made a bad call, and awarded me an honorary black belt, but it was too little, too late. I still hold wonderful memories from my years of Judo, but I never competed after that. I kept going to the YMCA, but mostly focused on volleyball and scuba diving lessons instead.

THE FOLLOWING YEAR, we sold our house on Laurier street and moved into the newly finished apartment building on Holmes Street. It had eight bachelor apartments, while the main floor would be our new residence. I assumed I was going to live there for the rest of my life, so I built it to last forever, maintenance-free. It had super insulated walls, eighteen inches thick. In addition to the wooden frame, I used cement blocks filled with zonolite, and an exterior of stone and bricks. I used terrazzo for the stairs and hallways, and added a sauna bath, as well as a sun deck on the roof. It was meant to be paradise, so I even gave myself an insulated and heated garage. For the kids, I added a playhouse in the backyard, complete with bunkbeds and toys.

I had considered making a treehouse, like I had when I was a child, but an event that spring made me think better of it. Sandra got it in her mind that it was Superman's cape that gave him the power to fly, so she tied a shirt around her neck and jumped off Mrs. Drummond's balcony. She did not fly, but she did break her arm.

ROBERT WYNGAERT

Our Apartment Building on Holmes.

We were so down to the wire with construction, that while the apartments were meant to be furnished, our tenants moved in on July 1st with nothing but the promise that the furniture was coming. It was an incredibly stressful time.

We had moved in a couple of months earlier, to get things ready, on May 1st, 1969. I remember the date because my brother-in-law, Bruce, helped us with the move. While we were carrying my very heavy bedroom set on the stairs, Bruce somehow broke his back. For months after, he had to lie flat on his back, hang on doors, and all kinds of therapies of the day. He still suffers from it, over fifty years later. I felt so responsible and guilty, that I was very much a killjoy whenever anyone tried roughhousing around me, or anything that might bring a second back injury to my conscience.

ONE OF OUR first tenants was a young woman named Anne Reid, whose siblings went to school with Danny and Linda. She worked at Sunlife Insurance, but was living on her own, so we got rather close. We even trusted her to bring Linda to church on Sundays when Barb couldn't.

A few years after she moved in, we introduced her to Barb's brother, Ronnie. We were thinking – and hoping – that they would hit it off. We were right, and before long, the two were engaged.

Sandra and her cousin, Sharon, both had crushes on Barb's brothers, with Sandra planning to marry Ronnie when she grew up. She was heartbroken when Anne told her about the engagement. That is, until Anne had a conversation with her about it. She told my kids to just call her 'Anne', not Auntie, because they were so close, like friends. It worked, and everyone was thrilled when Ronnie and Anne got married in 1971.

TO HELP EASE the financial burden of constructing the apartment building, I convinced Barb to participate in what I now know was a pyramid scheme. We began selling a line of skincare products called Koscot, which stood for Kosmetics for the Communities of Tomorrow. Although it required a 5000$ investment, you got your money back as long as you recruited one other person to sell the products. In order to recruit someone, you had to pay for them to attend an information session at a fancy hotel in Montreal. Barb completed a training program, so she could do the demonstrations, while I worked on recruitment.

    I did get my 5000$ for recruiting another poor soul, but I spent so much money sending people to the information sessions, and buying all of the products I was supposed to sell, that I ended up losing roughly 5000$ from the venture. By the seventies, Koscot was out of business and tangled up in a legal mess, so I was glad all we lost was money. Koscot was not my first attempt to supplement our income by being a salesman, which is not really in my skill set. At one point, I was an Encyclopedia Britannica salesman, and I even tried selling Amana freezers and food plans. Thankfully, I got the message after

Koscot and focused on businesses rather than schemes.

Regis, Danny, Neil, Trevor, Sandra, and Linda.

To make up for all of the stress and to celebrate being done with construction, Regis and I took our families on a vacation to New Brunswick. I discovered early on that vacations are something you need to take whether you have the money for them or not.

I'm not saying you should go into debt and live a lavish life above your means, but every once in a while, you need to disconnect from your daily life and recharge.

Regis and Gail rented a tent-trailer, while I borrowed a twenty-two-foot travel trailer from a friend at work. I was much more experienced with driving now, with my own cars as well as trucks and heavy equipment, but it was my first time pulling a travel trailer.

I don't remember much from the actual vacation. My most vivid memory from the trip is the drive home. While we were driving in the mountains, I was nearly falling asleep, but there was nowhere to pull off. In hindsight, this was a terrible idea and I do not recommend it, but Barb and I decided to switch drivers while we were still driving. Or rather, I decided, and Barb did as she was told. We managed the switch, but my trailer started to fish-tail, so we ended up with the trailer nearly hanging off the edge of a very deep cliff. I saw this and my heart stopped, as Barb and I rushed to get the kids out of the back seat. The trailer was still attached to our Buick Wildcat, but I somehow managed to unhitch it before the trailer plummeted down the cliff. It was so deep that we couldn't even see the trailer anymore, and couldn't salvage anything. I bet the trailer is still down there, but at least my family is safe.

The rest of the trip home was far from pleasant. I

had to figure out how to tell my co-worker I lost his trailer. In the end, the trip cost a lot more than expected, as I had to pay him the entire cost of the trailer, which I later found out, he also claimed from the insurance company. Needless to say, I never borrowed expensive things from friends again.

BAR-B-DELIGHT

NINE
1970S

"If you can dream it, you can achieve it."
			-Zig Ziglar

In 1970, the Quebec Government attempted to separate from Canada so they could form their own country. This still hasn't happened, but a tremendous amount of English businesses moved to other provinces and countries as a result.

My dream had always been to have my own business, so this was a perfect opportunity to look for bargains these companies left behind. I was always one to follow my dreams, and as Wayne Gretzky said, "You miss 100% of the shots you don't take." So, I found a piece of commercial land on Taschereau boulevard and made a ridiculous offer. They were asking for 7$ per square foot, and I offered 1$.

I was shocked when, within 48 hours, they accepted. I was also in a panic, because I never thought they would accept such a lowball number, and didn't actually have the money. To be honest, I was so terrified by what I had done that I asked Barbara to come to the notary with me, so she could refuse to sign the papers and cancel the deal. Surely if my wife said no, they wouldn't make me go through with the purchase?

Barb, who is my partner in everything and always supports me, knew that I was just letting my fear get in the way. She refused to get me out of it. She did say that I got myself into the mess, so it was up to me to get myself out of it, but I think that if I was really stuck, she would have done it. She just believed in me, even when I didn't.

I HAD a good job at United Aircraft, and the bank would have all the land as equity, so they gave me a mortgage and I became the owner of 70 000 square feet of prime real estate. I saw its potential, but looking at the land, all you could see was a large ditch with no access to the busy street it bordered. We had to drive up a bunch of side streets to get to it, which was not going to work for a business. We had a lot of work to do.

First of which was to decide what business I wanted to own. Although I got the land for a steal, the taxes were extremely high, and I needed to start making money as soon as possible if I wanted to keep it. One thing I could always bank on was that Barb was an excellent cook. At the time, ribs were really growing in popularity, but there was no restaurant that sold them on the South Shore. It just so happened that Barb had the most delicious rib recipe I'd ever tasted. We decided to open a restaurant called Barb-B-Delight Restaurant Incorporated, where we would serve ribs, chicken, and steak.

Bar-B-Delight during the construction phase.

Although we knew we were going to open a

restaurant, we were still a long way from getting there. Preparing the land for use was in and of itself a long-term, complicated endeavor. I had an old boss from United Aircraft, Jacques Bissonnette, who left to start a consulting firm, Soprin. His mechanical engineers and architects drew up all of our plans. I never would have been able to achieve my dreams without him coming to my rescue.

Once we had the building permits, my work began. One of our permits was so that we could close down the highway, after we put in the pipes, to hook our land up to water and sewage lines. We had to dig up the land to put in the pipes, then level it with thousands of loads of earth. Luckily, a contractor I had worked with before, Broadway Paving, had a lot of earth that they usually had to pay to dump in specially designated municipal lots. They were a godsend, as was Regis, who put in long hours of labor to help me out. Together, he and I constructed the bar fridges and all the light fixtures.

My friend Paquin did all of our plumbing, while I was the project manager. I found contractors to do the work I couldn't do, and figured out whatever I could. I poured concrete, did our floors and built the roof. We had stone walls in some places, with a stucco finish in others, and had to order special beams with steel plates from British Columbia for the roof. I assembled them myself, but had to hire a crane to put them up, as they were ridiculously heavy. I almost lost my arm while guiding the crane, when it got stuck between a heavy roof truss and the wall.

I wasn't the only one who was injured during construction. Near the end of it, my son, Danny, wanted to help us put up the light fixtures on the trusses of the roof. This required him to cross the wooden planks we put between them. I warned him to be careful and move slowly, but before I knew what was happening, he had fallen through to the floor, roughly fifteen feet below. He made it out with nothing more than a broken arm, but it took so long for them to see us at the hospital, that they had to re-break it before they could put the cast on.

IT WAS while we were building the restaurant that Guy Rouellan and I launched a Judo club at United Aircraft's Recreation Club. I was spending so much time on construction when I wasn't working, that I needed to be able to work out during my lunch breaks, or I wouldn't be able to work out at all. Plus, we thought a lot of the other men would enjoy it, and Guy was an amazing teacher. He was a big, tough guy who easily could have killed me, yet he let me throw him around in those classes, before I finally received my honorary black belt in 1972.

I tried to get Danny to love Judo the way I did, signing him up for classes at a local gym. Every week, he would leave the house with his uniform and come back hours later, but he never really talked about what he was learning. It took him longer than I was comfortable with to get his yellow belt, so I confronted him to see what was going on. He confessed that he didn't really like judo, so he had been lying to us about going to class, spending that time playing with Sharon and Sandra instead. I was sad that he wouldn't share my hobby, but I was trying to raise my kids to be strong and independent, to think for themselves, and not be forced into doing things they didn't want to do. I had hoped judo would help with that, but he clearly learnt the lesson some other way.

ROBERT WYNGAERT

My mother.

On the evening of August 29th, 1971, my dad came over and pounded on my door in a panic, saying my mom was very sick. By this point she was already bedridden, so it wasn't news, but the look on his face told me this was worse than anything she had faced before. He thought she might have had a heart attack, and wanted me to bring my oxygen tank over while he waited for the doctor to come. I was taking scuba diving lessons, so I grabbed my tank and rushed over. I tried my best to revive her any way I could, but it was to no avail.

She died in my arms of a massive heart attack, after having been there for me my entire life. I suddenly understood the pain Barb had gone through when she lost her mother years earlier, as I felt like I couldn't breathe. My mother had done so much for us. She was kind and loved by everyone, but I don't know if she knew how much I loved her, or what she meant to me. Looking back now, fifty years after losing her, I still have her picture on my desk, and look at it every day. I miss her so very much. One of my biggest regrets is that I never got to spoil her for all that she did for us, and all of the sacrifices she endured so we would never be without.

THE FUNERAL WAS a blur of sad faces and tears, but there was physical pain in my chest as I had to wrestle Linda from the coffin when she insisted she wanted to give her grandmother one last hug. It broke my heart, because I wanted that last hug just as much as she did.

MY MOTHER'S death was the proverbial straw that broke the camel's back. Up to that point, I was soldiering through, from United Aircraft to the restaurant construction to Canada Packers, trying to fit in Barb and the kids. I had also taken up part time work as a Gentleman Bouncer for Garda, providing security at various sporting events, and being a first line bodyguard for special guests like Robert Bourassa (the Prime Minister of Canada) and Colonel Sanders (of KFC fame). All of this to keep our heads above water, but I was sinking. Barb and I both were, because the more responsibilities I took on outside of the home, to build my career and my dreams, the more Barb had to handle at home, in addition to her full-time job, like maintaining the two apartment buildings. The busy-ness had kept us from noticing that we were burning out, but my mother's death brought it all crashing down.

We went to see a doctor, figuring he could prescribe us something, or tell us we were being ridiculous and to suck it up. Instead, he shocked us both by saying we were experiencing burnout, and needed to take a vacation.

. . .

WE HAD LET GO of Mrs. Drummond months before, since the kids were all in school. With no regular babysitter, we asked Suzanne Leduc, a woman who lived in our apartment building, to mind the children while Barb and I took my brand-new Chrysler 300 and drove to Florida.

It was our first trip with just the two of us since the honeymoon, and I don't think either of us realized how much we needed it until we were gone. We stopped in Fort Myers to visit Ken Bloxham and his wife, Marge, then continued on to Walt Disney World. I particularly enjoyed the Thomas Edison Museum we visited as well, but obviously, nothing can beat Disney. Barb was enjoying the trip a lot more before she got heat stroke, right about the time Suzanne called to tell us the children were not behaving. So, we cut our trip short.

While we had told Linda and Danny that Suzanne would be watching them while we were gone, it appeared that Sandra was unaware. Every time Suzanne told them to do something, like come inside when it got dark or to go to bed, the older children convinced Sandra, who was very independent, to say things like, "You're not my mother!" and "You're not the boss of us." It did not go over well with Suzanne, so the children were very glad to see us when we got home. That is, until we showed them our pictures from Walt Disney World. They did not appreciate us going to 'The Happiest Place on Earth' without them.

BY 1972, the Restaurant was built, so we applied for a liquor license before buying and installing all of the equipment. Pretty soon, we were ready to open, but still waiting on our liquor license. We were told that our request was under review, but we had invested every cent we had into this venture, and needed to start making money soon. We had a government representative handling our case, but after contacting him a few times to find out what was going on, he said that he was going through some personal finance problems. If we lent him some money, in cash, he would make sure our request went to the top of the pile. You hear rumors about governments being corrupt, but we quickly learned that the only way to get what we wanted was to grease their pockets.

Unfortunately, all of my money was tied up in the restaurant. I had even sold one of my apartment buildings to afford all of the construction. I asked how much he needed, and he told me five thousand dollars should get him out of his troubles. I went to my brother, Roger, who owned an Appliance store, and asked if I could borrow the money from him, explaining how desperate I was. Luckily, my brother agreed.

Caving in to his demands was clearly a terrible

idea, as we found out less than a month after paying him off. This time, he told us that if we gave another five thousand dollars, his supervisor would sign off on the permit. I was so angry, both at him and at myself. I never laid a hand on him, but I came close. He knew it was taking all of my self-restraint not to take my anger out on him.

The inside of Bar-B-Delight.

In the end, Bar-B-Delight was open for nine months before we finally got our liquor license. During that time, it was very hard to get customers and keep the business open. People were reluctant to come in, even though our prices were reasonable, because the building was so fancy and luxurious that it scared them away. Once we did convince people to come inside, a lot of them would find out we didn't serve alcohol and either leave or never come back.

THE RESTAURANT WAS TRULY a family affair. Barb's father was in charge of the ribs and chicken, which he would sometimes have to prepare in the middle of the night, in the basement, terrified of every unidentified noise.

Danny would help him out, sometimes even manning the fort on his own, while Linda would clear the tables with her friend Sonia Keleman.

Bobby, Barb's brother, was our cook, who stayed with us from the day we opened to our very last day in business, even though he was more than qualified to be a professional chef anywhere else.

Barb would spend her days making the desserts, then become our waitress in the evenings. She sometimes acted as a barmaid, but hated working down in the basement, so we tried to avoid that.

My sister Irene, and Barb's sister Carol, were our friendly waitresses who kept the customers coming back. Irene's daughter, Francine, would often help out as well, running to get me whenever a customer tried to leave without paying.

Barb's brother Ronnie did the breakfast shifts, until we realized it wasn't financially profitable for us to be open for breakfast, so he did deliveries for a while.

Though she wasn't involved in the day-to-day operations, Barb's sister Joan spent hours washing and ironing all of our tablecloths so we could continue to deliver a five-star service.

My dad would even rent out the restaurant at Christmas to host a big Wyngaert Christmas Family Party with his new wife, Antoinette.

As for myself, I was the host most nights, and I handled all the deliveries, the inventory, the orders, and anything that fell through the cracks.

ROBERT WYNGAERT

ON SATURDAY NIGHTS, Georges, Denise, Barb and I would go to local restaurants, to check out the competition. It was nice to revive our old tradition, as we used to all go out together on Saturday nights when the kids were little. Whenever I saw something other restaurants were doing that seemed to be successful, I would try to think of how we could implement it at Bar-B-Delight.

Georges had moved out of my parents' duplex a few years before, and one of his new neighbors was a man named Michel Blanchard. Mike was incredibly well-known in the community, as he got involved in everything. He was a retired RCMP officer now working as a sales representative for Esso, an Alderman for the city, and he worked with me as my partner at Garda. Not to mention that he was the one who played the trumpet for the Montreal Canadiens hockey games, whenever a player scored a goal. He never explicitly worked for us, but he went out of his way to bring his coworkers there after a shift, or groups after a meeting...he was our unofficial advertising department, and we were incredibly grateful.

With our permit in hand, we quickly built a bar in the basement, hoping we could make up for the lost time, and revenue.

TEN
1970S

"Protecting yourself is self-defense. Protecting others is warriorship."
-Bodhi Sanders

Once we had our liquor license, we opened a bar in the basement section of the restaurant to increase our revenues. The restaurant itself wasn't enough to cover our expenses, and while the bar did help, it also brought a lot of problems. It is common sense that alcohol can bring out the worst in people, but I never realized how many stupid things people do when they drink, until I owned a bar.

We had an organ player and entertainers, trying to keep up with our classy theme, but that is not how things always played out.

For instance, we frequently had a professional

wrestler, the Masked Destroyer, who would come to the restaurant. He was on a weekly wrestling program on television, and believed this gave him the right to eat and drink without ever paying his bill. He took advantage of his fame, insisting that he was bringing in business for us just by being there, and handing out autographed pictures of himself. I usually gritted my teeth and let it slide, but that night, I'd worked a double-header as a bouncer for the Montreal Expos at Jarry Park. I arrived at the restaurant and found him there. Again. Eating and drinking things he would never pay for.

I waited until he went down to the bar in the basement, then confronted him about his bill. He told me not to mess with him, bragging about what he did to the last restaurant owner who 'challenged' him.

I'd had enough of his arrogance, of working so many jobs, of the restaurant not making money...I couldn't take it anymore.

"Let's see who destroys who," I said, taking off my jacket.

I'm not proud of what came next, but after our 'altercation' he left and never came back. I don't think he wanted the media to know that a professional wrestler was beat up for taking advantage of a small business owner. It very easily could have gone the other way, but it wouldn't have painted him in a good light if he'd beat me up either.

· · ·

IT GOES without saying that I never used my martial arts training to provoke people, and I never took advantage of my abilities. I always relied on my skills solely as an insurance policy, to be used in defensive situations, to protect myself and others from injury. Most of them had to do with my business ventures, like renting bachelor apartments – one of them in a low-income area where collecting rents was not always easy, the restaurant, and the bar. I always made sure that I was physically fit, to ensure that our clients were safe in our establishments, and my family never had to worry.

ELEVEN
1970S

"The only person you are destined to become is the person you decide to be."
-Ralph Waldo Emerson

A few months after we opened the restaurant, I was working as a gentleman bouncer at an Expos Games when Gilles Desormeaux, my supervisor, told me there was a scout looking for 'tough guys' who could pass as police officers in a new movie called The Pyx. We both auditioned, and it just so happened that the night the scout was there, a fight broke out at the game, and I had to break it up. Apparently, the scouts came to see us because their scene would show a bar fight being broken up by police officers. I guess I looked like I knew what I was doing, because I was chosen to play Detective Clement in the film.

One thing I have learnt about the film world is that things often change. The bar fight I was supposed to break up never happened. Instead, they told me I would be getting shot and falling off a boat. I said that was fine, picturing my father's fishing boat. On the day we were supposed to film that scene, I arrived to see a gigantic ship in the St. Lawrence River. Thank God the current was too strong to film the scene that way, because I do not think I would have been able to survive a fall into the water from that height, even if there was no current. Instead, I fell to the deck, and they put out a pile of boxes for the others to fall onto. The guns and other weapons are also fake, but the fire that comes out to make them look real could definitely injure someone.

ROBERT WYNGAERT

Newspaper Clipping for The Pyx: Me, Christopher Plummer, Don Pilon, and Gilles Desormeaux.

The movie had some big names, like Karen Black, Donald Pilon, Yvette Braind'amour, Jean-Louis Rioux and Christopher Plummer. Mr. Plummer was such a nice guy. He would eat and hang out with us, talking like we were his friends rather than starstruck day players. He even asked me for some pointers on a scene where he had to punch someone, knowing I had a lot of experience in that area. I was so sad to hear of his passing, just as I finished writing this book.

At the end, I was invited to the wrap party, where all of the cast celebrated the end of the film shoot. It was really fun meeting all of these important people, after such an unexpected and exciting experience.

I WAS LATER CALLED to audition for another film, called Child Under a Leaf. It was once more for the part of a policeman, but I turned it down. I was already stretched so thin as it was, and my wife and children were more important to me than possibly pursuing an acting career. I was very happy with my position at United Aircraft and didn't want to jeopardize it, or the benefits it came with. I never regretted that decision.

I did, however, regret telling all of my friends and family to watch The Pyx when it came out the following year. The film was called The Hooker Cult Murders in other markets, which gives a better idea of what it is about. I especially got a lot of phone calls from the parents of children who went to school with mine, wondering why my children had told theirs to watch a movie with so much murder and nudity.

TWELVE
1970S

"Character cannot be developed in ease and quiet. Only through experience of trial and suffering can the soul be strengthened, ambition inspired, and success achieved."
– Helen Keller

Not long after we opened the restaurant, the hourly workers at United Aircraft Technologies went on strike, requesting higher pay and more benefits. In addition to striking, they frequently burnt police cars and vandalized the homes of some supervisors. They eventually settled after twenty-two months, but it was a very scary time for anyone associated with United Aircraft.

I was a salaried employee, so the strike didn't apply to me, but I was told that if I didn't come in, I would no longer have a job. Since my job entailed supervising the work of others, when the hourly workers stopped coming in, I had to cover for them.

I couldn't afford to lose my job, so I took on the responsibilities of all the employees under me. Or at least the ones that I knew how to do. Pratt hired scabs, and some supervisors went so far as to smuggle them into the plant with their personal vehicles, to protect them from the strikers. I know a lot of people were calling me a scab, but I didn't bring anyone in, I just worked a lot of extra hours and did a lot of additional tasks for my same salary.

I was one of the only supervisors who held a class one driver permit, so I was assigned to drive the heavy equipment for snow removal, as well as transferring parts and equipment to other plants. When the strikers set fire to the warehouse where United Aircraft stored the casting and engine parts in Montreal, I was also the only one crazy enough to risk my life driving an eighteen-wheeler from the warehouse to our plants.

In urgent situations like that, they picked me up in a helicopter at the helipad in front of Plant #5 and brought me to Plant #1, because there was no way I was getting through the picket lines with my car.

ROBERT WYNGAERT

Claude Labelle, me, and Guy Rouellan.

It was still extremely dangerous, so the Security team asked me what kind of protection I needed. Instead of one of the security guards, I asked for my Judo instructor, Guy Rouellan, to accompany me. He had black belts in both Judo and karate, so I knew he would have my back. They also decided that we should wear a wire, so they could monitor our activities, and send help if it was needed, as we didn't have cell phones at the time. They would have sent us with a police escort instead, but tensions were high, and it didn't make sense to endanger more lives and possibly escalate the situation if it wasn't necessary.

On one of those days, we were driving along Chambly road to bring a load of engine parts to Plant

#5. When we stopped at a stop sign, I looked around and saw we were surrounded by pick-up trucks filled with angry strikers, and goons looking for a fight. We alerted the police over the wire, but weren't sure what to do while we waited. We could have stayed inside the truck until they got close enough to cause damage, at which point we would be trapped. We'd seen the pictures of police cars up in flames, and it looked like the men outside were angry enough to want to put us out of commission, so we didn't want to risk it.

I suggested we go outside and stand back to back so we could protect each other, and possibly come up with an escape plan. I acted confident, but I was terrified.

As soon as we got out, one of the strikers yelled, "It's Bob and Guy!"

Some still looked upset, but the majority stepped back, and convinced the others to as well. Our reputations were well known around the plants, so they knew we had no choice but to drive the truck, or we would lose our jobs. It was a tremendous sign of their respect for us, and we both greatly appreciated it. By the time the police arrived, we were the only ones there.

ONE DAY, I was assigned to cover for one of my millwrights to assemble a steel structure from an overhead bridge crane. While I was trying to secure a steel beam into place, the beam slipped and fell towards my supervisor. Without thinking, I moved to push it out of the way, so it wouldn't hit anyone, and fell to the concrete floor twenty feet below.

Everyone rushed to help me, but I got up on my own, amazing them all. This is one more time that it was a miracle I did not die. Perhaps it was because of all the break falls we practiced in my judo training, or that my mission on earth wasn't over yet.

Although I kept assuring everyone I was fine, I was actually in a lot of pain, so I went to my car and drove to see my chiropractor. By the time I parked, the pain was excruciating, and I could barely make it into his office.

After he took some x-rays, he told me it wasn't humanly possible for me to have driven myself in the condition I was in. My whole spine was completely out of line, with four vertebrae needing adjustments. He told me I was very fortunate to be in such good physical shape, because my muscles must have supported my spine and kept it in place while I drove there. He recommended that I take some time off to help with the healing process, a few months at least. I took his advice in the sense that I resigned from Canada Packers, after fourteen years of being one of the Brown Brothers, but I am very stubborn, so I was back at United Aircraft after a week.

THIRTEEN
1974

"If you don't build your dream, someone else will hire you to help them build theirs."
-Dhirubhai Ambani

By July of 1974, I was risking my life for a company while my own business was falling through the cracks, so I made the difficult decision to resign from United Aircraft and devote myself full-time to Bar-B-Delight.

Because of the strike, local restaurants had been warned not to serve or deliver food to anyone still working for United Aircraft. Or for Garda, who was hired to protect the facilities from the strikers. Our restaurant was so close to bankruptcy, and I was already on the strikers' bad list because I drove the trucks, so I offered to supply all the meals United Aircraft and Garda needed, as long as they were the ones who came to pick the orders up. They agreed and gave us a purchase order that lasted until the end of the strike. It was a godsend. Our lifeline to keep the business running. My family and employees were kept very busy, and we received a monthly cheque that covered our operating expenses.

However, we were constantly on edge due to the many death threats we received from the strikers. They went so far as to call and say they were going to blow up the restaurant, with everyone inside it. Barb, who usually answered the phone, was a terrified pack of nerves. One time, I was the one who picked up, and happened to recognize the voice of the person threatening us. I called him by his name and told him I would hold him personally responsible if anything happened to the restaurant, my family, or any of my employees. He would have to deal with me, as well as the police. We never received another call.

I thought life would be easier and I would have more free time now that I was only managing the one business, without all of my other jobs. I didn't realize that owning a restaurant was 7 days a week, 365 days a year. Plus, you don't get paid by the hour, you get paid if you make it profitable. I didn't have the money to hire all of the personnel that would be required to run the restaurant I wanted ours to be, so I relied on my family to go above and beyond their tasks, knowing that I was paying them less than they deserved, or could be making other places. Everyone pitched in as needed. I know that I personally filled in as cook, barman, host, dishwasher, janitor, delivery man, restocking the kitchen and bar...it never ended.

FOURTEEN
1975

"Every strike brings me closer to the next home run."
-Babe Ruth

Nine months after I resigned from United Aircraft, in February of 1975, the strike finally ended, almost two years after it began. Gordon MacCaul, the plant superintendent, called me to see if I would consider returning to work for them at the newly-named Pratt & Whitney Canada. He knew I was busy with the restaurant and probably couldn't do it, but he offered me the position of General Foreman at Plant #2. This was a position I had been hoping to get for years, but every time there was a vacancy, I was passed over because I didn't have the basic qualifications – meaning an Engineering Degree or an M.B.A.

I agreed and went back, letting him think I was doing them a favor, without ever letting on how desperate I had been to return to work. I am sure their offer would have been much less if they had known.

WHILE RETURNING to Pratt gave me the job I wanted and opportunities to further my education through job-related courses, it also meant leaving Barb with all of the responsibilities of the restaurant, the bar, and the children.

This was too much for her, so we hired a manager to look after the bar. We chose Richard B., the man who sold us a lot of the kitchen equipment and other items for the restaurant. He was a young, retired policeman with a wife and four children. It seemed like a perfect match.

Barbara, Linda, Danny, and Sandra.

In December, after a long and busy summer, we needed a vacation. It was impossible with the restaurant, but Richard offered to manage Bar-B-Delight in its entirety while the family spent two weeks in Florida. It was such a relief to be able to travel all of us together, and leave our restaurant in the hands of someone we knew and trusted, who was intimately familiar with our business.

We flew to West Palm Beach just after Christmas. We had to leave extremely early in the morning, before the sun came up. I was used to flying because of Pratt, but it was the first flight for Barb and the kids. I know people these days wear comfortable clothes when they fly, but we got dressed up for it. And I don't just mean that we didn't wear our sweatpants; we went all out. Barb and the girls wore dresses, Danny had a nice vest, and I wore a suit, complete with an ascot tie. I didn't wear an ascot in my everyday life, but for some reason, I felt it was appropriate for plane rides. It seems so silly when I look back on it now, but at the time, we took it all very seriously.

We stayed at the Colonnades Hotel and I rented a brand new, light blue 1976 Cadillac Sedan. I liked the car so much, that I bought one for myself when I got home. The hotel was really something, with a staircase and two floors contained within our room. They had a family of ducks in the yard, and Sandra and Danny spent hours with them after Sandra discovered that they ate all of the warts she had on her knees.

Linda, Danny, and Sandra with the ducks.

We brought the kids to Walt Disney World and the Thomas Edison Museum, went on tours of the swamps to look for gators, we picked oranges...it was a lot of fun.

We spent one night in Miami, where Barb and I went to see The Platters in concert. We let the kids stay in the hotel room and order room service. When we got back from the concert, they wanted to know where we had been.

"We went to see the Platters," I told them.

Danny's face dropped, as he suddenly looked heartbroken.

"We didn't think you would want to come," Barb added, as shocked as I was at his reaction.

"I can't believe you went to have a bobo platter without us, when you know how much we love them!"

He got more upset when our immediate reaction was to start laughing, until we explained that the Platters was a group that sang such hits as 'Only You'. Bobo Platters were an Asian dish we often ate when we went to Miss Chinatown. We promised to take him for Bobo Platters when we got home, and the crisis was averted.

WHEN WE RETURNED from the trip and went to check on things at the restaurant, tanned and refreshed to get back to work, we found it all boarded up. I was in denial, giving Richard the benefit of the doubt, telling myself there had to be a logical explanation. It wasn't until we went inside and saw that all of our equipment was gone, down to the dining room chairs, that I faced the truth. While we were on vacation, the man we trusted to manage our business had betrayed us, selling all of our equipment and closing up shop. I wondered if that was how he got the equipment when he sold it to us in the first place.

I went to his home to confront him, but we weren't the only ones he betrayed. He had purchased a motorhome with the money, then left his wife and kids behind when he disappeared. She was broken-hearted and had no idea where he was.

YEARS LATER, his wife contacted me after finding out he was living in an apartment in Longueuil. She gave me the address and his apartment number, so I could pay him a visit. He was shocked when he opened the door and found me, but I took advantage of his surprise to push my way inside. He ran to his bedroom and came back with a handgun, that he brandished while accusing me of forced entry.

"If you don't leave, there will be blood on the walls," he threatened.

I had long ago written it off as a bad debt experience, so I decided the money wasn't worth my life, and went home.

A FEW MONTHS LATER, I happened to see him in a restaurant, sitting at a table by himself. I assumed he wouldn't have the gun on him, and if he did, he wouldn't dare use it, so I took a seat at his table.

He knew that without the gun, he wasn't going to get past me, so he told me that he would pay me back, and gave me twelve post-dated cheques of two thousand dollars each.

I was very happy with this deal. Although it

would only cover about half of what he owed me, it was better than the nothing I had been expecting. The first two cheques went through before he closed his accounts, and we never heard from him again.

CAMPING ALOUETTE INC.

FIFTEEN
1976

"Opportunity is often missed because it comes dressed in overalls and looks like work."
-Thomas A. Edison

Since reopening the restaurant would have required purchasing all new equipment and furnishings, for a business that was not profitable to begin with, we decided to cut our losses and sell it. Earlier, when trying to make ends meet, I had already sold off parts of my land to Kentucky Fried Chicken. This time, we sold to Rotisseries St-Hubert, but they only wanted the land. This meant we had to pay to demolish the restaurant we poured our hearts and souls into. I made a deal with a contractor so he did it for free in exchange for whatever materials they could salvage.

    I settled into my position at Pratt, and Barb went

to work at Kapetan, a local restaurant. It broke my heart, but it was also a relief, as our restaurant had been a failure, financially speaking.

People who met me later in life know me as a successful businessman, and would probably call me well-off, but that's because they never saw all the struggles it took to get me there. I spent most of my life working multiple jobs, trying any additional income streams I could find, failing time and time again at new business ventures before I 'made it'. When the kids were born, I took out a life insurance policy, that would pay off all my debts if I died. I told them the more debt I had, the richer they would be. The truth was that I believed in investing in yourself and your future. It stung, but I would rather go into debt trying to improve myself and provide for my family, than to scrape by without ever even trying to do better. Luckily, every failed attempt was a stepping stone, teaching me lessons so I would be prepared when the opportunity came.

IN MAY, Ken Bloxham called to see if I was interested in purchasing shares in his campground. Their permit to have it on the airstrip had expired, and they were now located in Saint-Mathieu-de-Beloeil, having purchased Camping Beloeil, that had been about to file for bankruptcy. He heard about us closing the restaurant, and wondered if I would want to invest in Kendan Ltd.

Years ago, I had tried to purchase a campground with Barb's cousin, Ray Bonin. We had even gone so far as to give a 5000$ deposit, but the owner died, and the deal fell through. Ken's offer was my second chance, but at this point in my life, I had no intentions of starting a new business. The restaurant had discouraged me, and I was resigned to just keep working at Pratt until I could retire. However, my accountant had warned me that the best way to avoid being taxed for Capital Gains was to invest in something new, so I didn't say no. Ken suggested I come work there for the summer, as a trial, but also so they could train me.

I no longer worked at Canada Packers, so I spent my nights and weekends at the campground instead. I worked hard, long hours, and remember being surprised by how little they were investing in the property. They held meetings to see if they should replace faulty doorknobs, which often led to me purchasing small items on my own, so I wouldn't have to deal with the meetings. Their mindset, which I later found out is very common, was to keep going with minimal investment, as long as they were making a return. My mindset, on the other hand, was to keep investing the returns back into the business, building it up to its full potential.

This was 1976, when Montreal built the

Olympic Stadium to host the Summer Olympics. We happened to be the closest campground to Montreal, which meant we got a lot of business and the company made a fortune. Before the start of the next summer I put everything I had, 130 000$, into purchasing a third of the shares of Kendan Ltd.

SIXTEEN
1977

"What you put into life is what you get out of it."
-Clint Eastwood

Over the Christmas holidays, we drove to Florida for another family vacation. Since we didn't have to worry about plane tickets, we brought Linda's best friend, Sonia. In retrospect, it might not have been the best idea to only get one hotel room for the six of us, but we managed, with the three girls in one of the double beds, and Danny on a cot. We were in Daytona Beach, but we still made the day trip to Disney, as Sonia had never been. The hotel, a Ramada Inn, had a restaurant that served freshly squeezed orange juice with breakfast, and I drank at least a glass every day, sometimes two. Danny, for his part, discovered the culinary delicacy of steak and eggs for breakfast.

We told him not to get used to it, but it was okay as a holiday treat.

THAT SUMMER, I put Barb and the kids to work from May to October. It was my second year at the campground, but my first as part-owner. Barb took the summer off from working at Kapetan to run the office, though she also found herself doing whatever was needed. Linda left her job at Roger's ice cream shop in order to help Barb out in the office. Sandra was heartbroken to have to stop babysitting Bobby and Moe's daughters; Karen, Donna, and Kathy. Her new job was taking care of visitors. We didn't have a gate at the time, so if the visitor didn't stop to register with her, she would have to chase them down through the park. Danny wasn't allowed to leave his job cutting the grass at our apartment buildings, but he got the added responsibility of helping out with the campground's maintenance, especially on weekdays, when I couldn't be there.

WE WERE ONLY in charge of the campground, as the previous owners still ran the general store, the snack bar, and the arcade. We had 250 sites, and rented them for 5.50$ per night, with the option of electricity, water, and sewage for 0.50$ each.

Now that I was part-owner, Ken and Dan became more like silent partners. They handled the accounting and stopped by occasionally to see how things were going, and to guide us as to what needed to be done, but they had very minimal involvement in the day to day operations. Most of the grounds work went to Jean-Marc Leblanc, who did everything from grass and repairs, to plumbing and electricity.

WHEN I WAS able to be there, mainly nights and weekends, one of the campers, ten-year-old Marco Bissonnette, followed me around like he was my shadow. When people asked who he was following, he would tell them I was his father. We both had dark features, so I think they believed him, although I hope his father never heard him say that. I don't know if he was interested in learning how to run a campground, or if it was just something for him to do, but he went everywhere with me.

THE OTHER OWNERS didn't want to invest any money into the campground, so I did what I could to improve it without spending too much on capital expenditures. Danny and I leveled sites, Barb painted picnic tables...I had big plans, and slowly but surely, I would make them come true.

By the end of the summer, Sandra and Linda loved their new jobs, as they were able to sunbathe when we didn't have customers, which was often. It was good for their tans, but very bad for business.

OVER THE WINTER, I spent my evenings taking business administration and microeconomics classes at Champlain College. All of my entrepreneurial endeavors had been failures up to that point, teaching me many lessons, but I thought it might be nice this time to learn in a classroom, rather than from my own mistakes.

SEVENTEEN
1978

"Think of adversity as an opportunity for growth."
-Unknown

Unfortunately, a series of external factors worked to ensure the campground would have terrible attendance rates, as well as revenues, for the first few years after I became a partner.

When Canada switched to the metric system, they had to change all of the exit numbers on the highway, to reflect their distance in kilometers rather than in miles. We had no warning of when this was going to happen, so we had already printed all of our promotional materials for the year when exit 64 switched to exit 105. All of our non-regular campers came in complaining about how hard it was to find us. Thank God for a Jehovah's Witness convention that nearly sustained our entire summer by bringing twelve thousand dollars in revenue.

ONE ADVANTAGE to business being so slow was that we were able to visit my niece, Johanne, and her husband, Dan, at Lake Connelly, which is about an hour from Montreal. Georges came as well, and Roger even brought his speed boat so we could go water skiing.

My brothers and I liked to show off, especially to each other, so when it was my turn to go water skiing, Roger decided that he would keep driving as long as it took for me to fall off. He drove around the Lake at full speed, so I only lasted a few minutes before wiping out.

When I hit the water, it was like landing on concrete which, as you may recall, I knew from experience. I lost consciousness and could feel myself sinking deeper and deeper into the lake. Luckily, the water was so cold that it brought me back to my senses. I quickly realized that I was in great danger of drowning, but one of the first things they taught me during my Scuba Diving lessons was to stay calm. It was very hard, but I tried my best not to panic.

ROBERT WYNGAERT

I don't know how long I was underwater, but my brothers were both very happy when I finally popped up. Everyone was so relieved that I had made it out without a scratch, until I gave them a big smile, to let them know I was okay – I had left my false teeth at the bottom of the lake!

EIGHTEEN
1979

"Always do your best. What you plant now, you will harvest later."
-Og Mandino

It was becoming difficult to manage the apartment building and the campground. We made a decision and put our home on Holmes for sale in 1979, including the furniture, since we advertised furnished apartments. I thought everyone would be happy to get all new furniture in the new house, but Linda and Sandra were very upset with me for quite some time, as their bedroom set had belonged to my mother.

We purchased a new house at 411 Tailhandier in St-Bruno, on the mountain. It was a beautiful, large house on a corner lot, but it didn't have a garage. I had grown used to, and slightly dependent on my heated garage, so I drew up plans and got to work building myself one before the campground got busy.

Since we were adding a garage, I figured we would also add an extra bedroom above it, instead of wasting the space. I even planned a circular, paved driveway in the front of the house, and a double driveway on the side, so we could accommodate ten cars.

I had just finished all the framework when a building inspector came to visit us. We showed him what we were doing, and he told us we had to stop construction immediately. Apparently, there was a new by-law that made it unacceptable to put rooms above garages. I could either lower the structure so it couldn't be used as a living space or tear the whole thing down. I was not happy, but I had no choice but to comply.

I WAS DOING VERY WELL at Pratt, continuously finding ways to improve how things were done, and taking as many courses as the company made available to me. My abilities also improved every time they entrusted me with more responsibilities.

Unfortunately, Pratt soon found out that I was the owner of a campground, which they considered a conflict of interest. I had always had another job, or business, almost the entire time I was working for them. After the restaurant, the apartment buildings, and Canada Packers, I found it interesting that the campground was where they drew the line. Luckily, I was only part-owner, so I assured them we shared the responsibilities and it wouldn't be an issue. They asked me to sign a statement ensuring that the running of the campground would not interfere with my position and responsibilities at Pratt. It was also implied that I would be closely monitored, and wouldn't be able to take days off unless I was deathly ill.

WE HAD A VERY DIFFICULT SUMMER, with an abysmal attendance. In the fall of 1978, Iranian workers had gone on strike and the U.S. deregulated oil prices, which led to oil rationing and shortages. It didn't affect Quebec as much as the States, where people had to line up for hours to fill their cars, but we were part of an industry that catered to tourists. With the high prices and long wait times for gas, very few people wanted to travel long distances. Especially not towing a trailer.

Our revenues were so bad, in fact, that Ken and Dan informed me that they would be filing for bankruptcy. For them, my investment had been a last-ditch attempt to salvage the company, but after a series of bad years, it was time for them to throw in the towel. For me, I had just invested every cent I'd made from selling the restaurant into this business, that they basically wanted to throw away. I had come into the camping business with high hopes, that I would work at Pratt until the campground became profitable, then I would retire and live out the rest of my life running a business that I could pass on to my children. I could see that we'd had a terrible couple of years, that it was a bad investment and I shouldn't have made it. But now that I had, I was not prepared to give up.

I begged them to reconsider, before offering to buy them out. I couldn't buy all of their shares at once, but we came up with a payment plan, so I could slowly acquire more and more of the shares as time went on, ensuring they would get their money back.

ONE OF THE first things I remember doing is purchasing a tractor with money I earned from working at Pratt. Whenever something required equipment, Ken and Dan would always pay someone to bring their own and do the work. They were both engineers, who saw the campground as an investment, but I was someone who worked my way up in the world through construction, manual labor, and heavy lifting. I knew that it would be much less expensive in the long run if I had the equipment to do the work myself. If I didn't put money into the campground—a lot of it – I was going to lose it.

MY FRIENDS CALL ME BOB

Sandra, Danny, me, and Linda in Jamaica.

In December, we went on our first 'all-inclusive' vacation. It was a far cry from the ones we go on now. The resort was called Go Bananas and was located in Montego Bay, Jamaica. Instead of having to carry your money around with you, all of the prices were in bananas, which you would buy at the office and wear around your neck like a really long necklace. Any time you wanted something to eat or drink – or even a souvenir – you simply unhooked the required amount of bananas, then retied your necklace.

While we were there, we went to see Mico Blanco. He was the limbo king, who would lie planks of wood across rows of pop bottles, set the wood on fire, then limbo under the length of the wooden plank. It was very impressive!

Barb and I participated in all of the activities. It was hard not to, with the three children cheering us on. We won an award for our reggae dancing, but didn't do so well at Find Your Husband. The game consisted of blindfolding all the wives, then letting them find their husbands by feeling all of the men in the line, which included young studs as well as the husbands. I wouldn't exactly call myself a jealous guy, but I may have uttered a few "Barb!"s under my breath when she lingered a little too long on the guy beside me.

Barbara trying to find me.

As we were there over Christmas, they had a Jamaican Santa ride in on a surfboard. We also went carolling around the hotel, holding candles, which made it extra hilarious when our 'animator', Spike, fell into the pool. We watched all the shows from our balcony, bet on crab races, and even participated in the scavenger hunt, which had us looking for things like cockroaches. I think we didn't find any on purpose.

It was a wonderful way to relax, recharge, and spend some time with the family.

NINETEEN
1980

"Family should be your number one priority."
-Robert Wyngaert

In March of 1980, we went to Florida and met up with Barb's sister, Joan, and her family. In addition to bringing two of their three children, Glenn and Lynne, Joan and Bob took in foster children, so even though our kids were teenagers, we had a good mix of ages. What I remember most of that trip was how Bob had recently discovered that some American quarters were made with real silver, making them worth much more than 25 cents, so we spent our days looking for them.

Danny, me, Barbara, and Sandra in Hawai'i.

Over the Christmas holidays, we went on a family vacation to Hawai'i. Even though we paid an arm and a leg for the direct flight, it still took us twelve hours to get there. Luckily, the unforgettable experience we had over the next two weeks made it well worth it.

We stayed at the Hyatt Regency, where we would sit by the pool and drink fancy drinks like Mai Tais, Blue Hawai'is, and Piña Coladas. These were very expensive, but we worked so hard during the year that I refused to worry about money while we were on vacation.

One day, they were filming a TV show at our hotel. I had no idea who or what Magnum P.I. was, but the kids went crazy over him, wanting to spend the entire day watching them film. I insisted we go do some sightseeing, but they were lucky enough to get pictures with Tom Selleck before we left.

We attended many shows, including Don Ho and Jim Nabors, the Kodak show, as well as a luau, which was delicious. It was so impressive to see everything they do with fire. We also went on tours, such as to the Dole Pineapple Plantation, and on hiking adventures to the top of Diamond Head Volcano. It was the first time I heard of chocolate dipped cockroaches, which were apparently quite the delicacy. Maybe that's why they had us hunting for them in Jamaica!

When we visited the North Shore, everyone except for Barb ignored the signs and walked along the beach, with the water barely up to our ankles. We knew how to swim, and it wasn't like the waves could be dangerous in such shallow water. Or so we thought.

In an instant, a giant wave came and carried us into the undertow. Danny and Sandra were carried out in the distance, so as soon as I caught my breath, I went after them.

Sandra was the youngest, so I went to her first, having to practically wrestle her to the beach. I hadn't realized that the wave ripped off her bathing suit, and she was mortified, begging me to let her die. It's hard enough to save someone who is drowning –

because they flail and drag you down – but it is even harder when the person doesn't want to be rescued. By the time I got to Danny, he was already on the beach, not very happy with me for saving her first. Luckily, we were all okay.

On New Year's Eve, the tradition was to have fireworks, which we enjoyed at first, but they lasted all through the night, ensuring no one would be able to sleep through the festivities. It was a wonderful vacation, but very expensive.

TWENTY
1981

"These tears need to be shed, wept into the earth where there is no hope of consolation. Sometimes a man has to cry alone."
-Edmond Manning

This year, I was presented with the United Technologies Award for Extraordinary Management Effectiveness, so Pratt and Whitney's concerns about my loyalty were clearly unfounded. It was a great honor for me to receive the award, and it came with a substantial increase in salary, as well as a 3000$ bonus, which helped make up for the trip to Hawai'i.

My father.

My father had been having a lot of heart problems, with almost daily angina attacks, but his surgery kept being delayed due to nursing strikes. We were thrilled when he was finally called in on January 18th, hoping this meant he would get back to his normal self. I was at home that evening when they told me that he had died on the operating table.

The surgery had been delayed so many times, that once they got to him, it was already too late. These days, it isn't hard to get me emotional enough to shed a few tears. Just talking about how grateful I am for my family will do it. Back then I was much better at holding it all in. My kids could have counted on one hand the times they saw me cry, and they wouldn't need all of their fingers. This was one of those times, but I didn't want my children to see me like that, so I said I was going to work at the campground, and left so I could absorb the news on my own.

His death hit me differently than my mother's had, because my father was a very different person. My mother had been warm and generous with her love and affection, but my father was less demonstrative. He would often say 'you shouldn't talk to say nothing', so his words were few and far between. He was hard on me, and it wasn't always easy being his son, but I loved him, and I knew that he loved me. More than that, I knew that he loved Barbara, as he would often give Georges and I approving looks, saying we did good and were very lucky, whenever our wives were mentioned.

Danny and Brenda Smith, me, and Sandra.

In April, we went to Myrtle Beach for two weeks to get ready for a busy camping season. Danny and Linda were too old to want to hang out with their parents, but Sandra came with us. We all took golfing lessons for the first week, before we were joined by our godson, Danny Smith, and his wife, Brenda, as well as my brother Roger, and his wife Kay. We would have a tee time of 6:30 am, as soon as the sun was up, so we could play our eighteen holes before enjoying a day on the beach.

. . .

ROBERT WYNGAERT

THAT SUMMER, my brother Georges came to work for us part-time to help out. I knew from Canada Packers that he wouldn't enjoy working on the grounds, so he worked in the office with the girls. At the time, we kept track of reservations and which sites were rented by a rather large map we hung on a corkboard wall. Small pins meant the site was occupied, while reservations got a sewing pin with a sticker of the dates on it. The map was color-coded to reflect which sites had which services, and was made out of regular paper, which came in handy when we made modifications to the sites, but it probably wasn't the most durable system.

After the summer Georges worked for us, we had to print a whole new map. Every time a customer came in with a comment on their site, such as 'muddy', 'pothole', 'noisy' or 'shaded', he would write it on the map, in pen or in marker. It was useful to know if the site had lots of trees, or if we needed to repair something, but many of the comments were dependent upon the weather, or who was camping beside them.

TWENTY-ONE
1982

"We cannot direct the wind, but we can adjust the sails."
-Aristotle

We went to Myrtle Beach in the Spring. Our son, Danny, was dating Sandra's good friend Liz Todd at the time, so the three of them joined us. Ronnie also came with Anne and their sons, Brian and David. Ronnie had a broken ankle, so we didn't play much golf, but luckily, we enjoyed each other's company We all had fun on the beach, as well as in the hotel pool, while Ronnie watched.

. . .

WHEN WE GOT HOME, we settled in for a much busier season at the campground. Not so much attendance-wise, but there was a lot more work to do. There was a lot of trial and error in the beginning, as well as many attempts to drum up business and make money. I had to pay Ken and Dan every April for their shares, which was long before campers arrived for the summer, so I came up with a promotion where campers received a discount if they paid in full before leaving in the fall. I wouldn't have made it through those years without people like my brother-in-law Doug, my nephew Danny Smith, and my brother Roger lending me money to tide us over until the season picked up.

AFTER YEARS OF ANDRE MIRREAULT, the old owner of Camping Beloeil, running the snack bar, the general store, and the arcade, we decided it was time for a change. Kids enjoyed the games, and we ate at the snack bar almost every day, but the store was a joke. The prices were ridiculously high, so the only people who shopped there were the unfortunate campers who hadn't brought a car to get into town. It was highway robbery.

I purchased all remaining assets of Camping Beloeil, a 70 000$ investment, but with a little revamping and fair prices, I was confident we could run the store at a profit. It came with a private residence, which I used as my private office. Since it had a bedroom, Barb and I also stayed there some nights in the summer, so we didn't have to drive back and forth to St-Bruno.

With the addition of a new gate at the entrance, visitors had to come inside the office to register, meaning that Sandra no longer had to run after them. We put her to work in the office, which was much busier now that it included the store and the snack bar. Not to mention everyone needing change for the arcade.

ON AUGUST 3RD, I was working at Pratt when I felt sick. I went to the washroom and found blood in my stools. There'd been a bit in them the day before, and I had dropped a case of beer from feeling woozy, but this time there was a lot of blood. I didn't want to wait too long like I had for the appendicitis, so I asked to have the rest of the day off and drove myself to the Montreal General Hospital. I parked haphazardly in front of the emergency doors and walked towards the entrance, but I passed out before I reached it.

When I woke up, they told me that I had a bleeding duodenal ulcer that had almost been fatal, and I was far from being out of the woods. I had already lost two-thirds of my blood over the past few days and needed transfusions and surgery immediately. They performed a gastrectomy, resecting my ulcer and saving my life. I could not believe that once more, the good Lord had decided to spare me.

I spent two weeks in the hospital, a week or so recovering, then went back to work. I told my secretary, Jeanette, how difficult it was for the employees to manage the campground office, the store, and the snack bar. I was contemplating getting rid of the snack bar, but that would mean our campers would have to drive over 10 kilometers to get to the nearest restaurant, Marie-Antoinette, in St-Hilaire. I was just sharing it as water cooler talk, but she offered to take it over with her daughter. We bought an old bus and moved all of the equipment into it so they could run the snack bar the following year.

TWENTY-TWO
1983

"We do not stop working and playing because we grow old. We grow old because we stop working and playing."
-George Bernard Shaw

In the calm before the start of another busy season at the campground, Barb and I decided to take a ten-day golfing vacation in Myrtle Beach. Once more, we went with Danny Smith and his wife Brenda. We took my beautiful Lincoln Continental Collector Series Limousine with a gold grille, which turned a lot of heads at work. Not just because it was a nice car, but it was the same one the president of Pratt drove, so people would do double-takes to make sure I wasn't him.

Danny Smith, me, Robert, and Cy.

We only stopped for gas and essentials, so with the four of us taking turns driving, we arrived in record time for days spent playing golf and lounging by the pool. On the last four days of our vacation, Barb's father met up with us, along with Ronnie, and a family friend named Cy. Ronnie, who missed Anne almost as soon as he arrived and wanted to go home early, was woefully surprised when we woke up to find Myrtle Beach covered in snow.

Barb and I throwing snowballs in Myrtle Beach.

The locals acted like they had never seen such a thing, so overnight, everything was closed. Golf courses, restaurants, movie theaters, gas stations...everything. All we could do was hang out at the hotel. Our golf game didn't improve, but we still managed to have a great time with the excellent company.

UPON OUR RETURN, I purchased the balance of the prime commercial land from Kendan Ltd. It was situated between the highway and the sites, so we thought it would be the perfect place to put a driving range for our campers. With the Vallée du Richelieu

Golf Course so close, it sounded like a sure thing. Unfortunately, it was a $100,000 investment that did not produce a good return. Apparently, most campers are not golfers.

Instead of being discouraged, we tried again, purchasing fifteen acres of wooded land behind the campground. Our plan was to promote Army Paintball Games, which were quickly rising in popularity. It was a way for us to offer another activity for our clients, and to increase our revenues with very little investment on our part, other than the land. We hit a goldmine! Not only did the campers enjoy it, but locals came all the time, venturing down to our snack bar for lunch. It was good for everyone's business!

AS THE CAMPGROUND GOT BUSIER, I found myself needing to take more vacations in the winters between them, using up more vacation days at Pratt than I ever had before. Barb and I left for three weeks in Florida.

Our first stop was with the Bloxham family in Fort Myers. Their house was just off the golf course of the Whiskey Creek gated community, so we got to practice our swings. We were slightly out of our element, as it was an executive golf course, making it very challenging. Still, we had a wonderful time.

Barb and I once more visited Walt Disney World without the kids, but they had been more than once by now. However, they hadn't seen the newly opened Epcot Centre, which I found very interesting. We treated ourselves and stayed in the Polynesian Village. It cost 115$ a night, but the linens were made of satin. It was expensive, but what an experience!

TWENTY-THREE
1984

"Ignoring things won't make them go away. It only makes it harder to face them when they finally come around."
-A. Meredith Walters

In 1984 I sold my Lincoln and downgraded to a Chrysler Fifth Avenue for $20 000. Clearly, the prices of cars were going up! About three weeks after I bought it, I was driving to work at Pratt, heading West on Highway 20. I noticed the vehicle in front of me was pulling a fairly large trailer, and thought, 'you're going the wrong way'. It was my first thought whenever I saw campers driving away from our campground. It was only when the trailer got unhitched that I started to worry, but by then it was already coming right at me.

I applied the brakes, hoping I could avoid it, and sighed with relief when I stopped inches from the trailer. Unfortunately, the 18-wheeler in back of me failed to do the same. His breaks took longer to kick in, so he crashed into the back of my new car. My driver seat, which was bolted to the frame, broke off so that I ended up on the back seat.

I managed to free myself from the safety belt and got out of the car as bystanders rushed to help me. I told them I was fine, but I couldn't help staring at my car, that was totaled, with smoke coming out of it. I took a few steps back, just in case it decided to blow up, and waited for the authorities, trying to digest the fact that I had yet again been in a traumatic accident, and survived.

After the police got my version of what happened, the paramedics insisted I go to the hospital to get checked out. I refused, explaining that I felt fine, and was already late for work as it was. They were reluctant, but they couldn't hold me, so they let me go.

It just so happened that Barb was on her way home from an appointment when she drove by the accident and recognized our car, so she picked me up and drove me to work. I had to lie and tell her the paramedics had cleared me, or she would have brought me right to the hospital.

I truly felt fine and had no pain when I left the crash site that day, but in hindsight, I should have listened to the paramedics.

ONE EVENING THAT SUMMER, we had a very bad storm. There were high winds and heavy rain while the campground was at full capacity. We were having dinner as a family, like we did every Sunday, when the wind brought down the main power line that was feeding our 550-volt transformer, as well as the main panels that supplied power for the whole campground. It was impossible to get an electrician on a Sunday evening, so I asked Linda's fiancé, Daniel Cavanagh, to help me out. There were a lot of Dannys in our family, so we usually called him Cazzie.

I knew it was a dangerous task, but I couldn't reconnect the broken mainline by myself. I needed him to hold the wire while I installed the birdie connector. As long as we were careful to not make contact with the other wires, or the steel pipe that was supporting the wires, we would be alright.

This was probably one of the stupidest things I have ever done in my life. I could have electrocuted myself, and my future son-in-law, getting us both killed. Thank God it worked out and the campground electricity was restored.

Linda and I on her wedding day.

Luckily, that risky night didn't deter Cazzie from joining the family. He and Linda got married on September 8th. The morning of the wedding, Linda stubbed her toe on a bureau while getting ready, effectively breaking it. She refused to see a doctor, or delay the wedding in any way. Instead, we taped it as best we could, and Linda pretended not to wince with every step she took. I have to admit I shed a few tears watching my firstborn get married and leave the nest, but Cazzie was a great guy, from a good family, and I knew he would take care of her.

As for Barbara, while Linda was on her honeymoon, she played the Teddy Pendergrass CD non-stop, so she could listen to Hold Me – which was Linda's first waltz – and cry. She eventually got over it, but it took a while.

IN THE FALL, Barb and I took a trip to Myrtle Beach with Roger and Kay. I was using my newly replaced Chrysler, while Roger drove down with his motorhome. Almost as soon as we arrived, I started having excruciating pains in my right arm and the back of my neck, residual damage from my car accident months earlier. Still, I kept playing golf and going to the beach, not wanting to ruin anyone's vacation.

After a week or so, I could no longer stand the pain, so I went to see a chiropractor. I went to see him every day that week, but to no avail. Ultimately, he recommended that I return home and go straight to the hospital.

You might be noticing a theme here, of me ignoring my body when it tells me I am stressed, of working through pain, and recklessly endangering myself in the name of being tough and strong. I hope you are also noticing that simple things tend to get complicated and hit me a lot harder than they should.

We had to cancel the rest of our vacation and returned home, covering 1740 kilometers in 19 hours, which did not help my pain. We drove straight to the

Montreal General Hospital's Emergency Room, but by then I was almost completely paralyzed on my right side.

I was admitted on November 2nd, and they soon performed a major surgery on my spine, specifically the R6 and R7 vertebraes, called the cloward procedure. It was very risky, as they removed pieces of bone from my hip, and cut my throat from ear to ear to get to the damaged vertebrae. They then placed the bones from my hip into my spine to secure it.

Even with the surgery a success, there was still a good chance I would be paralyzed, so I was advised not to move my head for 24-48 hours. They warned me that even in the best-case scenario, I wouldn't be able to rotate my head from side to side again. I would have to turn my whole upper body in order to look to my side. They considered it a minimum disability compared to having half of my body completely paralyzed, and I wholeheartedly agreed.

I waited until I was released to try and rotate my head. I did it very slowly at first, but continued doing daily head rotations, eventually regaining full mobility. I have kept it up to this day, over thirty years later.

Never doubt what determination can do.

UNFORTUNATELY, when I tried to bring my claim to the Société De l'Assurance Automobile, I was refused on the grounds that I didn't go to the hospital at the time of the accident, so they couldn't be sure that was when I got hurt. Upon release, I had a 7% loss of capacity on my right side, and there was nothing I could do about it. The only bright side was that it made me realize that all the money and power in the world cannot replace health. As they say, 'if you don't make time for your wellness, you'll be forced to make time for your illness', which I was.

TWENTY-FOUR
1985

"Success usually comes to those who are too busy to be looking for it."
-Henry David Thoreau

We were dealing with theft and vandalism, both at the campground, and at our house in St-Bruno. During the summer, Barb and I lived at the campground, and during the winter we were always in St-Bruno, leaving both homes unattended for extended periods of time. It was also getting busy at the campground, with the entire family travelling a half an hour each way after already working very long hours.

I figured it was about time that we sell the house in St-Bruno and move into the existing residence at the campground. We still had Sandra living with us, so I added a 40' X 40' extension to the existing residence, main office, and store. The only issue was that I only had forty days to design, plan, and implement the extension before the people who bought our house moved in. Not to mention the building permits.

It was no ordinary house that I designed, with three massive stone fireplaces; one in the dining room, one in the living room, and one in the garage. In addition to being able to fit all three of our cars, the garage would also be used as our recreation hall for parties. The campground was located in the suburbs, in an area that had many power failures during the winter months, and I didn't want my family to freeze. In addition, the building would house the washrooms, showers, and laundry facilities for the campers.

To achieve this almost impossible task of building the house in forty days, I had to use all of my skills from past experiences planning, scheduling and implementing. It also took all of my previous contacts, especially Paquin, without whom I never could have achieved it. I was stressed to my limit.

It required two shifts of tradesmen sixteen hours per day, seven days a week. Thank God I knew so many, but I still had to be on site to help them out, and to direct the project. Instead of traveling that year, I took my month of vacation time to see it through.

The house at the campground.

By July, the house was completed, and we were moved in. At Pratt, Royal Demers asked me to be in charge of his responsibilities as director of plant engineering while he took a week off. I was authorized to act on his behalf during this time. I was honored by the trust he put in me, and on Cloud Nine for the entire week he was gone. I couldn't help thinking of all the professional engineers and architects, or workers with MBAs and doctorate degrees that he passed up, choosing me instead.

THAT SUMMER, Linda took over the snack bar with Bobby. He already had a full-time job, so Linda was in charge of most of the day-to-day operations, with him bringing his daughter, Donna, to help almost every day. It was there that Donna would meet one of the campers, Dino Forbes, who would become her life partner, and the father of her two children. We were very sad to lose Linda in the office, but it was a godsend to have someone we trusted, who made delicious food, running our snack bar. I was proud that my daughter was following in my entrepreneurial footsteps of owning her own business.

IN THE FALL, Royal called me into his office to ask if I would consider taking a temporary position as Plant Superintendent. I would be replacing Gordie MacCaul until they found someone with the necessary qualifications to fill the position permanently. As in someone with an engineering degree.

Even though I knew it was way over my head, I accepted the position. My experience working with tradesmen and professionals in the past was certainly a big asset, as well as all of the courses I had been taking. I was continuously improving my education with

Management Courses at Concordia, and even the Dale Carnegie course, which taught me so much about Public Speaking and relating to people in a professional capacity.

THIS WAS the first year Barb didn't have to work at Kapetan Restaurant in the winter. The campground was doing well enough that once the season ended, Barb was able to spend her winters looking after the campground, which was much less busy. She deserved it after the crazy hours we worked all summer.

TWENTY-FIVE
1986

"Don't let schooling interfere with your education."
-Mark Twain

It took until 1986 for Pratt to find a qualified replacement for the Plant Superintendent. The man they chose, Yves Lachambre, was a brilliant mechanical engineer I had worked with before. He had the charisma of a leader, was career-driven, and had the ability to achieve success. I was sad to leave the position, but it couldn't have gone to a better man, and I was glad to work with him.

His promotion meant that his previous position as Senior General Supervisor was up for grabs, so I took on his responsibilities at Plant #1 and reported to him. I was receiving a lot of attention for filling in for and temporarily replacing senior management, but these 'promotions' never lasted. I had the knowledge and the experience to do the job, but I was lacking the required degrees to hold on to them once suitable candidates were found.

I had just been passed over for a permanent position, yet again, when Alex Gilliland, the Manager of Plant Engineering, told me I should apply for a Senior Project Manager position. I knew I didn't have the qualifications to hold the position permanently, but once more, I was assigned on a temporary basis, until they found someone better. Or at least with more degrees. Still, I was glad for the opportunity to prove myself, and I always learnt a lot from taking on these added responsibilities.

What I didn't know was that Alex had a trick up his sleeve that made this time entirely different; he had sent an application for me to join the Society of Manufacturing Engineers, based on my knowledge and years of experience. He waited until the application was approved to tell me about it, and I was shocked beyond words. It was all I could do not to burst into tears right there in my supervisor's office.

ROBERT WYNGAERT

SOCIETY OF MANUFACTURING ENGINEERS

This certifies that

ROBERT G WYNGAERT

being duly qualified was elected to the grade of

SENIOR MEMBER

in this Society an institution for the advancement
of scientific knowledge in the field of
Manufacturing Engineering

Being a Senior Manufacturing Engineer gave me the qualifications to officially be hired on a permanent basis in senior management positions. It was a significant achievement I never believed I would attain, considering my very limited formal education.

It was just a piece of paper when you got down to it, but I was so proud to join such a prestigious society. I was now allowed to legally sign documents as an engineer without needing someone else to sign off on them.

Still, I wasn't complacent in my position, or my studies. I continued to take every course and seminar from the society of manufacturing engineers that I could manage, to improve my knowledge, and for future promotions.

These courses came in handy when I was later

chosen to train the Corrective Action Team Leaders. As part of the Quality Plus Process, they were tasked to improve the response time, so we could correct deficiencies throughout our organization. It all worked out very well, and I was asked to write a few articles about the process, which were published in the Pratt & Whitney Internal News Bulletin. Alex even requested that I go with him to Halifax, Nova Scotia, as a consultant, to select qualified General Contractors to implement the construction of a new manufacturing plant. It was quite an honor.

ALTHOUGH THINGS WERE LOOKING up at work, moving to the campground meant that I no longer had anywhere to just relax and not stress. I went to work, where I loved the added prestige and responsibilities, but it could get stressful. Then I went home to a slew of new problems I had to take care of at the campground. My work life was hectic, not to mention the financial burden of running a business.

On the family front, in addition to running the snack bar at the campground, Linda graduated from Concordia University with a Bachelor of Arts, majoring in Economics. I was incredibly proud of her accomplishment, as she was the first Wyngaert to graduate university; a feat that wouldn't be repeated for quite some time. Sandra was doing well, working in the accounting department at Pratt, and dating a boy from Verdun named Jean-Paul Petrin. Danny, on the other hand, had many issues to deal with because of choices he had made. A lot of teenagers lose their way, and Danny had fallen into the wrong crowd, getting involved in drugs and other bad habits, that I just didn't know how to help him out of.

The stress of everything put together was becoming unmanageable, as so many of the problems were out of my control. If you've been paying attention, you know that my solution to problems like this is usually to ignore them and keep working until something forces me to stop. This time, it was a heart attack. Or at least the symptoms of one, that brought me to the intensive care unit in July.

My time in the hospital, as well as the months leading up to it, were a very dark period of my life. It got so bad that I seriously contemplated taking my own life. I was worn out and exhausted, and I couldn't see anything but continuous problems in my future, with no end in sight.

One of the planners in my department, Jean-Claude Poulin, came to visit me. He was one of the tradesmen who had helped me with the construction of my residence, and he recognized the signs of my depression, long before I owned up to them. He gave me a book by Og Mandino called The Greatest Miracle in the World, and told me it had helped him a lot when he was in a similar situation.

When the doctors finally discharged me, they put me on hypertension medication and told me I either had to change my life, or I would die. They might have been more delicate about it, but that was the general idea.

While I was recuperating, I read the book Jean-Claude gave me, then some other books by Mr. Mandino, also finding solace in the Serenity Prayer.

> "O Lord, grant me the serenity to accept the things I cannot change. The courage to change the things I can, and the wisdom to know the difference."

I was wasting so much stress on things I couldn't control, while ignoring the things that I could. I was in such a low point when I started reading them, but these books saved my life, giving me the hope that I could carry on. They changed my outlook on life, and helped me to make better choices in difficult situations, and with my life in general. They inspired me to be a better person.

I learnt not to pray for money, love, good health, fame, success, or happiness. You should pray for guidance, that you may be shown the way to acquire these things, and that is how your prayers will be answered.

I took all of this self-help and inspirational knowledge and wrote out letters to all of my nieces and nephews, sharing what I had learnt. I warned them to stay away from drugs, not from a place of preaching at them, but from a place of understanding. I told them what I had recently discovered, that the adversities they were experiencing would pass, and if they found a way through them instead of being overcome by them, they would be able to look back and laugh. I signed off with 'May God Bless You and Guide You'.

I also started writing letters to my family on their birthdays, instead of just giving them cards. Each letter would share all the milestones and adventures they had throughout the year, and be filled with what I hoped was wisdom and inspiration. Every time, I put 'May God Bless You and Guide You' at the bottom, with quotes to help them lead better lives. I sometimes worry they think it is silly, but they always seem to appreciate them. I have also been told by some of my nephews that they still have their letters to this day, and that they really helped them when they were going through hard times. If that is true for even one of them, then I did my job.

MY FRIENDS CALL ME BOB

I took the doctor's advice to change my lifestyle and take more vacations by purchasing my first motorhome, a 31-foot Bounder. It was 65 000$, but the freedom and getaways it provided were priceless. I began to take time out for myself, and to focus on my mental health, which I had always glossed over in the past. In addition to the works of Og Mandino, I fed my mind with Napoleon Hill's Think and Grow Rich, Dale Carnegie's How to Win Friends and Influence People, Denis Waitley's Seeds of Greatness, and especially Norman Vincent Peale's The Power of Positive Thinking. It truly encouraged me to be optimistic and grateful for what I had, because it could always be worse. I believe that these great authors played a big part in my success from that point on, and I thank them for the challenging and exciting life I continue to lead.

As for my son, he went through many rough patches, got lost and hit rock bottom, but then he found himself and turned his life around by going to rehab. He picked up many skills that other people his age never had the opportunity to, and capitalized on all of the experience he gained from working with me at the campground. Like me, he was never particularly good in school, so as my father did with me, I had him doing all of the manual work around the campground. He found his calling and was in his glory, doing anything mechanical, electrical, plumbing, or simply operating heavy equipment. He excelled.

Danny is probably one of the main reasons I continued to invest all the profits from the campground back into the business. We purchased a tractor, a golf cart, replaced electrical lines, and paved the main road. I obviously wanted to provide better facilities for my campers and more revenues for myself, but I needed to secure this stable career for my son.

WITH DANNY TAKING care of the grounds and the girls in the office, Barb and I were able to begin our new lifestyle of travelling frequently, especially once the camping season was over. We went on many summer getaways, then escaped to warmer destinations in the colder months. We planned to continue to travel like that for the rest of our lives.

TWENTY-SIX
1987

"One day your life will flash before your eyes. Make sure it's worth watching."
-Anonymous

In the spring of 1987, Barbara and I got the shock of our lives when we found out that she was pregnant. None of our children were planned, they were all happy accidents, but this was something altogether different. Our oldest child was married and our youngest was twenty-two!

Barbara had an aunt who was born to a mother of a certain age, and had the mental capacity of a seven year old as a result. Barb did not want to risk the same thing happening, but I was a catholic, and couldn't let her do differently.

We told the kids, who found it absolutely hilarious. One day we were at the dinner table, enjoying a meal together, when they all took out baby rattles to tease us. They thought they were pretty clever, but we weren't laughing.

At the time, Linda was working for a radio station, attempting to secure advertisements, and she hated it. Nearly every morning on her way to work, she would have to pull over onto the side of the road so she could throw up. We wondered if she could be pregnant, but she insisted it was because she hated her job so much that it was making her sick.

Before long, Barbara miscarried, which at this point in her life, she saw as a relief. Almost immediately after, we found out that Linda was expecting our first grandchild, which made a lot more sense.

SINCE BARB and I needed to travel for my health, Linda gave up the snack bar, so Bobby could run it with his sister, Carol, and Linda could man the office with Sandra while we went away. It was around this time that the Government told us we had to immediately stop the Paintball Games in the Woods. Apparently, it didn't comply with the zoning of the land, which we later found out was code for 'the Vallée du

Richelieu Golf Club is worried the golfers will be disturbed by what happens in the woods half a mile away'. The Paintball Games had been a lifesaver in the early days when we had no campers, but things had gradually started to pick up, and we no longer needed them to drum up business. It was sad for our campers, and the snack bar, but not as devastating as it would have been years before.

Me, Roger, Kay, Kenny, Al, Phil, Louise, Diane, and Barbara.

On the first weekend in June, Barb and I took our motorhome to Plattsburgh, where we met up with Roger, Kay, Georges and Denise. It was a lovely weekend trip, but there was a lake there with green water. The color wasn't so bad, but the broken beer bottles and pollution ensured that no one wanted to go swimming. Except for me. I can't say if it was because I was so eager to enjoy the summer, or if I was trying to show that it would take more than a bit of garbage to scare me, but I do remember that Barb made me shower before she would let me kiss her.

LATER ON THAT WEEK, when we were back home, my right leg took on this reddish color that Barb described as 'raw meat'. So, on June 11th, I went to Pierre Boucher Hospital and was diagnosed with cellulitis erysipelas-streptococcus group A, an infection similar to flesh-eating disease. They treated me with a very strong antibiotic, both intravenously and in pill form, for six days.

While I was in the hospital, I read a lot of self-help books and ones on positive thinking, but when my course of antibiotics was done, my leg looked the same. They concluded their treatment wasn't effective.

Their fear was that it would spread, so if they weren't able to get rid of it, they were going to have to amputate my leg. I could not let this happen. I read up and did my own research, discovering an article on tick bites. Apparently, they caused similar problems and could be very difficult to diagnose, as most doctors wouldn't consider it unless they saw a bite. I knew that I had been swimming in polluted waters, so I was relieved I figured it out.

I told my doctors, expecting them to give me the proper treatment so I could go home, legs intact, but they did not listen. They kept me on a course of treatment that was wasting precious time, wasn't working, and might be doing me more damage than good. I was not pleased.

As they had no intentions of changing the medication they were treating me with, I checked myself out of the hospital, against medical advice. I set out to find a doctor who would prescribe me a more effective drug to treat my disease, that I believed to be a tick bite, but it was no use. I went to three different doctors, and each one insisted I continue with the original antibiotic that wasn't working.

Every day, my leg got worse. I was desperate to find a doctor who would prescribe me another drug, even if it wasn't the one I suggested, just to try something different that might actually work.

On July 13th, I went back to my first doctor, Dr. Jean-Marie Martel, and begged him to look at the article I had read, showing him that it was from a medical journal. He was reluctant, but finally agreed to give me a prescription for a drug called Duricep, which they usually used to treat skin infections like Lyme disease.

By the time I went to my follow up appointment with Dr. Martel, I had made an unbelievable recovery. He could not believe how much I had improved. My energy was returning, and the raw meat look of my right leg had disappeared. He told me it was the first time in his professional career that a patient successfully recommended his own medication. If he is still practicing today, I am sure it wasn't his last.

I WANT to take a moment to say that in my life, I have been faced with the most incompetent doctors imaginable, but graced with the most incredible ones as well. A lot of patients go to doctors with crazy theories about what is wrong with them, so I understand not listening to every suggestion a patient makes. But I owe my leg, and possibly my life, to the fact that one doctor finally agreed to look outside the box and try something different. It took a hell of a lot of convincing. Someone less confident, or more polite, would have let the doctors cut off their leg. It is imperative that you advocate for yourself, because most of the time, no one else will.

IT WAS a slow and gradual journey to regain my health by exercising daily and body building with weights. It was a miracle that my leg was not amputated, but I think the huge quantities of the wrong antibiotic may have created problems with my immune system for years to come. Either way, I needed to get my body into top shape with Linda being pregnant. I was also promoted to a higher grade of Senior Project Manager, in recognition for my extraordinary effectiveness and value control proposals, which saved Pratt hundreds of thousands of dollars. I was on Cloud Nine.

CHELSEA RACHEL CAVANAGH was born on November 30th, 1987, making me the happiest man on earth. She was the greatest gift I ever could have wished for; perfect in every way. This miracle of life was the beginning of a new generation in our family, giving me a completely new outlook on life. Like her mother's birth years before, Chelsea's gave us a new purpose. We wanted nothing more than to experience the joy of our first grandchild growing up, and to witness all of her great achievements. We knew, even then, that there would be many.

MY FRIENDS CALL ME BOB

Me and Chelsea.

ROBERT WYNGAERT

IN DECEMBER, I had knee surgery so I could better take care of the campground, and keep up with Chelsea once she got to walking.

TWENTY-SEVEN
1988

"The difference between who I am and who I want to be is only separated by what I do."
-Unknown

My doctor recommended I find a way to lose weight to help control my blood pressure, so I joined Weight Watchers in 1988. Linda, Barb's sister Carol, and Danny's girlfriend Lynn joined as well. Lynn was the daughter of Mike Blanchard, who worked with me back in my bouncer days, and the kids all grew up together, so we were absolutely thrilled that she and Danny were dating. Barb and Sandra were already lifetime members of Weight Watchers, so we had a lot of support, and the added motivation of Sandra's upcoming wedding. Not to mention, Sandra would practically pull food out of our mouths if we tried to overindulge. My health continued to improve as I lost more and more weight. I never made it to my goal, but I got to 199 lbs, which was the lowest I had been in a while.

Me, Sandra, JP, and Barbara.

Sandra married JP Petrin on April 30th, with a reception at Hélène de Champlain. Contrary to the conventions of the time, Sandra had both Barbara and I give her away. I had never seen this done before, but Sandra felt that we both raised her, and both deserved to be up there with her.

Before the ceremony, their original priest was sent away, so the replacement had a meeting to discuss everything with her and JP. When Sandra mentioned that there were some AA members in the family and she preferred to not offer wine, the priest informed her that he had already ordered some, but that he would take care of it. Well, it seems that by 'take care of it', he meant that he would keep the wine for himself, and drink it before the ceremony. It was the longest wedding ceremony I had ever been to, and while Sandra had told him she was nervous and didn't want to say more than 'I do', he had her repeat every word, which made her even more nervous, as she kept giggling. So much so that she tried to put the ring on JP's wrong hand. It definitely didn't go according to plan, but the reception afterwards was wonderful. The food was delicious, and there were no broken toes, so everyone was able to dance and have a good time.

Back then, I had my doubts about JP, but over the years he has proven to be a reliable and thoughtful son-in-law, who is always ready to lend a hand and will bend over backwards to help us out.

IN JUNE, to help improve my public speaking abilities, I joined the Teleglobe Toastmasters International Club. It was a great asset for me, as more and more of my new assignments required expressing myself in groups of people. Sometimes rather large ones, such as when I was sent to represent Pratt & Whitney Canada instead of my supervisor, at a conference for managers from all divisions of United Technologies.

It was held in Hartford, Connecticut, and I was probably the only person in the group of sixty or so representatives who didn't have an engineering degree, or better. Due to time restraints, they randomly selected six managers to go on stage and report the cost of maintaining the facilities that came under their responsibility. As luck would have it, I was chosen to go first. Although I was well prepared and had all of my figures, there is no way I could have pulled it off without those public speaking courses.

IN SEPTEMBER, we took a trip out to Lac Labelle, where Danny and Lynn owned a cottage. Linda and Cazzie also came, bringing little Chelsea, who made every occasion brighter and more fun. The only way you could reach their cabin, which was on an island without electricity, was by boat, then up a wooden staircase on a hillside.

As the sun was setting and we called it a day, I was the one holding Chelsea to go back to the boat. They were still renovating, so there was no railing around the balcony to show you where the staircase was. Although it was dark by then, I was confident I was stepping in the right place, until I fell into the void. It was like the world around me stopped as I tried to protect Chelsea in my arms, hearing my daughter scream in a way you never want to hear a mother scream.

I rolled down the hill for what felt like forever, but it was also over in an instant. I immediately got up and checked on Chelsea, who was crying fiercely. We brought her to the hospital as fast as we could, given our location, and concluded that she had been crying from the shock. There wasn't even a scratch on her!

I, on the other hand, was a complete mess. I paid for it in the days to come, but I would have given my life many times over to protect that little girl.

Barbara, Chelsea, Cazzie, Linda, and I.

ROBERT WYNGAERT

In December, I went to hear Og Mandino speak in person at Place Bonaventure. I had fallen in love with his books, but hearing him in person made me even more inspired to continue on this path to live the better life of my dreams.

TWENTY-EIGHT
1989

"Don't back down just to keep the peace. Standing up for your beliefs builds self-confidence and self-esteem."
-Oprah Winfrey

We had left our Bounder in Florida for the second year in a row, and yet again, we experienced theft. Last year it was our bicycles that were missing, while this year we lost binoculars and got vandalized. Roger had bought a mobile home at Candlelight park the year before, so when the one across from him was put on sale, Barb and I jumped on it.

Barbara and I.

We were in Florida in April when Barb's father suffered a heart attack, and was put in critical care. She flew home immediately, while I joined her with the Bounder in a few days. Her father was a terrible patient, as he hated being alone. Someone had to be at his side the whole time he was in there. Thankfully, it wasn't long before Mr. Thompson was out of the hospital and back to his usual self.

AT PRATT, I was assigned to a major project; the dehumidification of plant #1. It had a factory floor of approximately one million square feet, but every time the temperature reached 90 degrees Fahrenheit, everyone inside had to stop working until it went back to safer levels. This resulted in millions of dollars in lost production hours, every year. They were happy to spend 15 million dollars to fix it once and for all.

I attended my first meeting to plan, direct, and implement the project with the chief of our mechanical engineering department, Guy Jobidon, and the consultant group, Pageau Morel. They had already been working on their design for many months, but when I looked at the drawing and specifications, I saw a lot of opportunities to make it better, or at least more cost effective.

I have noticed that even if a task could take fifteen minutes to do, if you give someone an hour to complete it, most people will take the whole hour. The same goes for money. If you give them a certain budget to accomplish something, most people will use it. I don't know if it is because I grew up fighting for every penny, or because I owned apartment buildings, a restaurant and a campground with next to no budget, but I always asked myself: How can I do this better? How can I be more efficient? How can this cost less money?

Sandra, Linda, and Danny with Brutus.

For instance, United Aircraft Technologies had a program called Value Control Proposals, where all employees were invited to submit cost-saving or problem-solving ideas. If the company thought your idea had merit, or if they implemented it, you would receive an award, which sometimes translated to a cash prize. The first time I won, we bought the family a St-Bernard dog we called Brutus. The kids weren't the best at taking care of him, and I didn't want Barb to be saddled with all of the responsibilities, so I found a way to automate some of them. I made Brutus a special trough, with a valve that linked to our water line, so he got fresh water simply by pressing his tongue down on the plate. I also put Brutus' leash on a steel clothesline, so he could wander the yard freely, and we wouldn't have to walk him as often. I worked hard, but I also worked smart.

This was posted around Pratt & Whitney around this time.

I REQUESTED MAJOR CHANGES, but my coworkers were not pleased by my initiative, and refused to change anything. I wrote a letter to Alex and explained to him that I couldn't manage the project the way it was designed. He told me this was insubordination and grounds for dismissal.

I probably should have shut my mouth then and played nice, now that I had voiced my reluctance. However, my word and my reputation were all I had, and I couldn't put them at stake for a project I didn't think would succeed. So, I wrote another letter, this time outlining my plan, and how it would save them millions of dollars. I staked my reputation and my livelihood on it, saying they could fire me if I was wrong, and implement their original design. Alex told me I was the most tenacious guy he'd ever met.

He discussed it with Royal, still the director of Plant Engineering, and the two of them tried, to no avail, to convince Mr. Jobidon to consider my proposal. According to him, his project had been approved by a top-rated consultant firm, so if any changes were made, his entire department would refuse to support us. This put Alex in a very difficult situation.

Luckily, Alex was a very intelligent man who had a lot of confidence in me, so he set up a meeting with the consultants, engineers, and president of Pageau Morel so they could review my proposal compared to theirs.

The president, Mr. Lefebvre brought me to fancy, expensive restaurants for our meetings, probably to convince me to accept their plans, but I held my ground. I believe Mr. Lefebvre was an educated man, who saw the benefits and value in my proposal, but couldn't let his team down, so he asked me to approve the original plans. I told him I would rather be fired on the spot than to approve their design. He got up, gave me a firm handshake and said he had rarely met a person like me.

I didn't know I had won him over until I arrived in our next meeting and saw that the drawings, specifications, and budget had been revised to implement my proposed design. I had to take full responsibility for the project, and accomplish it without the support of the mechanical plant engineering department, as Mr. Jobidon still didn't agree with my revisions. It was a lot of pressure, but I felt confident in the proposal, and was anxious to prove Mr. Jobidon wrong.

WE WERE lucky to have another busy summer at the campground, but Barb and I escaped in the motorhome many weekends, and even managed to spend a week at our new mobile home together in July.

Lynn, Danny, Barbara, Me, Ethel and Mike Blanchard.

Danny and Lynn got married on September 9th. The girls had been so upset that Barb didn't buy her wedding dress, so they couldn't wear it at their own weddings. To remedy this, Sandra bought her wedding dress, in the hopes that someone —such as her daughter – would one day wear it. Well, she didn't have to wait that long, because Lynn walked down the aisle looking beautiful in her sister-in-law's dress.

Our kids didn't live together after their weddings like I did with Georges, but it made me really happy to see how close everyone was, especially the girls. Lynn had started working for us at the campground, so having the three of them working together all summer made them more like sisters than sisters-in-law.

I was so happy to see all of my children happy and settled in their new lives. Linda, Cazzie and Chelsea moved into a new house in Beloeil, the town where Sandra was already living with JP. Sandra was expecting our second grandchild, and we couldn't wait to see Chelsea become a big cousin. Danny and Lynn had even purchased a home in Saint-Mathieu-de-Beloeil, less than five minutes from the campground. Things were going well for the Wyngaerts!

TWENTY-NINE
1990

"What doesn't kill you, makes you stronger."
-Friedrich Nietzsche

On April 11th, Sandra gave birth to a baby girl, Amanda Lynn Petrin, in the middle of a snowstorm. She was another bright spot in our lives, that helped me forget the stress of the dehumidification project. Chelsea was blonde, so people said she looked like Barbara, but with her dark features, Amanda looked like me. I owned it, even though JP insisted it came from him. Her hair quickly went very curly, so I reminded everyone how curly my hair was when I was a baby. Barbara and I were thrilled to have two granddaughters to spoil!

Me and Amanda.

The dehumidification project at Pratt took about a year to complete, from conception to implementation. As our deadline got closer and closer, my stress levels went higher and higher, until I had a heart attack on May 1st, the day we were supposed to put our new system to work. I was rushed to the Montreal General Hospital and underwent a coronary angioplasty to unblock my right artery. I spent twelve days in an intensive care unit, which was very stressful for everyone.

It was while I was in the hospital that I was told the system didn't function as planned when they launched it. On the day I was released from the hospital, my family wanted me to come home and keep resting, but I insisted on dropping by the plant so I could see what went wrong.

After reviewing the start-up plan of action, I noticed that the old ventilation and air systems were not disabled, as I had requested. I personally escorted one of our maintenance electricians to all the penthouses to ensure the old systems were put out of commission. They weren't needed with the new dehumidification system, so I had the fuses removed and the wires cut.

We restarted my new system and it functioned perfectly. It was quite a relief, but an even greater accomplishment. My plan saved the company millions of dollars, on a project that would save the company millions of dollars every year by completely eliminating the downtime.

After the new system had been running for a few weeks, the President, Dave Caplan, invited me to his office to thank me for implementing such a difficult project without even stopping production. He couldn't believe the results.

He brought me out onto the floor and said, "I believe the shop is more comfortable than my office!"

THIS ENTIRE PROCESS was a big advantage for my career as senior project manager, and gained me the respect of my supervisors, peers, consultants and subordinates. Even Mr. Jobidon!

It was one of the most significant events of my life. I want to say the respect meant more to me than the salary increase, but I don't want to lie, so I'll say it was a very close second at the time.

Now though, it is entirely the respect I earned and the pride I felt in the accomplishment that I remember.

I WAS SOON ASSIGNED to another dehumidification project, this time for Plant #5. They involved me from the very beginning, allowing me to contribute to the conception, as well as the implementation. I also got to define the plans to do the same in the warehouse of Plant #1. Their goal was always to eliminate down time, but mine was to complete the projects on time and under budget. I succeeded every time.

I no longer had to worry about proving my competence or working harder and longer to feel like I earned my salary. I had often experienced my own imposter syndrome, being the only non-engineer in the room, but I now felt like I belonged. We were all there to improve the efficiency of the company, so it could remain competitive in the market and earn world recognition for their gas turbine engines, and I was doing my part.

Building our retirement home.

Now that we had two granddaughters, Barb didn't like the idea of having our vacation home so far away from them. So, we sold our mobile home at

Candle Light Park and purchased 1.2 acres of lakefront land in Rouses Point, New York. It was the perfect spot, close enough to home that we would never be far from the family, but far enough away that the campground problems couldn't get to us, with beautiful Lake Champlain in our backyard. The land cost $47,000, and we hired a local General Contractor to build our dream retirement residence for $100 000.

Due to my experience dealing with contractors and writing specifications, I made everything very clear for him, including the delivery dates. However, I do not believe that his team understood any of my schedules or specifications. They were nothing like the tradesmen I was used to dealing with back home.

When I saw that they were never going to deliver what I wanted, I cancelled the contract. I still paid $100 000 for the man-hours and materials he claimed I owed him for, because I did not want to have any problems with him. It was frustrating to pay for a finished job when it was barely halfway done.

Once his team was out, I took over, not used to projects being off-schedule, over-budget, and with poor workmanship. I relied on old friends and family to help me finish the project. I am so grateful to Marco Bissonnette, Raymond Huard, Bobby and Moe, as well as my family, who were all instrumental in the building of our new home.

· · ·

ROBERT WYNGAERT

WITH TWO GRANDBABIES in the family, we made sure to truly celebrate the holidays, inviting the extended Wyngaert family over for a gift exchange on December 8th. Danny volunteered to be our Santa, and Chelsea and Amanda were so excited! The older kids kept trying to figure out who was playing Santa Claus or see if he was real, but Barb told me I wasn't allowed to tell them the truth.

In my defense, she probably confused them more than I would have by continuously calling our Santa Claus, 'Danny'. Every time, Sandra or Linda would remind her, "Danny isn't here, mum, he went ski-dooing."

THIRTY
1991

"At the end of life, what really matters is not what we bought, but what we built; not what we got, but what we shared; not our competence, but our character; and not our success, but our significance. Live a life that matters. Live a life of love."
-Unknown

By the beginning of 1991, Linda, Lynn, and Sandra were all expecting. It started with Linda, who was due in the Spring. Then Danny and Lynn announced they were due in the Summer. By the time Sharon, Barb's niece, shared her happy news, Sandra decided there was no way all of her closest friends were getting pregnant and having babies without her.

ROBERT WYNGAERT

Rikki

Rikki Christine Cavanagh was born on March 31st, the best belated birthday and Easter present I ever could have asked for.

Steve

Steven Michel Wyngaert was born on July 16th, the spitting image of his father.

Paul

Paul Ryan Petrin was born with the umbilical cord around his neck on October 30th. He gave us all a terrible scare, but thank god everything turned out okay.

It was so wonderful to have three grandchildren born so close together, discovering milestones and growing with each other, under the protective and watchful eyes of Chelsea and Amanda.

When the time had come for Sandra to go back to work after her maternity leave for Amanda, she realized she really didn't want to leave her daughter to someone else's care. So, she decided to be a stay-at-home mom when she wasn't working for us, and ran a family day care service. She started with Chelsea, got Rikki once Linda went back to work, then got Steve the following year. The five of them were biologically cousins, but they were much more like siblings. Watching them together was my greatest joy, as family is everything.

WE EVENTUALLY COMPLETED construction on our lake house, but we had to sell the Bounder motorhome to cover the additional costs. Barb didn't want to be away from the grandchildren for too long anyway, so we just spent a lot of weekends at the lake house, mostly accompanied by the kids and grandkids.

THE CAMPGROUND WAS GETTING BUSIER every year, but winters were pretty quiet, so Danny tried his hand at a woodcutting business. I let him cut the trees on our lands, destroying roughly fifteen acres for absolutely no profit. It was a failure, financially and as a business venture, but it was also a source of pride for me to see my son working so hard to accomplish something. I was finally beginning to see a return on my latest investment of the campground, but I went through a lot of failures and bad investments before I got there. It was nice to see my son taking on the same path, although I knew from experience it could be a long and very hard one.

AT PRATT, I was doing so well that they routinely assigned me the most difficult projects that other people didn't want to take. I was very touched by the confidence they had in me, but I sometimes wished I could just relax with one of the smaller, easier projects that didn't involve so much pressure. My current project was a ten-million-dollar expansion of Plant #5 for a new cleaning, plating, and waste treatment facility which should be completed within two years.

MY FRIENDS CALL ME BOB

Me and Rikki in front of the poster.

Whenever we went out with Amanda around this time, someone inevitably stopped us to see if she was the girl from the commercials. Our little granddaughter was a local celebrity thanks to her appearing in a series of commercials for the local malls known as the Fashion Centers. She did things like jump on a bed and learn to shave, each one more adorable than the last. As for the other grandkids, they didn't care so much about the life-size cutouts and posters as the fact that they'd been allowed to ride with Santa in the mall's Christmas parade.

. . .

ROBERT WYNGAERT

NOW THAT WE had so many babies around, we stopped the big group Christmas parties, and I played Santa, without a costume, just handing out gifts to everyone. To be honest, we spent most of the day getting the gifts out of their packaging and assembling them for the kids, but I wouldn't have it any other way!

THIRTY-ONE
1992

"What we call failure is not the falling down but the staying down."
-Mary Pickford

Barb and I went to visit Roger at his house in Florida in February, then came home and got to work on renovating the kitchen and basement at the campground, so Barb could get her double oven, and I could fix up my office. We also decided part of the basement would be used as the kids' playroom, now that there were five of them.

For Amanda's birthday, Barbara made her a bear-shaped cake. In addition to her share of wedding cakes, Barb made the most beautiful – and delicious – cake creations for our family. This was not the first time we got the bears, as it was Chelsea's favorite cake as well. What made this time different is that instead of a single comment from Bobby, as happened the previous year, everyone joined in. Barb started, telling the girls that they should kiss the bear. Danny told them it was the bear's birthday as well, so he led Chelsea and Amanda in a rendition of "Happy Birthday Teddy Bear!" I obviously played my part, egging them to give the bear a hug, finding it incredibly funny when they girls realized Barb would need to cut the cake so they could eat it. That's when it became less funny, as the girls started crying, refusing to eat it. Sandra accused me of starting it, but years later, when we watched the home movies, we were all shocked to see it was Barbara!

AT PRATT, I completed the dehumidification of Plant #5 and wrote an article in the Pratt news bulletin about it. We finished within our 4-million-dollar budget, and on schedule, thanks to my three-shift system of working on it seven days a week. Start to finish, it only took ten weeks, meaning we were done before the heat of the summer months could cost the company millions in mandatory work stoppages.

Irene and Roger in Florida.

In November, we went to Florida again, this time with Irene. While there, we decided to take a walk on the beach, to initiate her to the 'Florida Shuffle'. It's a dance move, named for the way you need to walk in ankle deep water to avoid surprising a sting ray. Irene didn't get the hang of it, as she suddenly screamed out before fainting. I thought she must be dead, as my heart stopped, and I rushed to her side. We called an ambulance, who drove right onto the sandy beach to get her. We had to follow the ambulance in Roger's car, waiting days for her to recover. She was very sick for weeks, even after we brought her home.

FOR CHELSEA'S BIRTHDAY, to avoid a repeat of the bear incident, we stuck to a ballerina-shaped cake, one that was clearly a picture, not someone the girls would get attached to.

THIRTY-TWO
1993

"You are never too old to set another goal or to dream a new dream."
-C.S. Lewis

I started my year off with a few trips to the hospital, though thankfully they were both planned. On January 28th, I had surgery on my knee, then on February 3rd, I got lasik surgery on my eyes. I am a strong proponent of investing in yourself, which comes in many shapes and sizes. For me it mostly meant investing in courses and my education, as I was constantly trying to make up for the fact that I never made it to high school when I was a child. As I got older, it meant investing in my retirement fund, and ensuring that Barb and I would be taken care of. Now, I was investing in my physical health and fitness, so I could continue doing the things I needed to do without being encumbered.

Me and Melanie.

Many years later, when my niece, Melanie, wanted to get that same lasik surgery, she came to me and asked for a loan. I saw that she was investing in herself, both in her health and in her confidence, so I decided to help her out. I lent her the money, but instead of having her pay me back with interest, I had her invest it with my daughter, Linda. My niece opened an account and started to send money into it every month, thinking it would go towards paying me back. After a year or so, she had saved the amount that I lent her, but instead of taking it back, I let it be the start of her investing in her own future. The initial amount may not have been that much, but she continued to send money into that account, as faithfully as if it were a bill, and was eventually able to buy herself a condo because of it.

My last project at Pratt was the expansion of Plant #5. Once more, I completed it on time and within budget, my reputation intact as I took an early retirement. Or at least I retired from Pratt, as I was going to be working as an independent businessman at the campground full time. And hopefully spending lots of time with my family.

Amanda, me, and Rikki after the blizzard.

We had quite the adventure in early March, when we went for a weekend trip to our house on Lake Champlain. On Saturday night, the news stations announced an overnight blizzard, with three inches of snow expected every hour. We debated leaving, but figured we would rather drive home after it passed instead of while it was raging.

This turned out to be a terrible idea, as the mountains of snow surrounding the house were nearly as tall as me the next morning. Our cars were completely buried, making it clear that no one was leaving any time soon. It was a country lake house, and there was the equivalent of an entire city block to get from the house to the road at the end of our driveway. Not something you can easily shovel by hand.

I knew that my neighbor had a snow blower, so I got bundled up and headed into the freezing cold and trekked through snow that came up to my waist across more than a hundred feet. Sandra, who started filming me almost as soon as I left, thought I kept looking back to pose and give her better angles, but in truth the wind was so cold that it felt like tiny knives digging into my skin, and I needed to turn away so I could breathe.

When I finally got to my neighbor's, he told me he would be glad to lend me his snowblower, only it wasn't working. I tried not to feel defeated as I set back into the blizzard, returning empty handed from my heroic mission.

After breakfast, I went out to shovel, joined by Cazzie, Linda, JP, and Sandra on rotation. Someone always had to stay in with the kids, and it was exhausting work. It took us nearly the entire day just to dig out the car and ten feet of driveway. The surrounding piles of snow were so high you could hardly see over them.

On Monday morning, we got up early to shovel again, as the kids really needed to get back to work, and I was in my last few weeks at Pratt. Thank God we saw a city snow plow and were able to convince him to clear our driveway once he was done with the main road. Still, our problems were far from over, as the city plow got stuck, and had to wait for a tow truck to get them out before they could continue plowing. Still, we eventually made it home, with photographic and video evidence to show their bosses it was impossible for us to have made it in sooner.

MY LAST DAY WITH PRATT & Whitney was, quite fittingly, March 30th – my fifty-fifth birthday.

ROBERT WYNGAERT

Mr. Abedda, one of my co-workers who painted the portrait of me you see in the background.

On April 2nd, my retirement party was held at Kenny Wong's restaurant. I had been to a few of these before, so I was expecting a dozen, maybe twenty-five people would come, we would have a delicious meal, then Barb and I would go home and get into the routine of running our campground.

Instead, I showed up and found 126 of my supervisors, peers, subordinates, consultants, tradesmen, and family members. Barb was there with the kids and their significant others, Georges came with Irene, Marilyne with Manfred, Bobby with Moe, Kenny with Louise...they all came to support me! I was shocked, not just that so many people had been invited, but that most of them had shown up, even with the terrible snowstorm we had that day.

I could never find the words to tell all the people in that room how much I appreciated their participation in such a wonderful celebration. I wish I could thank every single person who contributed to my success at Pratt & Whitney, both big and small.

Nicole Comeau and Muriel Leger, who did most of the work to organize the party, did a fabulous job, and really went the extra mile to make everything perfect, from the guest list to the decorations, the venue and the food. They even hired a professional photographer and assembled a photo album that they gave me several weeks after the event.

It seemed like everyone was sad to see me go, but wished me continued success in my future endeavors. All of the speakers had praise and compliments for me regarding my career, except for Mr. Leger, who told a story he found funny, but I did not. Apparently, he had asked Barbara what my best quality was, and she said I was a great provider. When he said everyone provides and that answer doesn't count, Barb supposedly said I had a quick temper. Which isn't a quality at all. I was not pleased, but everyone there laughed.

In addition to the photo album, I was presented with priceless gifts on the night of the party. There was a hand-painted portrait of me, a wood sculpture, a Brass eagle (Pratt's trademark), a painting of Plant #5 (the last project I managed), and a beautiful Canon Camera.

AFTER THE PARTY, Barb and I flew to Florida to visit Roger and have a nice vacation before a busy season at the campground.

Someone who didn't know me might have assumed that this would be my easiest summer yet, since I wouldn't have to juggle multiple jobs, but it was anything but. I finally had the time and energy to devote myself fully to the campground, making plans and implementing all of the ideas I had to make it better. Every year so far had been better than the last, but this year we broke records, increasing our revenues by 10%!

Some people commented on how lucky I was to have such a successful enterprise, but I told them, 'the harder I work, the luckier I get'. Being at the campground day in and day out also allowed me to see just how true it is that you can't succeed on your own. I never could have accomplished my dreams without the help of my beautiful wife, and my wonderful children, who not only supported me in my pursuit, but worked hard every day to make it a reality. They deserve a large chunk of the credit.

· · ·

IN THE FALL, I received a call from Jacques Bissonnette, the president of Soprin Consultant Firm. He heard that I retired, and after all of our dealings together, both at Pratt and with his firm for the restaurant, he was wondering if I would like to work with him.

It was an incredible offer. Before retiring, I wouldn't have dreamed of saying no to him, but I had big plans for the campground now. We were in the process of making a new storage area, where the spots would each have a number, and it would be fenced in for extra security. Jacques told me the project he was thinking of me for was to manage the construction of aircraft engine test cells at the Rolls Royce Facilities in Montreal, which sounded like a dream come true.

I was leaving for Cape Coral, to visit Roger, so I told him I would make my decision and call him back upon my return. As it turns out, we got back from Florida just in time for the birth of our sixth and final grandchild. Eric Robert Wyngaert was born to Danny and Lynn on November 17th, 1993.

ROBERT WYNGAERT

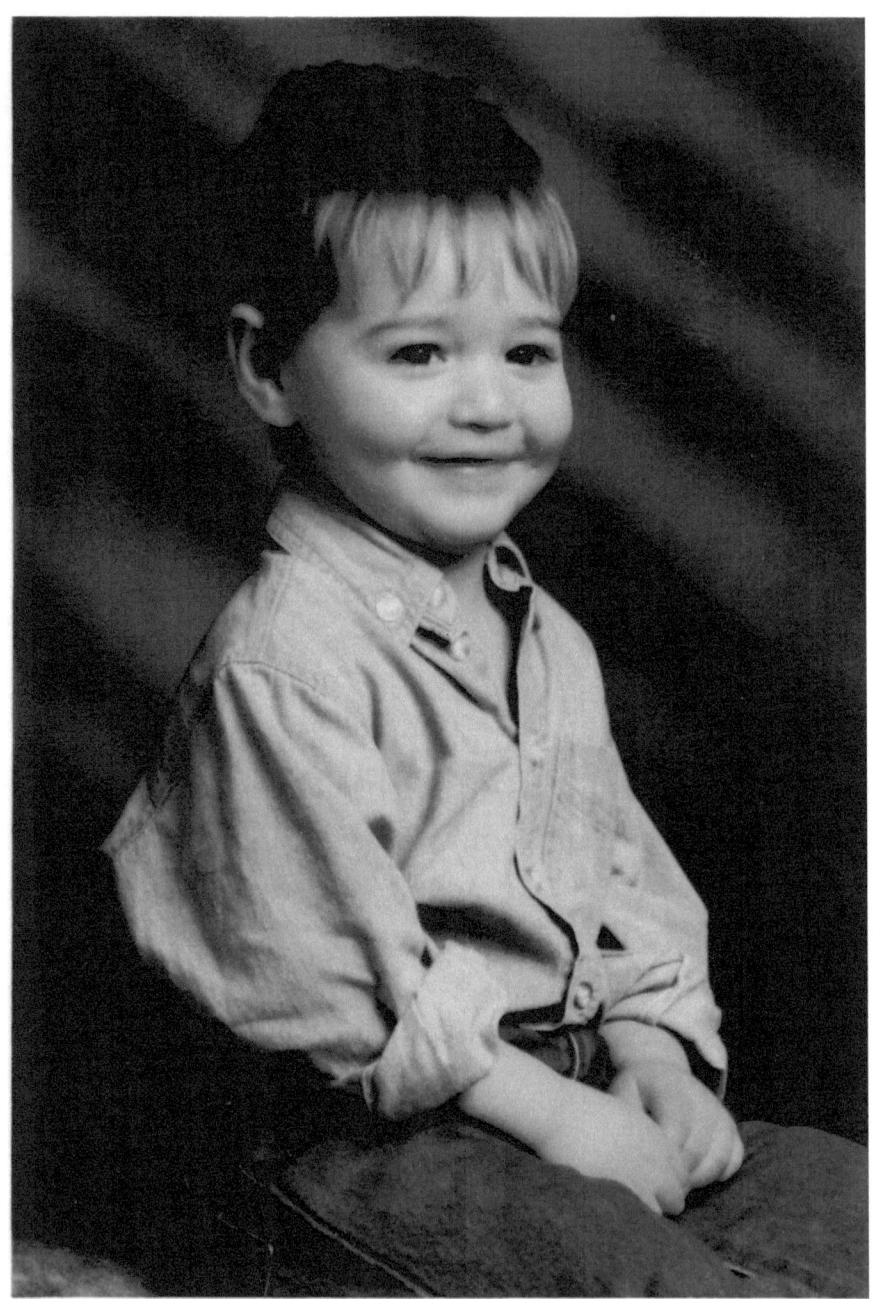

Eric

The creation of life has always given me a high, as I believe that family is the most important thing. I analyzed the pros and cons of Jacques' offer, and ultimately decided to refuse it. From a business standpoint, I was in the process of making a large investment in my campground, and I wanted to see it through. I wanted to bring Camping Alouette to another level by achieving a five-star rating across the board.

More importantly, I could see that I was building a family unlike any I had experienced before. I saw all three of my children, and all six of my grandchildren, on an almost daily basis. I was experiencing all of the milestones and moments that I was too busy working to experience with my own children. This was my second chance to be a part of their lives and to watch them grow up, and I didn't want to miss it.

Luckily, I thought of a mechanical engineer I had worked with before, who was more than qualified, and would definitely be interested.

THAT YEAR FOR CHRISTMAS, we all got a copy of Top Ten Teasers, the new game from Cazzie and Linda's company, Games People Play. I realized there was quite a lot of things I did not know, but it was a fun new tradition to play games over the holidays.

FULL-TIME CAMPGROUND OWNER

THIRTY-THREE
1994

"The purpose of life is to live it, to taste experience to the utmost, to reach out eagerly and without fear for newer and richer experience."
-Eleanor Roosevelt

As soon as the holidays were over, Sandra and her family moved to Burlington, Ontario, where JP had already started working at Petro Canada. His friend, Paul MacTaggart, who was a manager there, got him a job driving eighteen-wheelers. We were not used to being so far away from our baby girl, or our grandbabies. Luckily, they didn't like being away from us either, so Sandra and JP would drive over six-hundred kilometers each way, every three weeks, to visit us.

We missed them fiercely when they were gone, waiting all month for those weekends, that were always over too soon. Come Sunday night, Amanda would wrap herself around the legs of the dinner table, hoping that she would be able to stay. It was heartbreaking to watch her.

ONE TIME, Sandra and JP had to work in Ontario, but would be back within the week. They decided to let us keep the kids, so they could spend more time with their cousins, and with us. Amanda was ecstatic when she realized her plan worked and she was allowed to stay, but then she and Paul broke down when the reality set in, that their parents had left them behind.

She didn't wrap herself around the table anymore, but it was still just as hard to watch them leave. In March, when we went to Florida to visit Roger, we made sure to stop at Ronnie and Anne's for a day, and at Sandra's for two days, before going home.

ROBERT WYNGAERT

Rikki, Amanda, Paul, Chelsea, and Steve.

Barb and I finally became financially independent in 1994. In May, we sold our retirement lake house in New York for $200 000 and bought a 38-foot Friendship motorhome instead. The people who bought our house weren't able to secure a mortgage, so they gave me a $50 000 down payment, and monthly payments for the next few years. It was a nice surprise every time the U.S. dollar went up!

The sale not only brought in money, it also saved us all of the insurance and utilities that we had to pay year-round, whether we were at the house or not. Combined with my package from Pratt, and the campground's record year, this meant that we had the equity – or borrowing power – to invest in large projects.

After enduring a lifetime of stress and struggles, career challenges and financial crises, I finally felt like we had made it.

Barb was feeling under the weather one morning in June, so we let her stay up in bed and took care of things. Denise came over when she wasn't answering the phone and found her in bed, sweating and shivering. Barb was in so much pain that she felt like she was going to pass out, so Denise brought her to the hospital. She spent a week in there while they operated on her for diverticulitis. I did not like being away from her, but I guess it was payback for all of my previous stints in hospitals. Luckily, she came home to me as good as new!

MOST OF MY work at the campground was getting everything ready in the spring, and closing it down in the fall. Now that we had a motorhome, we spent every weekend of the summer exploring Magog, Ottawa, Quebec City...anywhere that was a few hours away from home. Barb and I made it to every State and Province in North America, with the exception of Newfoundland and Alaska. Georges and Denise often came with us in their motorhome, or we would meet up with friends or family members, depending on the destination. I felt like Barb and I deserved these mini vacations, but we were also assessing our competitors. Every campground we went to gave us ideas for how we could invest our resources to better serve our clientele, which was one of my top priorities.

. . .

WORKING for Pratt had taught me how to forecast and propose expenditures, but it also taught me that the person in charge isn't always the one with the best ideas. That is why I insisted on having Round Robin meetings at the beginning and end of every season, to get everyone's input. I would determine how much funds we had at our disposal, then we would all discuss what we wanted to spend them on. We would determine what was important, then prioritize what needed to be done immediately, making five-year plans to ensure growth.

I knew it was important that everyone felt pride in their work, and that they had a say in what was going on. In 1994, our funds went to creating more sites - thirteen of them pull-throughs, renovating the washrooms and main building, a new tractor, and trying to improve our drainage; a task that would resurface every time it rained. Other years we purchased land, army trucks, materials, anything that would help us develop more sites and accommodate our growing bank of customers.

One of our best investments was creating storage spots. We purchased 100 000 square feet of commercial land behind our neighbor, VR Dumont Inc., when they went bankrupt. It was right next to our existing storage area, so we expanded it to meet the growing demand for RV storage. It cost $75 000 to develop the land, but we got an additional forty storage spaces, which brought a return on investment within four years.

HAVING SO little formal education while I was growing up, I wanted to ensure that my children and grandchildren would never go through the same problems. So, for Christmas, in addition to a few gifts, I gave Linda, Danny, and Sandra some money for the kids, so they could invest it for their future education.

Looking back on this period, all I can remember is how ridiculously happy I was.

THIRTY-FOUR
1995

"You are the master of your destiny. You can influence, direct and control your own environment. You can make your life what you want it to be."
– Napoleon Hill

This year we did something different for our winter vacation. On January 14th, we set off on the longest trip of our lives – forty-three days in our motorhome. Our first stop was Milton Heights, a campground in Ontario, so we could visit Sandra's family in Burlington. We decided to kill many birds with one stone, so Ronnie and Anne came, as well as Donna and Doug, for a karaoke night. We stayed up very late singing, and started our vacation off with a bang!

We set off towards the warmth of the south, hoping to find a campground along the way. We had to stop at a rest area near Bloomington, Illinois after driving a thousand kilometers and finding that all of the campgrounds were closed for the winter.

The next morning, we drove to Branson, Missouri and stayed at Chastain's RV Park. We tried to go see a show, but when we discovered that most businesses were closed and they were expecting a major snowstorm, we decided to leave sooner rather than later.

We arrived in Memphis, Tennessee, and stayed at a campground within walking distance from Elvis Presley's home, Graceland. It was such a wonderful experience to visit the entire complex. I would recommend it to anyone who visits the area. I also feel like I have to mention Marlowe's, a local restaurant where we had an excellent meal, and great service.

THE WEATHER WAS a lot better by the time we got to Oklahoma City. We stayed at a KOA campground, where we were allowed to wash our motorhome. I say 'allowed' because most campgrounds restrict washing to their seasonal campers who can't move, because of the amount of water it wastes. After nearly four thousand kilometers though, the motorhome was in desperate need of some cleaning, so we stayed one night and took full advantage of the allowance before moving on to warmer areas.

WHILE IN TEXAS, we stopped at the Big Texan, a famous restaurant with a special challenge. If you can finish their 72-ounce steak dinner – complete with a salad, a shrimp cocktail, baked potato, and a dinner roll- within an hour, it is free. Very few have ever done it, which is why there are so few names posted on their board. Ours did not make the cut either.

We drove through New Mexico, then stayed the night at a KOA campground in Seligman, Arizona. We hit very bad weather conditions in the mountains there and saw many tractor trailers that drove off the road, like we had back in New Brunswick. It was a very bad day for me. I don't know if it was the stress of the weather, or PTSD from our past experiences, but I had chest pains and worried I was having another heart attack.

At long last we arrived in Las Vegas, where we registered to stay a week at the Circus Circus RV Park. The weekly rate was 100$, although I would assume that's the nightly rate these days. The Park was right on the strip and the weather was fantastic.

As soon as I parked the motorhome, Barbara set off for the casinos, honing her gambling skills while I washed our motorhome.

MY FRIENDS CALL ME BOB

After so many days on the road, it was nice to be able to relax and enjoy ourselves. In addition to gambling, most casinos offered some kind of nightly show that was free to watch. We walked from one to the next to see the Statue Show at Caesar's Palace, the Pirate Ship Show at Treasure Island, the Wizard of Oz Show at MGM, the fountains at the Bellagio...I am pretty sure we walked about ten miles every day!

I believe it was at MGM that I paid to have my picture taken and placed on an Adventure Magazine cover. They put my face over Indiana Jones' body, so it looked like I had been having adventures in the jungle. I may have played into this, so for the next decade, my grandchildren believed that I went on a safari and wrestled with alligators, lifted hippopotamuses, and became Tarzan. I was gone so long, and I never told them it wasn't true, so it took them watching the Indiana Jones movies as teenagers to put it together. I was sad to be discovered, but I enjoyed many years of my grandchildren arguing, "My grandfather's stronger than your dad" whenever the argument came up.

For the eight days and seven nights we were in Vegas, there was never a dull moment. We went to all the casinos, saw the car collection at the Imperial Hotel, a show at the Westward casino...we even attended a seminar on real estate properties in Colorado! That last one was a ploy to get tickets for Country Fever at the Golden Nugget Casino in the old part of Vegas. It was entirely worth it, as was Country Tonight at the Atlantis. Luckily, Barb won those tickets without having to sit through a seminar.

We left on January 30th and headed to Phoenix Arizona, but we knew we would be back soon. I have never seen such beautiful views as the landscapes in this part of the country. Sadly, we only stayed one night before going to El Paso, Texas, where we had dinner at the Iron Skillet, and stayed at the Samson RV Park.

FROM THERE IT got difficult to find campgrounds that were open, as we were heading North. We had to stay in a rest area just past Houston, with a long way to go before Roger's house in Cape Coral.

NOT WANTING to stop in another rest area, I drove almost day and night to get to Florida, only stopping for fuel and food. Barbara was not impressed, but I told her I was in my zone, and she didn't have to worry; I wouldn't fall asleep. Still, she sat in the passenger's seat to make sure.

WHEN WE GOT to Roger's, he wasn't even home. He had taken his boat to the local beach and wouldn't be back until late afternoon. It would have been nice to see him and Kay, but we were so exhausted that we crashed as soon as we got into the motorhome. We needed rest after driving ten thousand kilometers since we left Montreal.

ONCE ROGER and Kay got back, the four of us went to his favorite restaurant for dinner, Land & Sea, in Fort Myers.

Long road trips often wreak havoc on vehicles, so Roger repaired my generator, CB radio, and replaced a headlight switch while we were there.

THE NEXT DAY, my brother's best friend – who was also his nephew – Ken Doolan arrived. Most days, we would go for boat rides to various destinations to soak up some sun, as long as the weather cooperated. One of my brother's favorite places to bring us was the swap shop flea market. He insisted on getting his beefsteak tomatoes, eggplants, and other vegetables directly from the local vendors. I guess we got accustomed to fresh vegetables, growing up with my mom.

It might be because of Roger's love of fresh produce that Kenny assumed Roger had a green thumb at home as well. We woke up one morning to find Kenny watering the plants in the yard. This wasn't unusual, as Kenny was always trying to be helpful, but it was odd to find Roger laughing to himself while he watched it happen.

"What's so funny?" I asked my big brother.

He brought me over to one of the plants Kenny had already watered and had me touch the leaves.

"They're plastic," he explained, so Barb and I got a good laugh as well, with none of us telling Kenny until he was done with his task.

LUCKY FOR KENNY, we moved on to laughing at Barb by lunchtime. We went to Wendy's after hearing a commercial on the radio. They were having a promotion, where instead of bringing a piece of paper, you just had to say 'I'm a coupon' when you ordered, and the burgers would be 2 for 1. Kay and I sat at the table while the others went to order, making sure they knew what to say. Barb went first.

"Will that be all?" the cashier asked after her order.

"And two Frosties," she remembered, looking back to me for confirmation. I gestured to remind her about the promotion.

"Is that all?" the cashier asked.

"And I'm a coupon," Barb said reluctantly.

"You're a what?"

"A coupon."

"What do you mean?"

"It said on the radio, that if we came in and said we were a coupon, we would get a discount."

"That's not a thing," the teenager said, looking at my wife more and more like she thought she was crazy.

"It was on the radio."

"No, it wasn't."

Barb finally paid full price, and was not happy when she came back to the table with our food. No one had come to her defense, because it was so much easier to laugh at and tease her.

It was the first day of the promotion, so the employee hadn't been familiar with it, but Barb was right. Still, I couldn't convince her to try it again, although Roger tried, nudging her and saying, "Go on, tell them you're a coupon," every time we went out.

ROGER KNEW BARB LOVED CASINOS, so we also drove over an hour to get to Immocale Village, an Indian Reservation with a Gambling Palace. They also had a lot of CDs and Western-style clothing, so we did some shopping.

Barb and Kay even signed up for an art class, so while they were learning how to paint, Roger would shine up his boat, and I did the same to my motorhome.

In the evenings, Roger would usually let me select the restaurant, so I would try to avoid his regular haunts, choosing instead to bring them to fancy, expensive restaurants they would never go to if they had to pay.

FOR VALENTINE'S DAY, I suggested we go to Smithy's restaurant in Fort Myers. Roger always thought it was too fancy, but I thought we all deserved a treat. The food, the décor...everything was excellent!

After the meal, I thought it would be nice to take a calèche ride around the city. I thoroughly enjoyed it, but Barb did not. Our ride took us past a prison, where all of the inmates banged on the bars and called out obscenities as we rode past. Not quite the romantic mood I was going for!

A few days later, on the 17th, Sandra, JP, Amanda, and Paul arrived. We mostly continued the same routine, with a fast food lunch, a boat ride in the afternoon, and dinner at a nice restaurant in the evening.

One afternoon, the kids were playing in the driveway, trying to catch a salamander, when Roger had to go out somewhere. I can't remember the specifics, because the image burned into my memory is of Paul crouched over a red strawberry crate on the ground while Roger backed his car towards him. I yelled to my brother, even though I knew there was no way he would hear me, but Kenny had already appeared out of nowhere and banged on the side of the car to stop him. Paul was told to pay more attention to his surroundings, and Roger went off on his errand, but it took a while for my heart to get back to normal. I can't imagine what would have happened if Kenny hadn't saved my grandson.

BARB and I left Roger's and spent three days at Walt Disney World with Sandra's family. While Barb and I enjoyed ourselves every time we went, it was always more fun when we had young children with us. Magic Kingdom was just as exciting for us as it was for them, as they saw their favorite characters, and we saw their faces light up at it all. It was Amanda and Paul's first time at Disney, so it was particularly magical, but it would not be their last.

We rented a site at the Fort Wilderness Campground, which is a part of Disney, and Sandra's family stayed at a hotel. Every day, they would come see us early in the morning so they could take advantage of our early admission to the park.

AT THE END of their stay, they drove home to Burlington by car, and we set off in the motorhome, making a quick stop in Knoxville, Tennessee. The next day, we drove to London, Ontario. It was such a relief when we got into Canada, as I am always nervous crossing the border. I sometimes forget that we have a bottle of wine or some other alcohol in the motorhome, and I panic every time we go through. We parked the motorhome at the KOA campground, and spent the night at Ronnie and Anne's.

It is always a party there, with drinks and karaoke. Those Thompsons sure know how to sing! Their sons, Brian and David would sometimes stop by, but the boys weren't big on karaoke. Ronnie and Anne, however, were always excited to see Brian's son, Logan.

WE FINALLY GOT HOME on February 25th, after forty-three days and over 13 000 kilometers. It was a fantastic experience, but we were happy to be home. I would never have imagined taking such an extended vacation, but after my doctor told me I had to change my lifestyle, I was determined to take him seriously. I was definitely enjoying life more, but that included a lot of delicious food, which was something I might need to work on. It definitely made a difference to be travelling so often, and spending all of my other meals in the very capable hands of my favorite chef, my beautiful Barb.

After we hugged the kids and grandkids, we got to work planning our next long winter vacation! We were living life to the fullest!

· · ·

MY FRIENDS CALL ME BOB

IN ADDITION TO VACATIONS, I also implemented all of the improvements we planned for the campground, most of them based on our travels. I always made it a point to reinvest the net profits back into the business, so we could provide the best facilities in the most economical manner.

Thanks to all of my years at Pratt, and previous construction experience with my dad, I was usually able to get by with just myself, Danny, and our employees. This gave us substantial savings, and allowed our investments to go so much further than Ken and Dan could ever have imagined back when they owned it. We were quickly becoming a top-rated campground, building a reputation others in the industry strived to achieve, but we didn't want to become complacent with our success. I believe it is this drive I had, to compete with every campground I met on my travels, that was instrumental in improving campground facilities and utility services throughout the entire province of Quebec.

It usually came to an average of one hundred-thousand dollars per year in managed and capital expenditures, such as developing new pull-through sites, asphalting the roads, refurbishing the game room and playground, updating our maintenance equipment, motor vehicles and tractors, etc.

. . .

ROBERT WYNGAERT

AFTER A BUSY AND lucrative summer at the campground, in October, we went to a camping convention, where campground owners get together for workshops and lectures on best practices in the industry. They also have lots of suppliers who come to show you all of their new gadgets, but the most beneficial part is probably the conversations that happen during the breaks and meals. It is one thing to have a person tell you about an ideal, but it is quite another to share ideas with people who have real-world experience with the same problems you do.

Eric with Santa Claus.

In November, we took our usual trip to Florida,

then Christmas brought us a bonus gift, as we found out that Sandra's family would be moving home once the school year was done in June. It would be nice to have everyone together again. I think it is interesting to note that Chelsea and Rikki started auditioning for films and commercials this year, with Rikki even getting her picture on the Mega Blocks packaging.

THIRTY-FIVE
1996

"A positive thinker does not refuse to recognize the negative; he refuses to dwell on it. Positive thinking is a form of thought which habitually looks for the best results from the worst conditions."
- Norman Vincent Peale

On January 16th, I started having chest pains, so Barbara drove me to the Charles Lemoyne Hospital. They admitted me for observation as soon as I arrived, and reproached us for not calling an ambulance instead. Barb was not happy, as I was the one who had insisted on her driving me. Part of it was me absolutely not wanting to be brought to Pierre Boucher hospital, which was the closest, but I think I also thought that as long as I could arrive by car, it wasn't that serious.

MY FRIENDS CALL ME BOB

I was in the hospital for four days and diagnosed with angina. This time it wasn't the stress of my busy life that got to me, it was my weight. I was at my highest ever, 245 pounds.

I started reading a book by Oprah and Bob Greene, the Journal of Daily Renewal, and managed to get down to 200 lbs by April. To celebrate, we traded in our Friendship motorhome for a brand-new Scenic Cruiser. It was quite the expense, but after all the hard work we'd put in over the years, we deserved it.

On May 9th, I was driving our tractor down one of our hills, but it was going much too fast for my liking. I tried to press down harder on the brakes, but I realized that they weren't working at all. I didn't know if they were being difficult, or completely disconnected, and I didn't want to waste time trying to fix them as I gained speed. I knew the farther I went, the faster I would be going, and I didn't want to crash into anything of value, or – god forbid – anyone. So, I steered myself into a tree.

As you've probably come to expect from me, I got up and walked it off. That is, I walked from my crash site back to the main office and tried to go on with my day, but I was in a lot of pain. It turned out that I fractured a rib.

There was still a lot of work to be done to prepare for the camping season, so JP moved back from Ontario a few months early to help Danny get everything ready. It wasn't like I sat around and did nothing, but I did have to keep a slower pace for almost a month after the accident, before I could go back to my usual routine.

SINCE SANDRA WAS MOVING HOME, Linda began a new career as a Certified Financial Advisor, letting Sandra take over as General Manager of Camping Alouette. If only Linda had started this career earlier, I would have avoided many blunders, and been much richer!

For example, in 1999, Linda convinced me to multiply our capital gains exemption by giving each of my children shares of the corporation through an

Estate Freeze and a Family Trust. When I brought it up with my accountant, he told me that was something very wealthy people would do, but not a small business owner like me. Still, I imagined that it would be useful for the kids when Barb and I died. I have always trusted my daughter implicitly.

I BELIEVE that it is not easy to be successful. It requires a strong will and perseverance, because quality is never an accident. It is the result of high intentions, sincere effort, intelligent direction, and skillful execution. It represents the wise choice out of many alternatives. Throughout my career, my businesses, and my family life, I have always tried to make the right choices.

That is why it was so hard for me when the Federal government came to audit my business and personal finances. I can deal with deadlines and multimillion dollar projects, but this was the most stressful experience I had ever been through. After working countless hours and multiple jobs for forty years, they were combing through my receipts, saying I owed for unpaid income taxes on the business.

The auditors investigated every business and personal expenditure, inquiring about our credit cards, bank accounts, telephone records...they left no stone unturned. Everything was fair game, including where we went on vacation and how much we spent on each trip. They were ruthless. Luckily, I have always kept meticulous records of my projects and expenditures, and I had taken note of all of the contests I won at Pratt to pay for most of our trips, but none of it seemed to be enough for the auditors.

Eventually, they stopped asking for things, so we assumed they were satisfied and everything was settled. We usually left for longer trips once the camping season was over, but given how stressed the audit made us, we left for a month-long trip in the middle of August!

OUR PLAN WAS to drive out to Vancouver, stopping along the way to visit friends we hadn't seen in years. It was a chance to explore our beautiful country, and to see what the competition was up to.

One thing about travelling with me, that Barb absolutely hates, is that I am not one to enjoy the journey. I will have a destination in mind, and I might plan to stop at certain places along the way, but if the first place I want to stop at is three days away, I will drive the three days to get there before stopping. Obviously, I'll stop for fuel, food, and to sleep, but there is no sightseeing, sit-down meals, or anything relaxing about it, until we arrive.

So, although we 'stopped' in Lake George, Harrisburg, and Toledo, we didn't really stop until we got to Nappanee, Indiana. There were deficiencies on the motorhome that we wanted to fix while it was still under warranty, so we brought the motorhome back to the Gulf Stream plant.

The repairs would take longer than a day, so we booked ourselves a couple of nights in a fancy hotel with a swimming pool. We didn't expect there would be much to do or see while we waited, but the area turned out to be fascinating. There was an Amish community living there, so we noticed things like horse and carriage parking spots with troughs so the horses could drink, and a severe lack of alcohol in many of the places we ate at. Some of them did have beer and wine, but the waitress wasn't allowed to be the one to serve it. I was amazed by how skilled the Amish people working at the plant were, since they couldn't use electricity or any of the tools in their homes. The craftsmanship was incredible.

To this day, I also remember how delicious the food was. Everywhere we went, it seemed like everything was fresh and homemade. I never thought visiting a motorhome plant and an Amish community would be so interesting, but it was quite the experience.

Once the motorhome was ready, we moved on through Deforest, Wisconsin, and Fargo, North Dakota. It would have been nice if Fargo came before Indiana, or if the campground was made to accommodate large motorhomes like ours. As it was, a branch ripped a hole in the vinyl roof of our newly repaired unit. We were definitely not happy campers.

From there, we crossed the border back into Canada, so we could visit Danny Smith in Winnipeg. He and Brenda were no longer together, but we were able to meet his new wife, Karen. He gave us a sightseeing tour of Winnipeg from his car, and brought us to the marketplace, before we went to their house for dinner. It was nice to visit family we were once so close to, who now lived so far away.

Barbara, Alice, and Mary.

Next we went to Calgary, Alberta, after a pit stop at the Ponderosa Campground in Swift Current. I was surprised because their excellent facilities did not fit with their very low price.

In Calgary, we stayed at the Pine Creek RV Park. We called Mary and Pat House to let them know we had arrived, but they weren't home yet. Instead, we got to hang out with Mary's sister, Alice, while we waited. Apparently, this was the time to be visiting from Montreal!

Pat and Mary had sixteen people over that night, mostly their children and grandchildren, who we hadn't seen in years. We had a delicious meal in their beautiful mansion, with a spectacular view of the city.

My tow car needed to have a wheel bearing replaced, so we were going to be without a car for three days, until they offered to lend us theirs. More than that, while Pat went to work, Mary brought us on a tour of the Rocky Mountains. It was a wonderful experience! The breathtaking views, the gondola ride in Banff, a hike along the river...it left us with a treasure trove of unforgettable memories. I couldn't help but appreciate how lucky we were to have that opportunity.

Barbara, Regis, and Gail.

We left Calgary and headed for Edmonton on

August 30th to visit our once very close friends, Regis and Gail Lemieux. We had been the ones who introduced them to each other, and he had helped me on so many of my side hustles that I lost count. It had been years since we'd seen them, so neither of us could wait to get to their home in Wetaskiwin.

They acted as our tour guides, bringing us to the West Edmonton Mall, which was the largest in all of Canada. More than just holding hundreds of shops, it boasted an amusement area, a water park, and many other activities. We went on a submarine ride, watched people having fun in the wave pool, and enjoyed a lunch at the fifties themed Johnny Rockets. We had a great time, catching up and reminiscing.

Once we left the Lemieux, we drove to the Jasper

Athabasca Glacier Ice Land Center. They took us right into the glaciers with a giant snow coach. The view, and the entire experience, was mesmerizing.

We stayed at the Lake Louise campground while we were visiting the area. We didn't hike, but we rode the ski lift to take in a bird's eye view of Lake Louise, which was spectacular. As was walking along Bows River.

Next we made it to British Columbia, staying at the Wild Rose Campground in Hope for one night, before moving on to Caribou RV Park in Burnaby. We were there to see Monica Walls, who once upon a time was my little sister's best friend, Monica Maccabee. We picked her up at work and enjoyed a nice meal at the Thomas Cook restaurant in the Metro Mall. They had excellent lobster tails, and we made sure to have the best time sharing stories of our childhood and all the adventures we got up to since. Monica had been diagnosed with an aggressive cancer, so we knew this would be our last time seeing her, even as she smiled and waved goodbye to us. It was heartbreaking, but I was glad we got to have one last hurrah, for old time's sake.

OUR NEXT STOP was Stanley Park, but to be honest, all we saw was rain. It was constant, almost twenty-four hours, day in and day out. It was the worst part of our holidays, as we struggled to go sightseeing and do activities anyway. It either resulted in us seeing absolutely nothing through the rain, getting soaked in the attempt, or both.

ON SEPTEMBER 8TH, we arrived at Yellowstone's Edge RV Resort. The Yellowstone Park had almost been completely destroyed by forest fires, so there were many areas with hardly any trees. The lack of shelter meant we saw so much wildlife. Not just little things like squirrels, but we saw dozens of elk, a few deer, and even a handful of bison. At the time, I couldn't believe our luck, only in retrospect understanding that the deforestation caused by the fires had cost these animals their habitats. Thankfully, as with most habitats ravaged by disaster, life finds a way, and they eventually restore themselves.

We visited the Old Faithful Hot Springs and the canyon, as well as the sculpture of the Indian chief, Crazy Horse, carved into the mountainside. Not to mention a quick jaunt over the border to see Mount Rushmore's giant Presidential Heads. These were memorable highlights from the vacation.

We stopped in Iowa and Michigan, before spending a few days with Ronnie and Anne. We didn't have to stop in Burlington, as Sandra was waiting for us at the campground with Danny when we got home on September 15th. This trip was slightly shorter than the previous one, lasting 32 days and nearly 13 000 kilometers, but it felt good to be home!

Robert and Enid.

OVER THANKSGIVING WEEKEND, we hosted an eightieth birthday party for Barbara's father. Every year since he turned seventy-five, she insisted on throwing him a big party, arguing that it might be his last. We knew how lucky we were that he was still with us, watching his teenage great-grandchildren grow up, and we didn't want to take it for granted.

The family all got together in our old Arcade and we ordered BBQ chicken – nowhere near as good as the ones he used to make at our restaurant – and spent the day dancing, partying, and singing. He slept over, since his wife was in Rawdon for the weekend, then Barb and Ronnie drove him home.

WHEN I HEARD that the Camping Canada convention would be in Nashville, Tennessee, I immediately signed up for it, and planned another vacation around those dates. Barb and I left Sandra and Danny in charge of the campground and headed out in our motorhome.

We met up with Georges and Denise in Harrisburg, Pennsylvania, but after dinner, they left for Orlando in their motorhome, while we went to Tennessee.

We stayed at the KOA Opryland campground, hoping to catch a few country shows while we were there. We expected to meet a lot of campground owners, as it was a much bigger convention than the ones we usually attended, but we didn't think we would see any French Quebecers. Imagine our surprise when we ran into Normand Jacques, the president of Camping Quebec, and Maryse Catellier, the secretary.

We went for dinner together, where I had a fantastic 20 oz. porterhouse steak. I was very embarrassed when they wouldn't let me pay, but I promised I would make up for it.

On the first day of the conference, we attended the seminars with them, then Barb and I went to visit the Opryland Hotel. Everything was beautifully decorated for Christmas, with the most gorgeous decorations. We had a delicious supper at Beauregard's restaurant.

The next day, we introduced Normand and Maryse to the vendors that supplied us with the campground utilities that are not available in Quebec, like electrical boxes. I could tell by the look on their faces that this was how I was paying them back for that supper they paid on the first night. It was a game-changer, not just for Normand and Maryse, but for all of Quebec. We were the only ones at the time who were importing the necessary utility boxes specially designed for campground hookups, but after our introductions, the Camping Quebec Association imported thousands of units and made them available to all of their owners. It brought the Quebec camping industry to a whole new level.

We left after the convention and arrived at Candlelight Park on November 9th. Georges and Denise arrived that day as well, so we all went for dinner at Tropical Acres.

The following day, we got a surprise visit from Roger and Kay. We continued with them to Cape Coral, and settled in for our traditional visit, with boat rides and good food. We were living the life! We got home on November 20th, after eighteen days and over six thousand kilometers.

UNFORTUNATELY, Barb's father had been having a lot of health issues, and within weeks he needed someone by his side 24/7. Even though we had the big parties every year in case this happened, none of us was anywhere near ready for it when he passed away that November. He had been a constant source of love, support and encouragement for everyone who knew him.

From the moment I started dating Barbara, he became a close friend, offering advice and stories to me for the past forty years. For the grandkids, this was the first person they knew who died, and it was probably the first time they saw me cry. His death left a huge hole in all of our lives.

CHRISTMAS WAS hard for all of the adults, but thankfully, the children were too young to understand the loss. They were a bright light in all of our dark worlds.

THIRTY-SIX
1997

"The tests of life are not to break you but to make you."
-Norman Vincent Peale

We went on the trip of a lifetime in March. We had given everyone a little extra at Christmas, to make sure they could all afford a two-week vacation at Walt Disney World in Orlando, Florida. JP was taking a special computer course, so he wasn't able to come with us, but the thirteen other members of our family set out before sunrise for the drive. Barbara had pulled her groin a few days before the trip, so she was in a wheelchair. She didn't enjoy this, but the grandkids did, as it allowed them to skip a lot of lines, and gave them a place to rest when they grew tired of walking. The highlight for the grandkids was probably the breakfast we had with all of the characters from Winnie the Pooh, while I was very proud of myself for going down the Summit Plummet. It is a giant waterslide, where you are so high up that the people on the ground look like ants. It was an unforgettable vacation with my kids and grandkids all together!

Chelsea, Steve, Amanda, Paul, Rikki, and Eric at Disney in 1997.

When we returned from our vacation, the Federal Government announced that they'd completed their audit of our revenues. As I was under the impression we had settled the matter a year earlier, I was quite shocked to find out they thought we owed $250 000 of unpaid income taxes. There was no way this was possible, but unfortunately, the burden was on me to prove them wrong. I thought the stress was going to eat me alive.

BARB WASN'T DOING SO WELL around this time either. Losing her father really took a toll on her. She spent two months with bronchitis, and the coughing didn't let up for months afterwards. She was also diagnosed with high blood pressure, so she was glad to be able to get back to her exercise program once the bronchitis cleared. Every morning, she would walk around the entire campground, marking off if any customers arrived during the night, left early, or had unregistered visitors. Nothing got past her!

This was all done before she made breakfast for me, and whoever was working in the store that day.

IT TOOK months of negotiations between Revenue Canada and my Chartered Accountant, Jean Pilotte, before I was able to prove them wrong. Upon review, we settled on $48 000 to close the case. I probably could have brought it down lower, because I truly did not owe that money, but the stress was more than I could take, and my health was worth more than that.

MY FRIENDS CALL ME BOB

. . .

AFTER ALL OF the audit stress, we really needed another vacation, so Barbara and I headed for Myrtle Beach on September 5th. My brothers both came with us; Roger staying in a mobile home and Georges with his motorhome. We had excellent weather that made it a joy to walk along the beach and go swimming, for everyone except me. I was having chest pains and shortness of breath, so I couldn't keep up with the others.

True to form, I ignored my pain and tried to have a pleasant vacation. We went to watch Eddie Miles (the best Elvis impersonator I have ever seen), The Legends, Ripley's Believe it or Not, the Dixie Stampede, etc. We had a great time, but no matter how much I ignored them, my chest pains didn't go away.

AFTER MY BROTHERS and their wives went home, Barb told me I had to go to the hospital, to make sure I wasn't having another heart attack. I drove to the emergency department of the Grand Strand Medical Center for a consultation.

It wasn't long before Dr. Krates gave us the bad news; my tests showed three critical blockages in the veins leading to my heart. If he didn't operate on me, I would soon suffer a serious heart attack, and possibly die. Barb called our insurance company, and I was glad when they suggested I wait and have the surgery in Montreal. They recommended we fly, but I was pretty sure it wouldn't make that big of a difference if I drove.

Dr. Krates, however, didn't think I would last the time it would take to fly home, especially not without medical supervision. The insurance company finally agreed, and the surgery was set for the following morning.

IT TOOK ROUGHLY six hours for Dr. Krates to perform a triple bypass on me, after which I was put in the intensive care unit for two days. You can definitely see the difference from what Medicare gives you in Canada, versus insurance in the States. My room was like a hotel suite!

The evening before I was scheduled to be released, my heart stopped. All I can remember is hearing, "Code Blue", before I assume the doctors came and restarted my heart.

I woke up the following morning to a very terrified Barb, who was not pleased with me. As if it was my fault my heart stopped. Luckily, Linda had flown down to be with her.

IT TOOK two more days before I was discharged. Barb, Linda, and JP were all there to pick me up. I wasn't going to be able to drive back to Montreal, so Roger drove up with JP and Kay to drive the motorhome while JP and Linda took turns driving his car. I was incredibly touched by how they all dropped everything to be there for me and help me out.

ONLY SIX DAYS after undergoing major surgery, I was doing pretty well, even going on short walks. My family took this as an excellent sign, and decided we would go for supper at a restaurant in the mall. Their theory was that I had to eat anyway, so I might as well join them instead of eating alone in the motorhome. Believe me, this was not a good idea. I was exhausted just from sitting there, and practically had to be carried home. It was much too soon for me to venture out to restaurants.

JP AND LINDA drove home after the restaurant incident, but the rest of us stayed another week so the doctors could make sure I didn't have any complications from the surgery. I refused any future invites to go out, and spent the following days improving my condition before my next appointment. I was doing good, so Dr. Krates gave me the okay to go home.

Roger was the only one who could drive the motorhome, but we were all in a hurry to get back to

Montreal, so he insisted on only stopping for fuel. We got there on October 1st.

It was another close call on my life. I think the stress from the government audit was the main cause, so I took it as a lesson to live each day as if it were my last, and to take every day one at a time.

THIRTY-SEVEN
1998

"There is always a storm. There is always rain. Some experience it. Some live through it. And others are made from it."
- Shannon L. Alder

In January, Quebec had its biggest ice storm in centuries, shutting down 80% of the main electrical grid and leaving most businesses and residences without power for twenty-two days. Montreal was declared a disaster area, with millions of people without heat, or power. In an essay once she was back in school, Chelsea called it, 'The Time Quebec Froze Over'. As it was, we were among the lucky ones, because I had equipped my home with three wood burning fireplaces, plus propane gas to heat our hot water tanks, and two generators to keep the kitchen and television running.

The fourteen of us – Barb and I, the kids, and grandkids – stayed in the house at the campground. I wasn't yet fully recovered from my triple bypass surgery, but together we were able to keep an eye on the campground, and keep the fireplaces running 24/7. We had more than enough wood, but it had to be brought into the garage to thaw out before we could use it. We went through roughly a cord of wood and forty liters of propane every day. Thanks to the campground, the fourteen of us lived pretty much the same as before the storm, although in closer quarters. We even let strangers use our commercial washrooms and showers, as so many people were without hot water.

Danny and Lynn lived close to a police station, so they were the first to get their power back. The past few weeks had been like a fun vacation for the kids, with movie rentals, new toys, and sleeping on the floor with their cousins like a sleepover party. Poor little Steve cried, "It's not fair. Why do we have to go home first?" when they left.

ONCE THE INITIAL fallout was over, we had to clean up the mess and repair all of the damage caused by the storm. Luckily, since we were in the disaster zone, we received government support to get up and running again. We were assigned eight employees from the unemployment roster - Danny and Sandra among them - for five weeks to remove all of the broken trees and branches. It was a giant task, but we were able to open in the spring, only slightly worse for the wear.

Me and Barbara at our fortieth anniversary party.

ON APRIL 10TH, Barb and I headed to Kenny Wong's to celebrate Amanda's birthday. Boy, were we surprised when they brought us to a large room filled with all of our closest friends and family. Barb, who thought it was a surprise party for me, was shocked when she finally understood that it was for our 60th birthdays, and 40th wedding anniversary. Even Father Jerry, our local priest, was there so we could renew our vows. Then, after a delicious meal, we sang karaoke and danced the night away!

IT WAS around this time that Lynn was diagnosed with breast cancer. She went through chemotherapy, as well as radiation therapy to make sure they removed it all. We hoped and prayed that she would make a full recovery, and thankfully, she went into remission. Barb and I got her a wig with real hair, so she could feel more like herself while she waited for hers to grow back.

AS FOR MY HEART, it was doing better, and I was getting daily exercise, as well as weekly vita-flex massages from a professional, Bob Mariasine. He would bring his massage table and do it at the house, even convincing me to buy an inversion table of my own. I have to admit, I was open to anything that would keep me alive and healthy.

MY FRIENDS CALL ME BOB

· · ·

WE MADE a lot of new purchases at the campground, and took advantage of the storm's damage to redo some of our original infrastructure, like our walk-in fridge, counters, shelves, windows, and roof. We had to replace many hydro poles and electrical lines.

I also commissioned a beautiful conference table from a famed Belgian woodworker in the neighborhood. I made it round, like King Arthur's Round Table, with enough room for twelve to sit comfortably.

THIRTY-EIGHT
1999

"One cannot think well, love well, sleep well, if one has not dined well."
-Virginia Woolf

I had big plans for the campground in 1999, notably replacing the public washroom facilities in our wooded area, as well as our 'E' section. The renovations were necessary to maintain our five-star rating. We were one of only eight to receive top marks, out of the 780 campgrounds registered in Quebec. Our planned expenditures for the year always took into account what would maintain our rating, what would bring in more revenues, and what would make our customers happy.

Barbara.

I got into full renovation mode, working on the washrooms in our main building to start. I still needed to work out the architectural, mechanical and electrical plans for the new washroom facilities, so I figured it would be nice to do them in Florida. I had just purchased a 38-foot motorhome, a Monaco Diplomat, so Barb and I took it for a test drive!

Sandra, JP, Amanda, and Paul met us there on February 27th. They'd purchased the two-week Park Hopper Plus for Walt Disney World, which allowed them access to all of the parks, as well as to skip some lines. We didn't have Barb's wheelchair this time, so the passes were definitely appreciated!

After a week or so, Barb and I announced we

would be heading to Roger's for a few days, while they finished off their passes. Amanda had a tendency of getting car sick, and Paul thought it would be more fun to travel in our motorhome than in their parent's car, so they asked to come with us instead. Roger was thrilled for the company, but it would take years for the kids to live down the fact that they'd turned down a few days at Disney to spend time going on boat rides and to dog races with us. Luckily, Sandra and JP found a nice Belgian couple to buy their passes, telling them all about their Wyngaert friends back home. However, they pronounced it 'Wing-hart'.

Me, Eeyore, and Barbara.

We returned to the cold of Montreal and got straight to work rearranging the shelves in our convenience store and building the new washroom facilities. In order to maintain our five-star rating, we needed to have a certain number of washrooms and showers per so many sites, but I also wanted them to be modern; something you would expect to find in a hotel rather than the middle of the woods.

We only had a couple of months to complete the projects before the season came into full swing. All the demolition and construction was carried out by my staff, with the exception of the bricklaying on the exteriors, which I contracted to Yvon Lapolice, one of our campers. He did the work with Marco, who you might remember as the little boy who used to follow me around when I first purchased shares in the campground.

We finished the projects in May, just before the campground got busy. Barb and I needed a vacation after all that work, so we spent a weekend in Plattsburgh with Roger, Kay, Fay, and Bruce. It was fun to travel with my baby sister and old football buddy for a change!

Me and Barbara at Le Continental.

That summer, we discovered what would become our favorite restaurant, Le Continental, in Quebec City. Their cuisine is Franco-Italian, but the major selling point is their flambé dishes, and the Caesar salads they make right at your table. After the meal, no matter how full you are from all the delicious courses that came before, you have to find room for their Brazilian Coffees and Crêpes Suzette! We brought most of our friends and family there over the years, and recommended it to every single camper who was headed for Quebec City.

Barbara and I in Shediac.

We also spent two weeks exploring the East Coast, mostly with Roger and Kay. We visited New Brunswick, Prince Edward Island, and Nova Scotia. It was another wonderful vacation for the books, and I can say with certainty that I never ate so much lobster in my entire life!

NOW THAT THE campground washrooms were all modern and new, Barb convinced me to redo the one on the main level of our house, between the kitchen and the dining room. We removed the bathtub and put a marble counter surrounded by mirrors, with a chair and fancy magnifying mirror. Somewhere nice where you could sit to put on your makeup. Although to be honest, I don't think I ever saw Barb use it as such. Bobby's wife Karen was definitely a fan though, as she teased that she wouldn't come to our Christmas supper unless she could get ready in that bathroom.

Bruce and Fay.

We honored my heritage for our Family Suppers this year, making them Belgium themed. Instead of having the girls just dress the same, I ordered them all yellow aprons, with the Belgian flag in the middle. We served stove-vry and a selection of traditional Belgian appetizers, just like my mother used to make. The Belgian waffles were a big hit!

Me and Barbara.

For New Year's Eve, we had a big party in the garage. The children spent most of the night in the basement, but we got everyone together just before midnight, so we could all do the countdown together. I wasn't one to buy into the whole Y2K, end of the world, everything is going to crash theory, but I didn't think it made sense for anyone to risk flying on January 1st. Still, if it was the end of the world, I was glad to be spending it with all the people I loved most.

Luckily, nothing happened at midnight, except for more partying and celebrating, with a buffet table filled with Barb's cooking and Denise's sandwiches.

ROBERT WYNGAERT

Eric, Rikki, Amanda, Chelsea, Steve, and Paul.

THIRTY-NINE
2000

Camping Alouette Inc. is a respected, successful Company. We want to make it better for our customers, our employees and for the community in which we work. Our goal is to be the recognized leaders in the campground industry.

-Camping Alouette Mission Statement

BY 2000, we had increased our yearly profit reinvestment from roughly $100 000 to more like $250 000. This was mostly because the campground was bringing in more of a profit, but we were also building a reputation, and we wanted to keep it up. We were top-rated not only in Quebec, but with all of the

American camping associations: Good Sam's Club, Woodalls, AAA, etc. We made it a part of our Mission Statement to be recognized as leaders in the camping industry.

In light of this, we focused on 'revamping' everything, to make our roads, landscaping and signage fit better with our five-star branding. There was a house in Beloeil where the trees were all shaped as different things, so we asked the owner, Guy Bernard, to come and do something with our hedges. He turned them into trains, deer, an owl, a squirrel, and Big Ben, with new additions as the years went on!

We hired two new employees this year; Chelsea, who'd done a few shifts with her mother last year, and Amanda, who was starting completely from scratch. I started my granddaughters out with the same salary I'd given my daughters back when they started working, which wasn't much. However, I kept a close eye on them, and gave them raises as they were able to take on more responsibilities. It was important for me to be able to provide this opportunity for them, to never have to look for a job, and to have a stable start in life. I didn't want them to have to worry about things like being laid off the night before their wedding, or having to decide between a transfer to a different province, and being without a job.

Even more important was that they learn a good work ethic and the proper skills, so whichever job they chose in the future would be open to them. They worked hard, long hours, with a smile, and made me proud every single day. By the end of the summer, they were both making more in a couple of hours than I had in a week at Daniel Kiely's. It wasn't long until Rikki, Steve, and Paul were working at the campground as well.

Linda, me, Rene Raiche, Lynn, Sandra, and Barbara at Camping Quebec.

I don't know if there is any link, but that fall at the Camping Quebec convention, we won the award for best customer service! I made it a point when training my staff to always greet the customers with 'Hello, how can I help you?", and Sandra continued the tradition, urging the employees to greet every customer like they were valued and important, no matter how busy we were.

This year, our theme for the family suppers was Hawai'i. We liked to keep the themes secret so we could surprise our guests, but the family always knew, because Barb spent weeks, if not months, trying out recipes. Barbara's sisters who lived in the area; Joan, Carol, and Marilyne, came to our house every Friday night for karaoke. The kids would usually hang out in the basement, but sometimes they would come up with us, and we would let them sing a few songs. On one of these Fridays, Amanda sat between the Thompson sisters, who started a conversation about how much fun the supper would be, with all the pretty decorations. Poor Amanda, who didn't know the theme was a secret, told them all about the Palm Trees, Hula Dancers, and Pineapples we had planned. It took years, if not decades, before we trusted her with another secret.

Barbara, Linda, Lynn, and Sandra.

At the end of the year, in addition to my usual planning for campground expenditures, I made Barbara a proposal for future vacations. I had big plans for weekend trips closer to home, longer road trips in Canada and the States, as well as flights to Europe and the Caribbean. After most of my life spent making plans to build up my career and wealth, I was now making plans to live my life and enjoy it. Obviously, I wanted to ensure that we could maintain our way of life, but never at the expense of the things that made it worth living. My main priorities were now to make our campground the best in Canada, but more importantly, to support and guide our children and grandchildren, so they could succeed as well.

FORTY
2001 AND 2002

"Whether you think you can or you think you can't, you're right."
-Henry Ford

I went through a phase where I had absolutely no motivation. I had many ideas and dreams I wanted to accomplish, but I could not find the energy to plan them out and implement them. I sat down and thought of things I could do in the short term, as well as long term, to bring back my drive and ambition. Part of my attitude was possibly based on the fact that I kept trying to get the permits to build a recreation hall at the campground, but kept getting refused by the city.

Well, after making my list, I decided that instead of continuing to try and get their permission, I would start building now and ask for forgiveness later. I did not want to give them the opportunity to tell me my rec hall was a safety hazard that had to come down, so I built it going above and beyond all the safety rules and building codes. I used commercial trusses, made everything thicker than it needed to be, and even surrounded the interior of the building with a shoulder-level brick wall to prevent any fires. It was as sturdy as rec halls come, and attached to a state-of-the-art RV Wash. I had used many of them during my travels, but our Canadian climate gave an open-air RV wash a limited time of operation every year. So, we made ours fully-enclosed; the first of its kind in all of North America, as far as I know.

Our recreation hall and RV Wash.

Obviously, the city wasn't happy. Contractors were told they couldn't work on the project, since we didn't have a permit, so I had to rely on my own employees, and close friends.

Eventually, my case was brought in front of a judge. I knew I would be in trouble, but I prayed they wouldn't make me tear it down.

Luckily, the judge took our side, apparently wondering why every other campground was allowed to build a rec hall, yet they kept refusing me. I knew that the city wanted to get rid of us so they could build houses and make a lot more in taxes, but I obviously couldn't use that in my defense.

I wasn't there for the trial, but I found out the outcome when the mayor of St-Mathieu-de-Beloeil called and told me to come and get my permit. It sounded like the words were physically painful for him to say. I knew I would have to pay for it in the future, but for now I had my hall and my RV wash. I was happy!

ROBERT WYNGAERT

Me and Barbara.

We put the hall to good use, starting that May, when we hosted a Country Western Festival. It was supposed to be an opportunity to bring in more revenue, but we ultimately found it to be a lot more trouble than it was worth for the business. However, from a personal standpoint, the Wyngaerts had a great time, as it reignited our love of country music. We quickly found a teacher and started Line Dancing Lessons. Our hall was the site of many weddings, birthday parties, anniversary parties...the girls were excellent at decorating for all of my events, but Lynn really went above and beyond to make any party extra special. Her Halloween parties were legendary, with ghosts, skeletons, and even tombstones!

Me, Sandra, Lynn, Danny, and Linda.

THANKSGIVING WAS RATHER special this year, as we suddenly lost power in the middle of the afternoon. The turkey was in the oven and we needed way more stovetops and ovens than a generator could handle, so we rallied. Each of the girls took a few things to their houses so we could finish the cooking, then we all came together for the meal. It felt like an ironic, yet divine intervention when the power came back just as we were sitting down to eat by candle light.

. . .

IN OCTOBER, we went to the Camping Quebec convention, pretty confident that we would be coming home with the Award for Innovation we submitted for. I couldn't imagine what any other campground could have done to compete with our fully equipped recreation hall and never-before-seen RV Wash. We were also the first in Canada to have wireless internet on most of our sites, thanks to JP.

I was flabbergasted when someone else went up to claim our prize. I looked to Sandra and Linda, to make sure I heard right. They shrugged, as if to say "we tried our best", but they were also crushed. I can't even remember what the winner's innovation had been.

It wasn't until the end of the night, when they announced the Campground of the Year, that they shocked me by calling, "Camping Alouette!"

Apparently, they read the proposal Sandra submitted for the Innovation Award and decided we deserved better. I was overwhelmed by happiness and pride for everything we had achieved since purchasing a run-down plot of land. I had a passion to be the best in what we do and to meet all of my objectives. I wanted to maintain my basic principles of loyalty and honesty.

Barbara and I at Camping Quebec.

Barbara with our Dynasty motorhome.

At the end of the season, Barb and I purchased a 2002 Monaco Dynasty, our biggest and most expensive motorhome. It was 42-feet, fully equipped, and cost more than most houses. However, it was on my bucket list, and even Barb was thrilled with the Whirlpool bath she got to relax in, and the washer/dryer combo. It also gave us an excuse to plan another family trip to Walt Disney World, all fourteen of us.

Barbara, Linda, Sandra, me, Eric, Amanda, Rikki, Chelsea, Lynn, and Steve at Disney in 2002.

Things were going well for us financially, so once we got home from Disney, I focused on what I believed would be my legacy; the Wyngaert Estates. I purchased land on one of our hills, bordering the golf course, and made plans to build a gated community where my family would live; Barb and I, the kids, and someday the grandkids. I designed a block plan to present to the city for approval, along with details, and a schedule. I was so encouraged when they told me it looked like a good plan and should be approved at their next meeting. I began to clear the land, to provide space for the houses. I planned to have nine lots of an acre each.

ROBERT WYNGAERT

Bob Smith and Joan at our Ireland-themed Supper.

MY FRIENDS CALL ME BOB

Ronnie, Marilyne, Bobby, Joan, Donna, Doreen, Carol, and Barbara at our Texas-themed Supper.

FORTY-ONE
2003

"Two of the greatest gifts we can give our children are roots and wings."
-Hodding Carter

In the Spring, Barb and I went to visit Ronnie and Anne like we often do, but this time, Brian had a new girlfriend he wanted us to meet. Instead of just having her over for supper while we were there, he thought it would be funny to play a trick on her.

We usually parked our motorhome at a campground, but slept at my brother-in-law's whenever we were in town. This time, we were too early in the season for our usual spots to be open. Being campground owners, we absolutely hated seeing people camping in parking lots, because we know what it can do to business, but we had no choice. So, we were parked in the London Flying J when Brian pulled up with Nancy.

"I wonder what it looks like inside one of those," Brian said, getting out of the car.

"It must be beautiful," Nancy agreed, looking at the fancy brown motorhome.

"Why don't I ask them if we can take a look inside?"

"No, you can't do that," Nancy argued, dismissing him.

"If we don't ask, we'll never know."

"Brian, you can't," Nancy said, afraid now that she saw he was serious.

"Worst they can do is say no."

We couldn't hear their conversation, but we saw how uncomfortable Nancy was as she tried to convince Brian not to disturb us, and then how upset she was when he didn't listen.

When Brian knocked, we sent Ronnie and Anne to hide in the bedroom, then I went to answer the door.

"I'm sorry to bother you, but would you mind if we came in to see what it looks like from the inside?" Brian asked me with a smile.

"Of course, come on in!" I said, stepping aside so they could walk up. Nancy looked torn between her anger at Brian, and wanting to see. To be honest, I probably would have let them come in, even if it wasn't my nephew. But then I would have been the one whose better half was shooting daggers at them.

We walked through the living room and the kitchen, then I showed them the bathroom, which was the most impressive part. I opened the door to the bedroom, where Ronnie and Anne were waiting with smiles.

Nancy didn't seem to register that they were there, and then she looked so confused until Brian introduced us to her. She hit him playfully on the arm for tricking her, but the rest of us had a good laugh. We should have known, right from this first time meeting her, that she would liven up our parties for years to come.

THE SUMMER BROUGHT a lot of changes to the campground, some visible and others not. Our internet was very slow, relying on antennas and modems that we rented out to campers. You would think they were coming camping to escape from work and enjoy nature, but our clientele was the kind that appreciated us cutting down trees so they could get a better wi-fi signal. Which we did, removing a grassy wooded area to make 'wooded' RV sites in its place, for those who wanted to feel like they were camping, while enjoying modern amenities.

As far as the internet, JP and Paul installed fiber optics so the entire park had reliable wireless internet. It was quite the investment, but worth it for our campers.

AT THE END of the season, instead of going on a road trip, Barb and I took a flight to Europe. We had chosen Paris as our theme for the Christmas Suppers, and decided to go see it in person.

Paris was different from any other place we'd experienced before. It seemed like everyone there was slim, smoked, and carried a cell phone. I'd had a phone in my car, back when I was working at Pratt, and thought I was pretty cool at the time, but I couldn't imagine wanting to allow myself to be reached 24/7, no matter where I went.

I loved the architecture, and how 'old' in Paris meant thousands of years, rather than the hundreds of years when referring to Quebec buildings. Even how the buildings are narrow in the front, then expand out to fit the streets. Barb enjoyed how fancy everyone dressed.

We spent a day exploring the Louvre, but I easily could have spent three. It was so interesting to see the artifacts of how people lived in the past.

We were both shocked to see how many animals were allowed in restaurants, and how we had to pay to use the washrooms, which were subpar compared to ours, sometimes consisting of nothing more than a hole in the ground.

We left Paris to visit Belgium; the land of my ancestors. We visited the Manneken Pis statue and purchased a few small brass replicas for souvenirs.

The evening we were scheduled to return to Paris, there was an incident that delayed the train. By the time we got to Paris, it was early morning, so the metro wasn't running yet. I tried to find us a taxi as we walked towards our hotel, which was roughly six kilometers away. We didn't get far before running into a police road block.

It wasn't until the officer approached us, hand on her gun, asking what we were doing in such a dangerous area, that we found out it wasn't safe.

I explained to her about the trip to Belgium and the train delay in French, but my Quebec accent was very different from her Parisian one. She asked where we were from, correctly pegging us as lost tourists. I told her we were from Quebec, and it was our first time in Europe, so she offered to take us to our hotel in their Paddy wagon, as they were taking down the road block.

It was quite the experience!

The officers all asked about things in Quebec, insisting that they would love to visit our country. I told them to look us up if they ever did!

With the Manneken Pis Statue in Belgium.

We came home and got ready for the Christmas suppers. In honor of our theme, we even asked our hedge guy, Guy Bernard, to turn one of them into the Eiffel Tower.

We let Chelsea and Amanda help serve this year, so they took turns acting as our doorman, waiting for the cars to pull up, then opening the door to let them in. We had them in black coats and top hats, with white gloves, and made sure they pointed out the Eiffel Tower, in case the guests hadn't spotted it. Diane, a camper who took care of our flowers, made another tower for us to have inside, using Styrofoam and Christmas lights. The girls took pictures of all the guests in front of it after we handed them their berets. We'd bought a lot more knickknacks during our travels, so all the staff wore Paris Bistro aprons and chef hats. I think it was our best year yet!

Sandra, Linda, Amanda, and Lynn.

FORTY-TWO
2004

"Dance like nobody's watching; love like you've never been hurt. Sing like nobody's listening; live like it's heaven on earth."
-Mark Twain

Amanda, Rikki, me, Paul, and Linda.

After Sandra and Linda raved about their experiences at All-Inclusive resorts, we decided to take a family vacation to Breezes Punta Cana, so we could all go together. Lynn turned us down, saying that if it didn't have a washer and a dryer, she wasn't interested. It was why she had stayed at a hotel while we all stayed at the campground in Disney. Chelsea's best friend, and our beloved lifeguard, Jessica came with us, and our friends Tony and Sonja Vanderzon were waiting for us with two of their children when we arrived on the night of February 28th.

They already had the lay of the land, so when they saw our bus drive up, they greeted us in the lobby with drinks. Tony brought me a drink that was so fancy, it was on fire! I took a sip of my flaming drink, unaware that you were supposed to blow it out and let it cool down before putting your lips on the glass. My lips were blistered for at least a week.

Our first day there was rather cloudy and not as sunny as we would have liked, so most of us explored the resort and drank in the lobby, but the girls spent their day in the hot tubs to 'keep warm'. In the evening, we went to the Mexican restaurant, and I discovered that I like the 'Tex Mex' version of Mexican food, not the authentic kind.

The following morning, Barb came with me to eat breakfast at 7 am. We got into a routine where we had an early breakfast, I would go to the on-site spa, then I would have coffee and maybe a little snack while the others finished their breakfasts. This particular morning, it took forever for them to join us. Eventually, we found out that Rikki had gone to the doctor's because her entire face was swollen. She was diagnosed with Sun Poisoning, given a shot of Benadryl, and told to avoid the sun for the next 48 hours. That was much easier said than done in the Dominican Republic, so she and Amanda stayed in their room (that they shared with Chelsea, Jessica, and Paul) during the day, only coming out at night.

The resort's entertainment was in a coliseum-like theatre, where only the stage was covered from the elements, but the shows were wonderful. They had an entire team of dancers, but they also had variety show nights, or competitions like 'Mr. Breezes', and a weekly karaoke night that we all participated in. Before the show, they would have the children do a little activity, which Barbara loved to watch, even though our grandchildren were all grown up. Then they would teach everyone the club dance.

It was truly paradise, to be in the sun with my family, drinking all the fancy drinks and enjoying delicious meals without having to pay anything extra. We were such a large group, with five beautiful young girls, so all of the animators knew us, and often sat to eat their meals with us. I participated in more activities than I ever had before, with dancing lessons, Beach Olympics, Water Aerobics, Water Polo...you name it, we tried it.

It was during the second week that we told one of the animators about Chelsea being a dancer, taking ballet and jazz since she was a toddler. We thought it was just fake enthusiasm when he asked her a bunch of questions, until he invited her to dance in one of their shows later on in the week. I think Chelsea wanted to relax and not make such a big deal of it, but we quickly convinced her to say yes. She rehearsed for a couple of days with the dancers, then blew us all away as a pink spotted white cat in their production of Cats. I had been watching her dance shows for years, and knew she was talented, but I was amazed at how it took her less than two days to look like she had been dancing with them for years. I was so proud, telling everyone who would listen that she was my granddaughter.

OUR RESORT HAPPENED to have a trapeze at it, which almost everyone tried out. My back was acting up, which definitely wasn't helped by the dancer who liked to jump up into my arms every time she saw me, so I sat this one out. JP, however, really enjoyed it, and participated in one of their shows. He was rather good, but I think we were too busy giggling at his lime green spandex outfit to notice. It's funny that he could trapeze without getting hurt, but pulled his hamstring while fetching an out of bounds volleyball.

The restaurants were absolutely delicious, and

we discovered the magic of crème brulée. The French restaurant was our favorite, because of the food, but mostly because they would break hotel rules and seat us before our entire party had arrived. As someone who considered people late when they arrived on time, it was very difficult for me to wait for the grandkids, who usually left their room at the time we were supposed to meet at the restaurant.

I WAS AMAZED to find they had Grand Marnier, which I love, but is very expensive, so I ordered it all the time. We had read up before coming on what the common tipping practices were, but we may have overdone it, because they would go above and beyond to give us the best service imaginable. When one bar ran out of Grand Marnier, waitresses would run to another bar to get some for me, often without me even asking.

There were vendors along the beach, selling all kinds of jewelry, alcohol and souvenirs. Their favorite advertisement was, "Cheapy, cheapy, almost free!", which we still use to this day to describe a bargain. I wandered there on my own one day, and came back with a souvenir for Danny, that everyone thought I paid way too much for. To prove it to me, they had me watch as Cazzie bought the same thing for less than a third of what I paid. I told them I didn't mind, that I was so much more fortunate than these people, but they still made it a rule that I wasn't allowed to go there on my own anymore.

It was a marvelous vacation, and even after two weeks, we were all sad to be leaving. None more so than Jessica, who spent our last night crying as we said goodbye to all of the animation team.

ONCE I GOT BACK to work at the campground, I had plans to build a large garage, where we would be able to repair our equipment, and store it in the winter. Unfortunately, we were having problems with the city, so I let it go and extended a plateau area to the storage instead. We didn't need to fence it in, as it was so far removed from circulation, and we even kept it graveled. We charged the same price whether it was asphalted or not, so it didn't make sense to spend the money on asphalt when the demand was there either way.

SANDRA'S FAMILY was going to renovate their house, but when the architect told them it would be smarter to move, they decided to build their house on the Wyngaert Estate instead. They moved in with us at the beginning of the summer, while we started work on a fancy, cement house for them. Sandra designed it to be the house of their dreams, with grand staircases, walk-in closets, reading nooks, a wine cellar, an in-law suite...it truly was a mansion.

As far as the summer went, we hardly noticed a difference, as they were usually there every day for work anyway. There was a motorhome in our storage that went into foreclosure, so we accepted the unit to make up for the unpaid storage fees. Once it was sanitized, JP and Sandra moved into it while Amanda took the spare bedroom and Paul slept in the basement. Amanda listened to me as I sang to her and told stories of my youth in the mornings while Barbara took to making her lunches (Paul preferred to buy his). After hearing that red grapes make you smart and improve your memory, Barb added it to her grocery list so she could put them in Amanda's lunches every day. Whenever we were on our vacations, she would ask Lynn to drop off a lunch for Amanda, since she was making them for Steve and Eric anyway. The kids were definitely spoiled!.

In November, I was invited to a special evening for the Richelieu Valley Chamber of Commerce, and was honored to receive their 'Grand Richelois 2004-2005 Award' for my contributions to the local economy.

WE WERE VERY nostalgic this year for our Christmas supper theme, so we went with Traditional Christmas. We had roasted chestnuts, 'Christmas' soup, and everything we would have dreamed of having for Christmas when we were little.

FAMILY VACATIONS HAD BECOME our yearly tradition, so we went to Mexico, at the Occidental

Grand Flamenco Xcaret, for the Christmas holidays.

The week before we left, we went to Thailand, one of our favorite Asian restaurants, with the usual Tuesday night gang. Georges received a fortune cookie that read, "You will soon come into a lot of money." Since the entire family would be on the same flight together in a few days, Georges assumed this meant we were going to crash. As someone who didn't really enjoy flying to begin with, my stress levels went through the roof. However, when I told my children about it, they said, "As long as it happens on the flight home."

Barbara, Chelsea, Eric, Rikki, Steve, JP, Sandra, Paul, Amanda, Linda, Cazzie, Lynn, and I.

The grandkids were old enough not to believe in Santa anymore, so I would usually wait until there was a big enough pile of presents under the tree, then bring a chair upstairs to let them know we were opening the gifts. It came in handy this year, as we left on December 25th, spending Christmas day in an airport instead of at home, but at least we were all together.

It was wonderful to have everyone there, but this resort was a lot less fun than Breezes. We were so used to being roped into all of the animation team's shenanigans, but this time we had to convince them to do the pool aerobics. Half the time they cancelled it, saying it was too cold, and the other half they led the exercise from outside the pool. While Breezes constantly had volleyball and water polo games going on, here we had to ask them to set up the net so we could play, which was usually more trouble than it was worth.

The nightly entertainment, however, was wonderful. Every night, we got to listen to Joanne, a Canadian expat, sing with a piano accompaniment. They even had a popcorn machine to keep us supplied in snacks.

One night, we were all listening to the piano and enjoying our drinks for hours after dinner. When we finally got up to leave, Lynn tried to put her shoes on, but for the life of her, she couldn't.

"My feet are so swollen my shoes don't even fit!" Lynn said, showing us her feet.

We all laughed until Linda put her shoes on and tried to follow, but nearly tripped over her own feet. Once Danny caught her and she steadied herself, we realized that Linda and Lynn had brought the same pair of shoes on vacation, and Lynn had tried to put on Linda's size 7s, while Linda was floating in Lynn's 9s. We laughed about it for days!

The girls were pretty excited when they ran into an actor from the Xmen movies, but I was much more interested in the Xcaret Park. Our resort was situated next to a cultural park which I would compare to a Mexican Disney. I think they called it an amusement park, but it was also a nature reserve, with wild animals both on land and in the ocean. There were recreations of traditional villages, and I was mesmerized by the 'Ha: Breath of Life' show we got to see in the evening. I was expecting fire dancing, like we saw in Hawai'i, but I was not expecting a game of field hockey where the puck is on fire. Or for all of the statues that surrounded us to come to life and participate in the show. It was absolutely magical!

We spent another day snorkelling in underwater caves, which was more incredible than I could have imagined. I had been snorkelling before, but nothing compared to the snorkelling we did on this trip. One moment we were in complete darkness, and the next we were bathed in light from a tiny opening in the ceiling, sometimes having to swim underneath to get to the next section. Back at the resort, we barely had a beach, which was inconvenient for us, because we loved walking the beach in the mornings and the afternoons, but there sure were a lot of fish! Cazzie got a terrible sunburn on his back because he went out snorkelling every day with a water bottle filled with bread, and spent hours swimming with what looked like thousands of fish.

One of our last days there, Sandra's family, as well as Linda and Chelsea, spent a day as Dolphin Trainers. They went behind the scenes at Xcaret and learnt about the dolphins, stingrays and manatees, even getting to swim with them. Cazzie, Rikki, and I went to meet up with them at the end of the day, when they each took turns being pushed through the water by a pair of dolphins. Pressing a nose to each foot, the dolphins would lift them out of the water, so it looked like they were standing up and gliding over the surface of the ocean. We were enthralled just watching it, until it was JP's turn. They were all given 'uniforms' for the day, and the shorts mustn't have fit properly, because almost as soon as JP came out of the water, his bathing suit pants came down, showing us everything. It was definitely not what any of us were expecting to see that day.

FORTY-THREE
2005

"You can have it all. You just can't have it all at once."
-Oprah Winfrey

We decided we preferred flying to hotels with the family rather than driving alone in the motorhome, so we sold it. We only received half of what we paid for it, making it a terrible investment financially. Cars and motorhomes usually are, but the memories we made traveling over the past two decades were worth it.

After hearing all of our stories, Ronnie and Anne were also looking to try an all-inclusive vacation, so we thought it would be fun to go the four of us together. When we saw the Sandals Royal Bahamian resort was 65% off, we immediately booked for April 2nd.

Getting there wasn't easy. Our flight was delayed and they left our bags outside in the rain all night, so we arrived in Bahamas at 4 a.m., exhausted, with our bags soaking wet. When we got to our room, however, we assumed Sandra must have secretly paid for an upgrade, because it was gorgeous. As it turns out, the upgrade was complimentary. After paying for upgrades we never got at other resorts, it was a welcome change.

We were worried when we read that Sandals doesn't allow tipping, since it greatly contributed to the excellent times we had on our previous all-inclusive vacations. We tried to tip the man who brought our luggage to our room – under the table – but he refused, explaining that he would be fired if he accepted it.

As it turned out, the service was above and beyond our wildest dreams, even without tipping. It was only for a week, but Sandals became the standard through which we measured all subsequent vacations.

We were so impressed by their chocolate buffets and a la carte breakfasts, which we had never seen before. Most all-inclusives will offer buffets for all the meals, with a la carte suppers at some of their restaurants that require reservations. At Sandals, if you want, you can spend the week without ever setting foot in a buffet. They also don't allow anyone under eighteen, which meant we never once had screaming children at supper or playing in the hot tubs. Although I loved our trips with the grandkids, it was nice to be 'couples only' sometimes.

One of the days of our trip, the four of us ventured out to the Atlantis resort. The Thompsons found refuge in the casino, while Anne and I explored, eventually finding a movie theater on the promenade, where all the movies were free. By the time we got out, Barb and Ronnie were still at the machines.

We spent hours exploring the little shops they would set up on some evenings. It wasn't necessarily that there was so much to see, but Anne liked talking to all of the shop owners, asking them about their lives and their families.

Ronnie, Anne, me, and Barbara in Bahamas.

Back at the campground, we were working hard, building Sandra's house. We were still going off of a verbal permit, but it hadn't caused any problems yet. When Hydro Quebec told us they couldn't put in the electricity without an address, we directed them to the city, who gave us 3451 de l'industrie.

The house was taking shape, so you could walk the halls and recognize all of the different rooms. The windows had arrived, and the entire structure was built by the time the city advised us to stop any further work on the house.

We were incredibly confused, but apparently,

our permit had been denied. After a verbal approval, months of construction, and hundreds of thousands of dollars, they were going back on their word.

There had to be a misunderstanding, so we went to the mayor, who told us we could get our permit as long as we closed the campground. They saw it as a win-win situation. With the campground gone, they could build a housing development, which we'd already started.

I was so discouraged. We had built the campground from the ground up over the past three decades, and now they were making me decide between my family business and the family legacy I wanted to build upon it. Unfortunately, the Wyngaert Estates were intrinsically tied to Camping Alouette, and I did not want to have anything to do with this manipulative and treacherous municipality. We abandoned Sandra's dream house and started listening to the offers people made to buy the campground.

WE STILL WENT on our weekend getaways, now to hotels instead of campgrounds. We would usually stay within a few hours' drive, like the Hilton Hotel at Lac Leamy, weekend trips to Quebec City, and several trips to London and Niagara Falls. We made it a point to eat in the best restaurants, and took the time to enjoy the area, such as local vineyards, since we didn't have a campfire to sit around.

OUR FRIEND RON D'ERRICO, who did the paving at the campground, invited us to his place on Lac Toro. We slept in his cottage, went for drinks at a hotel nearby, and even went on a boat ride. I had known Ron since my early days at Pratt!.

UNFORTUNATELY, Roger was diagnosed with Alzheimer's Disease around this time. We had noticed small things at first, like when he got lost going to places we knew well, or needed my help to install his satellite. You see, Roger was incredibly gifted at repairing any kind of motor or appliance. It was like he just looked at them and immediately knew how they worked. Which was why it was so heartbreaking when he came to the campground to repair one of our dryers, took it all apart, then couldn't figure out how to put it back together.

BARB HAD her own health scares after eating some wild rice. She was in very bad pain all night, so we went to the hospital and found out it was a flare up of her diverticulitis. She needed surgery to remove a chunk of her intestines, and was in the hospital for ten days. We found out she is very entertaining when she is on morphine, as she hallucinates. She commented on the flowery wallpaper to Denise, who was worried as the walls did not have any wallpaper. Denise told the doctors, who lowered Barb's dosage. It was the first time we saw her on these drugs, but it would not be the last.

Linda, Evelyn, Sandra, Mary-Anne, Brigitte, Anne, and Victoria.

In September Linda and Sandra accomplished the incredible feat of walking sixty kilometers in one weekend to raise money for breast cancer. I am so proud of them!

ROBERT WYNGAERT

. . .

IN OCTOBER, we went to the camping convention as usual, but this year was extra special. They always have a theme for their parties, and this year, since we were at the Manoir Richelieu in Charlevoix, it was olden days. As in 1800s, Victorian Era costumes for everyone. We sent in our sizes and got our outfits when we arrived, so some of us were happier than others. I got to wear a top hat and a three-piece long suit, complete with an ascot tie, which I hadn't worn in years.

Barbara, Me, Sandra, and Linda.

This year, Barb actually paid attention to one of our daytime sessions, since Linda was running it with Maryanne Hoelsher. There is a lot of financial planning we never even considered before she went into that field, so she booked a spot at the conference to share her knowledge on things like family trusts with the rest of the campground owners. After Barb was done supporting Linda, she went back to the casino, where she won 1000$!

Barbara, Georges, and Denise.

ROBERT WYNGAERT

WE HAD some fresh blood at the Thompsons supper this year, inviting Barb's cousin Ray and his wife, Linda, while Carol brought her daughter, Wendy as her date. Our theme was Mardi Gras, so we got our granddaughters silly hats and had them imitate the animated fool we had as part of the decorations.

FORTY-FOUR
2006

"Letting go doesn't mean giving up, it means moving on."
-Unknown

On January 1st, we continued our tradition of all-inclusives with the family, but this time, Sandra, JP, and Paul stayed home at the campground while the rest of us went to Ocean Sands Beach and Golf Resort in Punta Cana. We were glad to have Jessica with us again, as well as Lynn's brother, Paul Blanchard. He'd worked at the campground for years, so he was also a part of the family.

This time was much more like Breezes, although the resort was so big that we couldn't always be together. I think Paul Blanchard enjoyed his first time vacationing with us as much as we did, joining in for volleyball, water polo, and many other activities.

We tried another snorkeling excursion, but it was very different from the one in Mexico. Punta Cana has a large ship that is wrecked just off the coast. You can't see this from the shore, but there is a huge 'cage' under the water with sharks. It is quite the maze to get inside, so when the man in charge of us saw that I was having trouble, he said, "Come granddad, I'll help you," and guided me through. I was used to being called granddad, but I don't think he meant it in the same way my grandkids do.

Apparently, I wasn't the only one having trouble, as the girls went back up to the boat long before our time there was done. When I asked them why they left, they explained that Paul Blanchard cut himself on the cage when he was going in, and they didn't want to be near the shark when it realized there was fresh blood in the water.

My back was acting up again, which wasn't too bad, until we went on a banana boat ride. The girls went parasailing, so we thought it would be fun to watch them from the water, but the boat was going so fast and taking sharp turns, that I flew off. It would have been fine, as I was used to it with my brothers, but for the life of me, I couldn't get back on. Cazzie had to help me up, and once the fear sets in, you don't want to fall off again.

. . .

IN FEBRUARY, we met with professionals to prepare the documentation necessary for the eventual sale of the campground. It was very hectic, as we had offers coming in one after the other. We'd had offers ever since we built up the campground's reputation, but had never entertained them like we were now. It took time to analyze each one.

ON MARCH 5TH, we were getting ready for another busy season at the campground when I received an emergency distress call from my brother, Georges. He was convinced that he had throat cancer, but the doctors here weren't agreeing with him, so he flew to Las Vegas to get a second opinion at the Mayo Clinic. Barb and I took the first flight out so we could be there for him and his wife, Denise, who was a basket of nerves.

The specialist assured Georges he didn't have cancer and the symptoms were in his head, but Barb and I were still glad we went. Georges' fear and paranoia would have driven them crazy if left unchecked, but as it was, we spent a week there with them, distracting them and helping them get over their ordeal.

NOW THAT THE Wyngaert Estates had fallen through, Sandra and JP were looking for a new house, as they couldn't stay with us forever. It was a wonderful experience, having them so close, but none of us ever thought it would go on this long. We went to many open houses, before they ultimately decided to build a house in a new development in Beloeil, less than five minutes away from their old house.

Fay, Barbara, Kay, Anne, Roger, me, and Ronnie in Atlantic City.

IN JULY, Barb and I went to Atlantic City, forty-eight years after we first went for our honeymoon. This time, we stayed at the Tahj-Mahal Hotel, and could afford to go into any shop or casino we wanted. We even got to participate in a version of 'The Price is Right'!

When we got back from the trip, I was shocked to see that my weight had reached 240 lbs. I decided to do something about it, hiring a nutritionist to meet with me on a weekly basis, and eventually got back down to 199lbs by the end of the year.

IN OCTOBER, I refused a large offer from Parkbridge, a company that owned many RV communities throughout Canada. We liked the idea that Parkbridge would keep it as a campground, and that they had so much experience in the broader camping industry. We even liked Dave Rozycki, one of the owners we met with, but we felt our campground was worth a lot more than they offered.

ON NOVEMBER 20TH, GEORGES' wife Denise had a quadruple bypass surgery at the Montreal General Hospital. I was no stranger to major heart surgery, so I tried to assuage her fears before she went under, and we all checked on her once she was in recovery. We even got her a bracelet, although I'm not sure I understand how jewelry helps you recover from surgery. Denise has been a part of my family almost four times longer than she was out of it, and has been a constant friend and travel companion to us for over fifty years. She means the world to us, so we wanted to make sure we went there to show her.

ROBERT WYNGAERT

. . .

IN DECEMBER, Sandra went to the hospital for a complete hysterectomy to treat the endometriosis she'd been suffering from for years. It was heartbreaking to watch her as she wobbled in pain, walking slower than an eighty-year-old, but it was the knowledge that I couldn't do anything to help her that killed me. I can ignore my own pain for days or weeks, even months, but I constantly tried to call her an ambulance, because I couldn't accept that nothing could be done to help my baby girl, when she was clearly in so much pain. That was the hardest part for me, but for her, I think it was the doctors who told her, one after the other, that this was all in her head. That she was exaggerating her symptoms and should go on with her life, working through the pain. Instead of feeling supported and cared for, Sandra felt shame, so she spent so much of her time those years apologizing to us for being an embarrassment. No matter how many times we told her we loved her and were concerned about her pain, not about our pride, she didn't listen.

This year for our Family Christmases, we chose Las Vegas/Casino night as our theme. It was an exceptional year as far as how many weekend trips we took, and so many of them included casinos. It also gave Barb the chance to put whatever she wanted on the menu, and gave us an activity we could all do after dinner. We ended up doing karaoke, as we always did, but it was a lot of fun.

THE NIGHT after the Wyngaert supper, we attended another big event, the fiftieth anniversary of Broadway Paving. It was a night of dinner and dancing, with some surprise old friends. We obviously knew Ron D'Errico and his family, but they put Barb and I at a table with Ron Buswell, and his wife, Angie. He had worked under me at Pratt, what now truly felt like a lifetime ago. I have never regretted retiring from Pratt, just as I was starting to climb the corporate ladder, but it is always nice to be reminded of who I once was.

FORTY-FIVE
2007

"Don't cry because it's over, smile because it happened."
-Dr. Seuss

Lynn's cancer came back. In another example of the medical system failing, every time she went in and described her pain, sharing her fears that it was cancer, they told her it was a herniated disk, or something equally innocuous. Losing weight and getting massages were their recommended treatments, until they saw the spots on her lungs and realized they'd been wrong.

BY THE SPRING, Lynn seemed to be doing better, so I brought the entire family to Quebec City for

March Break. We left on a Thursday and went to Michelangelo's for supper, taking advantage of how close it was to walk there without having to worry about a designated driver.

On Friday we went for supper at Le Continental. It was the first time for many of them, and I was so excited to share the experience with them. Cazzie and Barb wanted French fries, as usual, so there were plates of fries put across the table for everyone. I personally love their potatoes and seasonal assortment of vegetables, but I have to say the fries are also tough to beat. One of my favorite parts of the Continental, other than being treated like a beloved regular, is spending hours eating delicious food with the people I love.

We went home on Saturday to give the girls some time to pack. Barb had wanted to go on another vacation, but I had no interest in travelling, so I said I would pay for someone to go with her. I wasn't expecting everyone to volunteer! In the end, Linda, Sandra, and Lynn took me up on my offer, while Chelsea and Amanda paid their own way. They tried to make me jealous, so I would regret my decision, telling me all about the food, the sun, their slumber parties, and inside jokes, but I was fine at home alone. I had to get the campground ready, and the less planes I had to go on, the better.

They were shocked to see how beautiful the renovated store was when they got home, and I was proud of what we had accomplished.

CHELSEA WAS STUDYING SCIENCE, and Amanda was planning on becoming a doctor, so when the BodyWorlds exhibition came to Montreal, the three of us, and JP, went to check it out. I have always been fascinated by how the body works, and it was incredible to see what's going on underneath our skin, with all the muscles necessary to perform simple tasks. They also had animal bodies, which was so interesting!

ON MAY 6TH, Lynn was admitted to the hospital. They'd been administering chemotherapy treatments, but things were not improving. At first, she was in good spirits, figuring out how to watch her tv shows on a computer (before Netflix went digital), but we could see that she was not doing well. The cancer was in her lungs and her bones, making it hard for her to breathe, and she was in constant pain. After a few weeks, she asked if she could go home to be more comfortable, so we made sure she had everything she needed to make that happen.

. . .

IN THE MIDDLE of the night between May 30th and 31st, we got a call from Danny saying Lynn took a turn for the worse, so an ambulance was bringing them to the hospital. We rushed there to meet them, while Sandra and Linda went to his house to look after the boys, who were still sleeping.

Ethel and Mike, Lynn's parents, joined us at the hospital before she took her last breath.

WHEN WE TOLD Steve and Eric, they decided that they still wanted to go to school, so the other grandchildren went as well. Danny and Linda went to make the funeral arrangements, while the rest of us sought the comfort of each other at the campground.

By lunchtime, all of the grandkids were there with us as we tried to process what had happened. Lynn wasn't the first person I loved who died, but she wasn't like my parents and Barb's, she was like my child. Only forty-four years old, with two children still in high school. It wasn't right, and it didn't make sense.

OVER THE NEXT FEW DAYS, we planned her funeral, making program booklets, folding pink breast cancer ribbons, bringing the boys to buy suits...it was a period of intense darkness. We tried our best to put on a brave face for the boys, encouraging them to go to the movies with their cousins, but nobody was even remotely okay.

We had to cancel the first aid course we were supposed to have that weekend, and closed the entire campground on June 4th, the day of the funeral. We still had campers, but every store employee, every grounds worker, every longtime camper...everyone was at the church. We had a group, West Coast Connections, that came every year, and completely forgot to warn them or have them pay their bill...we just shut down.

The funeral was held at the Our Lady of Fatima Church, where most of the family went every Sunday. There were so many people there that they didn't even fit inside the church. Every seat was taken, people were standing in the back, and once the service was over, we saw that there were people waiting outside and in the hallways. Lynn was loved!

LOSING her changed everything in our family. For years, we had developed a flow at the campground, with Sandra tackling days, Lynn working nights, and Danny handling the grounds. In one fell swoop, we lost Lynn, Danny went into a depression, and it took a very long time for any of us to feel okay again. It didn't help that for years, campers would come in and ask us, "Where is Lynn?" or the office staff would pull out a storage contract and start crying when they recognized her handwriting, while the client looked on in confusion. The frustration that had pushed me to sell the campground before was nothing compared to the grief that showed us we couldn't go on like this anymore.

WE HAD A STRING OF OFFERS, and people who came close to buying the campground, but they all ultimately fell through. After a few more close calls, we got into negotiations with Parkbridge, who were still very interested.

EVEN WITH THE possibility of an impending sale, we treated the campground like it would stay in our family for generations. In July, we drew up plans to hook up to the newly installed municipal sewer system, which we had been fighting to have for the last twenty-five years. We used one of our campers, Roger Gauthier, as our excavation contractor, because I like supporting the people who support us. Plus, we knew he had a vested interest in the project. He estimated it would cost $140 000, which was steep for something none of the campers would necessarily notice, but it was a lot cheaper than the alternative.

Years before, there was an issue with the septic system at Camping Lac du Repos, so the owner went into the septic tank to fix it on his own. His son-in-law was waiting outside, so when the owner stopped responding, his son-in-law went in after him. Within minutes, the two of them, as well as a camper who tried to help, all died from the toxic fumes inside. After watching the pain and sorrow that family went through because of their septic system, any amount of money to get hooked up to the municipal sewer system was worth it.

PARKBRIDGE LIFESTYLE COMMUNITIES finally came to their senses and realized they did not want to miss out on the opportunity of a lifetime with Camping Alouette. They presented us with a new offer, which was more reasonable, but still less than I believed the campground was worth.

We analyzed it, then made a list of all of the campground's assets to show them how much more they were getting than what meets the eye. Sandra typed it all up for me, using the MasterCard commercial format. After listing all of the assets and their worth, she wrote, "Our five-star reputation: Priceless." She also included, "Add a million to your offer, and consider it our counter-offer" more to be funny than because we meant it, as we were sure nobody would settle for a million dollars over their offer price.

We were absolutely shocked when they accepted.

Suddenly, the campground was sold, but we hadn't really intended to accept it. I talked it over with my family, as well as trusted professionals, and we decided it was in our best interest to go through with it. Not because we'd inadvertently agreed to it, but because I was tired of the physical labor and mental stress the campground involved, and none of my grandchildren planned to take it over.

We didn't believe the sale was real until the papers were signed, as we had gone through many offers and verbal agreements that fell through, often at a heavy cost to us.

IN OCTOBER, for our health and for a change in scenery, we spent the weekend in Mont Tremblant. On Saturday, Sandra, Linda and their friend Brigitte came up so the four of us could go for a hike. Barb spent the day with Georges, Denise, Jean Pilote, and his wife, Louise.

During the hike, Sandra was the only one who brought a bag, so we all put our stuff in it, including water bottles and snacks. It was a lot more difficult than I wanted to let on, but I was saved from being the focus of everyone's concern when Sandra passed out at the beginning of our climb. We figured she must be hungry, so were in the process of putting pieces of banana in her mouth when she woke up. She insisted she was fine, but we were not convinced. I took the backpack from her and we kept going, but we made her go first, and I don't think I took my eyes off of her, just in case. Afterwards, we all went out for a nice supper, then the girls went home, and Barb and I enjoyed the rest of our weekend.

ON NOVEMBER 15TH, we met at our lawyer's office and signed the papers, making it official. I sold Camping Alouette, the business I operated for over thirty years with the help of my family. After signing, our lawyer hinted that it was customary for the buyers to take the old owners out for a fancy meal to celebrate, so we went to Vargas for a very long lunch.

IN THE FOLLOWING WEEKS, I felt so many mixed emotions. The campground was not only a place where we all came to work, it was also the place where we enjoyed countless parties with family and friends...it was home. Because of this, and the fact that we didn't want to have to go through the trouble of moving, we negotiated with Parkbridge so we could live in the house for the rest of our lives, rent-free.

ROBERT WYNGAERT

Camping Alouette in the Eighties.

Camping Alouette when we sold it.

On November 24th, Barb and I went to Cuba with Sandra and Linda. I joined in on their Girl's Trip because I needed a vacation after all the stress of the past year. We were very well treated at this Riu. One of the waitresses would reserve our table for us at the show every night. She is the one who gave us the catchphrase, "Thank you very much, enjoy your drink!" She would tell us we tipped so much that it was two for one, and we didn't have to tip again the next time.

This trip wasn't as relaxing for Sandra, who had trouble reaching her family, and a sinking feeling that something was wrong back home. It turned out that JP's father had passed away a couple of days after we left, but they didn't want to needlessly ruin her vacation. He'd had a few heart scares, like me, so while the Petrins mourned, it was a sobering wake up call for me. Some of JP's family stayed a few extra days, so we were able to catch up, offer our condolences, and thank them for decorating our house for Christmas while we were away.

Brian, Nancy, me, Sandra, and Barbara.

On December 7th, Barb and I went to Champlain College with Sandra, JP, Paul, Rikki, and Steve so we could watch Amanda in her school's production of The Coronation Voyage. Chelsea and Rikki weren't the only ones who took after their grandfather in the movie star department!

OUR THEME for the Christmas Suppers this year was Thailand, in honor of the restaurant, and food, we enjoyed so much. Barb tried out a multitude of recipes, as she always does, and every one was delicious. Still, we decided to outsource things this year to give her a break, and encourage a local business. Jessica, our bonus granddaughter, had a boyfriend whose family owned a Laotian/Cambodian restaurant called Pho Vietnam, so we hired them to do the catering.

We went to have lunch there one day, to make sure Jessica was right about the food being delicious, and it exceeded our expectations. While they didn't have all of our Thai favorites, they had many succulent dishes we were eager – and grateful- to discover.

Amanda, Linda, Chelsea, me, Rikki, and Sandra.

We had the Thompsons over on the 15th, confident that we'd organized an evening to remember. Since we didn't have to worry about making the food, we went all out with the decorations, even buying fish! We'd all had a tough year, so it was important that we try and raise everyone's spirits.

JUST A COUPLE OF DAYS LATER, Barb and I purchased our riverfront dream home facing Mont-Saint-Hilaire, in Beloeil. It had been JP's father's dream house, the one he said he would buy if ever he won the lottery, and selling the campground was our version of winning the lottery. Our niece, Johanne Wyngaert, went above and beyond to save me time, energy, and money, even if she wasn't earning a commission.

WE HAD my family over for our Thailand themed Christmas on the 22nd, then celebrated our family Christmas a few days later. There was a gaping Lynn-shaped hole in the day and in our hearts, but we tried to make the best of it, especially for the boys. In addition to the gifts we got the grandchildren, we gave each of them a certain amount of money for them to buy something special to commemorate the sale of the campground. I knew too well that we tend

ROBERT WYNGAERT

to let the big moments pass us by without noticing, so I wanted to make sure everyone did something to honor the role the campground had played in our lives.

RETIREMENT

FORTY-SIX
2008

"Life is short and it is up to you to make it sweet."
-Sandie Delaney

To celebrate the sale of the campground, and because it was now our tradition, we went to Punta Cana's Grand Paradise on January 3rd. Linda, Cazzie, Chelsea, Rikki, Danny, Steve, Eric, Amanda, and Paul had all been there for a week already, and weren't impressed, so we set our expectations very low.

It all went downhill as soon as we got to the airport. Right off the bat, our flight was delayed for ten hours due to mechanical problems, so Barb and I spent an entire day in the airport. Once we arrived in the Dominican, we saw that the others hadn't been exaggerating the hotel's issues. They had been calling

Sandra for days to try and get a refund, but were told that at least Barb and I were in the new section. That is to say, the resort was advertised as 'newly built', but in reality, some of the rooms hadn't been renovated in decades, some of them were mid-renovation, and others had been built on a deadline in darkness. I don't mean that like they did such a terrible job that it must have been done in the dark. I mean that when we walked around at night, we saw employees painting and installing light fixtures under the cover of darkness. While we couldn't always see them, we definitely heard them, drilling and hammering all hours of the night. Not to mention the drains kept getting blocked, which flooded our rooms every time it rained.

I've had heart attacks on vacations that were better than this one!

That being said, it wasn't all bad. Everyone except for Barb, Chelsea, and Amanda went out for a snorkeling trip, where we got to see beautiful fish and enjoy a nice boat ride. I was careful to never venture too far away from the boat, as I had recently seen Open Water on the plane, a movie about a couple that gets left behind on an excursion and are faced with sharks in the middle of the ocean.

Luckily, Sandra worked her magic and we all got the hotel fees refunded, so we only had to pay for our flights.

. . .

ON JANUARY 18TH, Barb and I took our new Cadillac to Lac Leamy for a family getaway to celebrate the sale of the campground. We all arrived at different times, then had to eat at the casino restaurant in shifts, because they didn't have enough room for all of us.

I was so excited to introduce them to the executive lounge – with fresh-baked cookies every night – and their incredible pool. It was half-inside, half-outside, so even in the dead of winter, you could swim under the stars. It was heated, of course, so we would sometimes get out and roll in the snow, making it extra warm when we got back in.

We missed Danny at supper, since he was called back to the campground, as well as the grandkids, who went to meet a family they had gotten close to during our Punta Cana trip. As for Barb, Sandra, JP, Linda, Cazzie, and I, we ate at the Baccara restaurant, which is incredibly fancy. It's the kind of restaurant where they wait until everyone's meal has been served, then a group of waiters come out so they can all lift the cloches to reveal the food at the same time.

Every course was delicious, but dessert was something else. We wanted to try everything. Our least favorite was the decorative flowers, but the rest more than made up for it. It wasn't until the waiters came back to offer us more coffee and their faces dropped, that we realized something was wrong.

"You ate the flowers?" they asked.

"Yeah, there were some chewy parts, but it wasn't bad," Cazzie said, not wanting to criticize their food, after everything else was so tasty.

The waiter was silent for a bit, before saying, "That must have been the glue." He admitted that they were meant as a decoration, not to be eaten. Nothing was toxic, so we would be fine, but boy were we embarrassed!

ON SUNDAY we all went home, just in time for our dance lessons. I wanted to have a big party this year, as it was my seventieth birthday and our fiftieth wedding anniversary. I thought it would be fun to have everyone waltz and foxtrot across the floor. Our friends, Tony and Sonja joined in as well, but I have to admit, I was surprised when Amanda, Rikki, Steve, and Paul all signed up with us. To be perfectly honest, I think Paul did better than anyone else in these classes. To this day, if we forget the steps, he and Sandra are the ones we will go to!

Ronnie, Joan, Doreen, Donna, Barbara, Carol, Marilyne, and Bobby.

On March 29th, we had our birthday and anniversary party at Helene de Champlain. So many people showed up, and after a delicious meal, we spent the night dancing away to Nightshift, a live band, before going home exhausted and happy.

My favorite part was when the grandkids got up and surprised us with a wonderful speech, turning our life into a fairytale. Some of the facts were off, but the sentiments and the magic are all true:

"Once upon a time there lived a beautiful princess in

MY FRIENDS CALL ME BOB

a magical city called Rosemount. This princess, let's call her Barb, lived with her father, her mother, her 5 sisters, and her 2 brothers. Their castle was a small one but that only brought them closer together. Being the second oldest it was only normal that she made sacrifices in order to take care of her younger siblings and for the family's finances. She always dreamed of meeting her Prince Charming and living a carefree life.

Meanwhile, in a quaint rural village, lived Prince Charming, but most people call him Bob. His castle stood alone with a white picket fence and was home to his parents, his 2 brothers and his 2 sisters. Although he was the youngest of the three princes, he was always the one called upon to defend the honor of the family.

At the sweet young age of 15 it was arranged that Barb would accompany Bob to the banquet. Having never met, they were surprised at how easily they got along and how quickly they fell in love. Unlike most fairytales which end when the prince and princess meet, the story of Bob and Barb is only just beginning.

Unbeknownst to Barb, Bob befriended the King hoping that when the time came he would approve of the match. The princess felt neglected as her prince charming no longer spent time with her, but passed many a moments on the balcony drinking ale with the king. The princess began to make alternative plans with her evenings and spent them with other gentlemen callers. The prince felt he was losing *the princess* and so he had a magician engrave his heart on his forearm. Her name appeared. The princess's older sister, Joan, and her suitor, took it upon themselves to encourage reconciliation, as they knew all along that the couple were soul mates. She took her sister's advice.

It was not a waste of time that the prince befriended the king, because when the king's carriage collided with a tree, and then Bob's carriage impaled the king's, it was convenient that they were on such good terms.

On the 7th day of June in the year of 1958, they were wed and became King and Queen of their own Kingdom. The family of two quickly grew to include, our parents, Linda, Danny, and Sandra. Life was not always easy but it was always an adventure. In order to achieve financial independence by becoming entrepreneurs they purchased dwellings that they rented out to fellowmen while still working for other kings, and even starring in the movie, The Pyx. Expanding their endeavours, they branched out into the cosmetic industry by buying and selling Koscot products. Because Barb was such a wonderful cook, Bob felt it was unfair to keep all that talent to himself, and so he opened an eatery called Bar-B-Delight in honor of his gorgeous bride. Owning an eatery that was open 365 days a year took a toll on the King and

Queen's family life which they held very dear. Consequently, they sold this business and put their profits into Camping Alouette, the beautiful 5 star campground that gave them the financial freedom they worked so hard for. The campground reign was the longest and the most prosperous, not only for the business but for their personal lives as well. It was during this time that they welcomed Danny, as Linda's husband, JP as Sandra's husband and finally, Lynn as Danny's bride. They also welcomed Chelsea, Amanda, Rikki, Steve, Paul, and Eric, their 6 wonderful grandchildren. After 31 years of owning and improving what became the best campground in all the land, they received an offer from Lord Park Bridge that they couldn't refuse.

Through the years Barb found her Prince Charming and the carefree life she always dreamt of. Her castle was now much larger, perfect for entertaining her family and friends, bust most importantly, her 6 grandkids who are: good-looking, smart, caring, hard-working, talented, and who make all the obstacles they went through worthwhile. We got our modesty from Granddad. And they all lived happily ever after. As we know, along with every fairytale is a moral. For this particular fairytale, which we all know is based on a true story, the moral is not that the princess dreamed of love and found it, but that it is important to work hard as a team in order to make your dreams come true. It also helps to have people around who are willing to lend a hand as well as a strong support group that is your family. Grandma and granddad's home is where the heart is. We love you guys. Congratulations on your golden years and we all hope to live a fairytale with as much love and adventure as yours has been and will continue to be. Here's to the next chapter!"

Roger, Fay, me, and Georges.

I HAD BEEN surprised when my beautiful sister, Irene, and her entire family were absent. The following day I found out that she hadn't been doing well, then took a fall and was currently in the hospital. Things were not looking good, but the kids hadn't wanted to worry me until after the party.

MY FRIENDS CALL ME BOB

Barb and I visited her on the Sunday, which happened to be my birthday, before we enjoyed a nice family supper. I am so grateful for that visit, and for all of the times I treated my sister to fancy restaurants, as she died on Monday, March 31st, putting a damper on Rikki's birthday.

The funeral was on the Friday, and I couldn't help but remember the previous Saturday, when I saw most of the family under much happier circumstances. We could tell Roger's Alzheimer's was getting bad, as he kept asking us, "Where's Irene?"

THIS HAPPENED to be Danny's birthday, so after the funeral, Barb and I took him and his new girlfriend, Josee, to Quebec City to celebrate. We had a delicious meal at the Continental, and I did some unusual shopping. Every time we came to Quebec City, we passed an Inuit Art Museum, with beautiful sculptures and paintings done by Inuit artists. I always found the items inside incredibly beautiful, so I decided it was time to treat myself. It was my birthday, after all!

We had a beautiful new house to decorate, so I purchased two bears sculpted in marble. They are unique in the world, which I believe makes them priceless. I have never seen any that even come close to mine. Even today, I can't believe how lucky I am to have them.

AS THIS WOULD BE my first summer in my adult life that I didn't have to go to work every day, I decided to get into golfing. I joined the Beloeil Golf Course and took lessons from Daniel Talbot, the club's resident professional. Joan and Bob were members at Chambly, so I would often go there to play with them, Ray Bonin (Barb's cousin), and Don Burke (a friend of Bob Smith). The Beloeil Golf

Course had a minimum spending limit, so although I didn't play there as much as I should have, I brought people there for supper almost every week, whether we played golf or not.

Roger.

On May 10th, Roger's doctor advised him that he would no longer be able to drive. He was very upset, so he decided to get out of the car and walk the rest of the way home.

Roger was found on a sidewalk that evening. He'd suffered a massive heart attack, but I was able to go to the hospital and see him before he passed away at 3:30 am. It happened to be Mother's Day, so we went out to celebrate with the family, but my heart definitely wasn't in it. My big brother, my hero and protector, was gone, and I just couldn't believe it.

His funeral was on Barb's birthday, and I was tasked with giving the eulogy, but no words could express how much he meant to me. Roger was my inspiration, showing me that if you work hard and build something for yourself, you can accomplish incredible things.

He used to work for Eaton's department store, and they would get rid of any dented or broken appliances. Roger, with his gift, would bring them to my garage and repair them, then sell them for a sizable profit. He turned his gift into Metro Appliance, and all of the businesses that came after.

In less than a year, we had lost Lynn, the campground, my sister, and now my brother. It was a dark time none of us would ever want to repeat, but I was grateful I had such a close-knit family to fall back on.

After this, we were finally able to move into our house. It was bittersweet to leave the house we'd lived in the longest, that our grandchildren had grown up in, but we were never going to be able to enjoy our retirement if we still lived at the campground. People came by all the time, wanting propane or to be let in after hours.

Other than Barb and I, everyone was still working at the campground, so we were leaving our home, but they still had their extended playground. Plus, Sandra negotiated so Danny could stay in the house instead of us, keeping it in the family.

. . .

IT WAS the beginning of a new life that we hoped would last a long time. We got a million-dollar view of Mont-Saint-Hilaire and its unbelievable daily changing view, with the Richelieu River flowing below. Each and every morning, I could watch the sun rise above the spectacular, indescribable views from my kitchen window.

We discovered that the view changed with the seasons, as well as with the weather. Some days the world would be filled with rain, while others it was a winter wonderland covered in a blanket of snow. I thought we would miss the bustle of the campground, but our street was very busy, with a lot of people who walked by every day. Barbara worries all winter, watching people walking or ski-dooing on the river, but come spring, the birds return, as well as the beautiful green grass, flowers and trees. In the Summer, we get to see the nature of things in full bloom, after a long and hard winter.

Apparently, a lot of people die soon after they retire, because they lose their sense of purpose, but I made sure this wouldn't happen to us, constantly finding new projects to work on. I set out patio furniture and cleaned the grounds so Barb could enjoy the outdoors, and got to work on renovations. They never stopped. On the exterior, I removed some large trees to provide more parking spaces, added outlets, and Jean-Guy Raymond helped me build a dock for my newly-purchased boat. On the inside, we renovated all of the bathrooms. Jean-Guy Proteau, my niece's ex-husband, installed a suspended ceiling in the solarium so I could transform it into an upstairs living room. I ordered custom-made blinds so we could choose how much sunlight we wanted to let in, and how much privacy we wanted to have.

On June 4th, my niece's son, Daniel Proteau, did an excellent job renovating the perimeter of our pool. He even added a giant stone fountain with a large brass blue heron bird, who keeps guard on the swimmers below, while simultaneously pouring water on them. He also installed a large stone at the base of the solarium, and a custom-made iron fence and gate to secure the property. I am so happy to have friends, and family, who are talented like that.

ON JUNE 29TH, everything was set and we were able to go on our first boat ride. We decided to name the pontoon Lynnie, after my daughter-in-law, and it put a smile on our face every time we saw it. I decided to take a page from Roger's book and had the boat leave every Sunday at 1 pm. That way, even if you weren't invited, or couldn't make it for lunch, you knew that you were always welcome if you showed up on my dock at 1 pm on a Sunday. Which many people did. Our first ride had my family, as well as Joan, Bob, Marilyne, Tony, and Carol. Throughout the summer, they would be our regulars, but they were often joined by others, such as Ronnie and Anne, Brian and Nancy, Georges and Denise, Diane and Al, Ken and Lou, etc.

. . .

MY FRIENDS CALL ME BOB

ON AUGUST 4TH, Linda decided to move in with us while she searched for an apartment. Chelsea and Rikki were going to be sharing a condo in Montreal while Chelsea studied Anatomy and Cell Biology at McGill, and Rikki was at Dawson. I felt a tightness in my chest, watching my grandbabies move out, looking so grown up. However, the week after they moved in, they called me to help fix their toilet for them, proving that you're never too old to need your granddad!

ON AUGUST 16TH, we had a repeat of the double wedding situation from 1956, but this time it was two of our great nieces, and there was no way we could attend both. Laura Smith, Danny and Brenda Smith's daughter, was marrying Justin Barfett in London, Ontario, while Stephanie Klein, Suzie Graham and Danny Klein's daughter, was marrying Josh Bartlett in Syracuse, New York. We got the invite to Laurie's wedding first, so Barb and I went there, while Sandra and Linda went to Stephie's. We made the eight-hour drive with Carol and her boyfriend, Greg, then I took them, as well as Tony, Marilyne, Ronnie, and Anne, to a nice restaurant called Le Petit Prince.

After the meal, and for most of the weekend, we entertained everyone in our hotel suite at the Best Western. The wedding was excellent, and it was wonderful to spend a weekend with so many Thompsons!

IN SEPTEMBER, Amanda won the Bob Gibson Memorial Scholarship, for employees of Parkbridge and their children. It is always hard to hand over something you have dedicated so much of your life into building, but Parkbridge was truly a company with the same values as me. I was so proud that they recognized how talented my daughter, Sandra, was, as they promoted her to Regional Manager at the end of her first summer. She was in charge not only of the campgrounds they had already purchased in Quebec, they trusted her to do the research and find more properties for them to purchase. It was a huge responsibility, orchestrating mutli-million-dollar deals, but with her knowledge and experience, they couldn't have found a more qualified person.

THAT FALL, the stock market crashed. I was so glad that, thanks to Linda, Barb and I had effective tax planning in place, and our finances were taken care of. We had invested the proceeds of the campground sale in a diversified portfolio under Linda's management, and she put a plan in place to pay me dividends that would replace the income we had been receiving from the campground. Unfortunately, taking our money out when the markets were so low would have bled us dry.

Thank God I had taken some money out to purchase my dream home before the markets crashed. I had enough money to buy the house outright at the time, but Linda recommended that I open a line of credit, just in case.

Well, that line of credit came in handy when the value of my portfolio was falling every day, with nothing but bad news on the economy. As Linda suggested, I used my line of credit for cash flow, to stop the bleeding of my capital until the markets rebounded.

In the meantime, she sold my investments and bought similar ones the same day to crystallize the capital losses. I was able to carry these losses back against the gains that I had on the sale of the business the previous year, which resulted in a sizeable tax refund. It was a scary and unpredictable time, but in the long term everything worked out. Looking back, I am so happy that I had Linda's guidance and expertise during this tough time. She made the best of what could have been a nightmare!

I WAS SO THRILLED with our new house that I never wanted to leave. I was happy simply staying there and inviting friends and family to enjoy it with me. Barb, however, still loved to travel, especially in the winter, so she went on another Girls Trip in November. She, Linda, Sandra, and Amanda went to the Beaches resort in Turks and Caicos for a week. They chose the location, then decided they would try Sandals' affiliate company, but Beaches is entirely geared towards children. When they came back, just in time for Chelsea's birthday brunch, they showed us all of their pictures with the characters from Sesame Street.

JP had taken advantage of their absence to go on a cure I recommended for him, where all you eat is water with lemon juice, cayenne pepper, and a bit of maple syrup. It was supposed to clean out his system and help him on his new venture to improve his health, which included a new workout program as well. Chelsea's birthday brunch was his first meal in a week, so he thoroughly enjoyed the cinnamon rolls and breakfast foods! Personally, I enjoyed seeing Chelsea and Rikki, who only came once a week now that they shared their apartment in the city.

WE WERE SHOCKED to find out that JP had a heart attack when he went home that night. Apparently, the combination of his cleansing cure and exercise program dislodged a piece of plaque from one of his arteries, sending it to a smaller one, and the decadent brunch sealed the deal, completely blocking the artery so his heart was cut off. They had to go in through his groin to remove the blockage, effectively saving his life.

Amanda, Rikki, Linda, Chelsea, and Sandra.

We didn't really feel that into the Christmas spirit this year, especially with half of my family missing for the Wyngaert supper, so we stuck to Traditional Christmas as the theme and just made turkey.

FORTY-SEVEN
2009

"Whoever has a heart full of love, always has something to give."
-Pope John XXIII

We kicked off the New Year with a trip to the Hilton Hotel in Lac Leamy to celebrate Sandra's 44th birthday. We left on the Sunday and stopped for a delicious lunch at Red Lobster on the way. We spent the afternoon gambling before an exquisite meal at the Baccara. This time we didn't embarrass ourselves by eating the decorations, although – to be honest – I don't recall them bringing us any.

On Sandra's actual birthday, we spent the day going back and forth between the casino, the inside-outside pool, and our hotel room. After one of our swims, Amanda and I went to the sauna. It started out okay, but the longer we stayed in, the hotter it got. I'm the type of person who will never give up first, as you've probably noticed. Unfortunately, my granddaughter was the same way. More than once, Sandra came in to tell us we should get out, but each time, Amanda and I both told her we were fine and could stay in there all day. I think it was a combination of the fact that we were about to pass out, and Sandra telling us we would miss our dinner reservations that convinced us to get out, at the same time, both of us still insisting that we could have stayed much longer.

THIS NEXT EVENT isn't something I participated in, I really just watched it happen, but I still believe that it is worth mentioning. After living through the segregation and racial divides of my youth, I got to see Barack Hussein Obama, an African American man with a Kenyan Father and a Muslim middle name, inaugurated as the 44th president of the United States of America. CNN is often running in the background at our house, and although I joke about the 'breaking news' that consists of the same stories they've been repeating all day, this was a moment I was proud to be able to see during my lifetime.

Barbara, me, and Sandra.

In February, Barb and I left for Sandals Cuba with Sandra and JP. Linda had already been there and told us it had all of our beloved Sandals amenities, but with a slightly more affordable price. They had been twice, and given the DJ a hard drive with all of Cazzie's karaoke songs, so we were treated good from the start. We spent the day in a cave, and enjoyed the manager's cocktail, where Barb and I won the contest of who has been married the longest. When they asked Barb our secret to staying together so long, she forgot the word for 'communication' and instead told them it was 'orientation'. She was adorable, turning the bingo wheel instead of picking a number when they asked her to, resulting in the papers flying everywhere, and to them keeping us on the stage much longer than anticipated. They upgraded our candlelit dinner for two to a dinner for four, nestled in one of their wine cellars, with our very own musicians serenading us. For days after, people would cross our path and say, "Hi Barb!" because she was so entertaining. She made an impression!

IN MAY, Chelsea graduated from McGill University with a Bachelor of Science. I can't even tell you what Anatomy and Cell Biology means, other than that my granddaughter is one of the smartest people I know, and she will do amazing things. We had a family supper to celebrate, but I knew this would not be the last degree she would earn.

IN JULY, Linda introduced us to a man she was dating named Rudolf Beck. It was sad for all of us when she and Cazzie got divorced, as he had been a constant part of our lives for so many years, but our main concern was always our daughter's happiness. We knew it wouldn't take her long to find someone new, as she is a beautiful catch, inside and out. I believe Rudy is the luckiest man in the world to have met her.

THIS SUMMER, I started taking golf more seriously. It was my second year as a member of the Beloeil Golf Club, so I continued taking lessons from professionals, and actually put it to practice rather than simply using my membership for the restaurant. I played over fifty rounds of golf, even breaking 100 twice! Realistically speaking, golf was the only sport I could play at my age to keep active, so I wanted to take advantage. Not only in the summers, where Ray and I tried out all the golf courses within driving distance, such as Bromont, Chambly, Rouse's Point, etc. I also chose vacation spots with the understanding that they had a golf course nearby, and that I would play a few rounds.

I didn't like traveling in the summer, and I still don't, because my yard is like paradise, a riverside dream, with frequent visits from our family. Be it boat rides, campfires or family suppers, Barb and I are usually surrounded by the people we love.

SOMETHING I HAVEN'T REALLY COVERED MUCH is religion. I mentioned it a few times when my children are little, but I haven't gone into how diligently Barbara kept her promise to raise our children Catholic. I go to church for the big events, but Barb is at Catholic Mass every Sunday; the Protestant putting the Catholic to shame. For a long time, Barb, Linda, Cazzie, Sandra, JP, Lynnie, Chelsea, Rikki, Steve, Eric, Amanda, and Paul were in church every Sunday, with the girls serving as Altar Girls. Their attendance became less regular once the kids reached high school, but Linda and Barb still went consistently, which is how I ended up attending a barbecue at Annette and Fred Tardif's. It was for Noreen's birthday, with over thirty members of their church's congregation. I accidentally enlisted myself to join Dick Shea's curling club, but thankfully, after a failed first practice, he didn't hold me to it.

IN OCTOBER, we decided to introduce Melanie to all of our favorite Gatineau places, on a weekend trip with her and her grandparents. We all went to a dance show at the casino, which was terrible. It was so bad that Melanie, Barb and I walked out, leaving Georges and Denise to finish it alone. Thankfully, even with the bad show, Melanie loved it!

ROBERT WYNGAERT

Tony, Bobby, me, and Ronnie.

This year, for our Christmas Suppers, we did things a bit different and had the best year yet! Usually, we choose a theme and keep it a secret, guarding it with our lives. Or at least we try to. This year, our theme was the Roaring Twenties, so we figured it would be more fun if we let our guests know ahead of time, so they could come in costume. Well, they went all out! In the invitations, we included a password for our speakeasy, so everyone came in flapper dresses and suits, ready to enjoy some bootlegged liquor. We had 'Wanted' posters with my face on them, as if I were Al Capone, and since Chelsea is such a talented dancer, we let her come up with a routine for our flappers. Sandra, Linda, Chelsea, Amanda, and Rikki all danced it together, then taught it to whichever guests wanted to learn it.

Marilyne, Anne, Barbara, Karen, and Carol.

My favorite part, however, was halfway through the meal, when JP and Paul barged in – dressed like 1920s FBI agents – to arrest me. JP had decided to stop shaving that fall, so he had a full, dark beard that made some of our guests not recognize him, and wrongfully assume the setup was real. We all had a good laugh about it afterwards, and it is still the Supper to Beat in terms of theme.

FORTY-EIGHT
2010

"They say life flies, but you are the pilot."
-Unknown

Most of our grandchildren went to Cuba in January, and when they returned, a lot of things were different. Amanda's foot was in a cast from a speaker falling on it their last night, Rikki was dating one of Steve's best friends, Thomas, and Paul was seeing Rikki's best friend, Samantha.

A COUPLE OF DAYS LATER, we went to Osteria to celebrate JP getting the position of Manager at Camping Alouette. Sandra had been taking care of our campground, as well as all of Parkbridge's Quebec properties, and they finally decided that being Regional Manager should be her full-time job, rather than just a second full time job to do on top of her other one. The office manager position was given to Amanda, who'd been putting in the hours and taking on extra responsibilities for years. Even though Camping Alouette was no longer owned by the Wyngaerts, our experience and knowledge of the industry ensured that it was staying in the family!

AS PER MY tradition of spoiling my big brother, Georges, we celebrated his seventy-fifth birthday in Quebec City with Johanne and her husband, Paul Messier, at the Continental. It was to celebrate, but also to trick him so he wouldn't suspect the surprise party Johanne threw him the following month. She had twenty-seven members of his family and closest friends. It wasn't quite the surprise she was hoping for, however, as Denise warned him, fearing he would have a heart attack if it truly was a surprise!

DURING THE SUMMER, I was once more a member at the Beloeil Golf Club, but I spent most of my time playing at other golf courses, especially Chambly, where my friends were all members. My last game of the season was on September 10th, as I went in for knee replacement surgery on the 13th. I'd been suffering for years with bad knees, getting cortisone shots and the like, but I decided it was time to do something more permanent. It was a very invasive procedure that would require months of rehabilitation. I spent five days in the Lake Shore General Hospital, and six months afterwards, recuperating. All of my life, I have always been very active, so it was difficult for me to have to take things easy. Even at the age of seventy-two, I was used to physical work, maintaining my yard, handling renovations, and helping my son install granite slabs throughout our property.

ON LABOR DAY WEEKEND, Barb's sister, Joan, had a lot of visitors in town, so they all came to our house. It was Joan and Bob, their son Danny, his oldest daughter Laurie with her husband Justin and newborn twins (Nolan and Greyson), Danny's youngest children, Jordan and Madison, as well as Glenn, Sue, and Brandon. We wanted to go on a boat ride, but the weather was cold and rainy, so we stayed home, and the kids spent the afternoon in our heated pool. After supper, we had a campfire in the backyard.

It was the perfect day, and I am so glad we got to have it, as Bob Smith died on October 15th. I lost my brother-in-law, my friend, my golf partner/instructor...he had been an ally for me in the Thompson family for the past fifty years.

Ronnie and Anne came to stay with us for the

funeral, and we tried to do what we could for Joan, offering to host everyone at our house afterwards. The funeral was on October 18th, and it was crowded, but I believe even more people came over after, at least forty-five of them, to reminisce about our times with him.

ON NOVEMBER 20TH, Barb and I went to the Sandals in Emerald Bay with Linda, Rudy, Sandra, and JP. This was our first all-inclusive with Rudy, and I think he was nervous, so he and Linda booked different dates and flights, so our trips would overlap, but not be the same.

It was extra special, as the entire resort had butler service, meaning there was an employee whose job it was to cater to our needs. Samson and Anthony would reserve our pool chairs and cabanas in the morning, as well as our restaurants, get us drinks, unpack our luggage...all the things that no human actually needs another to do for them. We even had vouchers for him to iron our clothes!

Linda, JP, Sandra, Barbara, and I.

One day, our butler prepared a special, romantic bath for Barb and I. The bath looked so inviting with all of the candles, bubbles and flower petals! There was even a plate of fruits, cheeses, and chocolate for us to snack on, and bottles of champagne and wine, to make sure Barb and I were both taken care of. I sat on the ledge to ease myself in, as we weren't used to taking baths together, without realizing that I accidentally sat on one of the candles. I nearly hit the ceiling I jumped off the candle so fast. It was a lovely thought, but I wouldn't be taking any fancy baths in the future. I still have the mark!

When it came time for Rudy and Linda to head home, they absolutely had to have lunch at the Drunken Duck, even though it opened at 2 and their shuttle left at 3, which would be cutting it close. Luckily, they made it through lunch, grabbed their stuff from Sandra's room, and made it to the shuttle only a few minutes late.

Those of us who were staying went to the pool and were relaxing when we saw a couple that really looked like Linda and Rudy approaching us. The closer they got, the more we realized it was them. Apparently, Linda had been so frazzled and in a panic because they were late that she accidentally took Sandra's wallet instead of her own. Sandra went back to her room with Anthony, the butler, who biked back with Linda's wallet. They ended up taking a taxi to the airport, where they luckily made their flight.

Samson had been our favorite of the butlers up to that point, as he was the one who brought us fruit and mimosas to take our pills every morning, as well as pizza or nachos in the afternoon, but Anthony's heroics definitely bumped him up a notch!

AFTER THE HOLIDAYS, Barb and I decided to experience our first cruise, rather than our regular all-inclusive vacations. After all, Joan swore by them.

Then again, she didn't drink, so having to pay for her alcohol wasn't a deterrent.

We had our flight out of the Plattsburgh Airport, so on December 28th, Barb, Sandra, JP, Amanda, and I went out for lunch with Georges (after a yummy snack from Denise), and had him drive us to the airport so we wouldn't have to leave the car in the parking lot. Our flight kept getting delayed, because the plane was still in Florida. Apparently, it was really cold over there, to the point that the wings were frozen and covered in ice. You can't fly like that, and the Florida airports don't have anything to de-ice them like we do, so they put the planes in the sun and were waiting for the ice to melt. It was not a good start to my vacation, and we weren't too thrilled with the idea of going to a snowy Florida.

I was already frustrated, when a child decided to pull the fire alarm instead of pressing the elevator button. Or so we found out hours later. All we knew at the time was that the fire alarm was going off, and we had to evacuate the building. We had already gone through security, which included a thorough patting down for me, due to my knee replacement and heart surgeries. Our coats and boots were all on their way back to Montreal with Georges, so we froze outside for at least an hour while the firefighters made sure there was no fire inside. Once they cleared the building, we had to throw away all of the drinks we had just purchased, and I was once more brought into a different room to be patted down. And they wonder why I hate flying!

Thankfully, the hotel was very nice. We stayed at the Peabody, which had ducks, like the Colonnades we stayed at when the kids were little, only these ones were inside the hotel, and could often be found riding the elevator. The most impressive for me was the tv screen in our bathroom mirrors, with soft lights to guide you to the bathroom at night!

The five of us had left Montreal early, so we could enjoy the sun before the cruise, but we were met with the coldest temperatures I've ever experienced in Florida. Luckily, Orlando didn't close down like Myrtle Beach had!

We spent our first day walking around and picking up some last-minute things we would need for the cruise. We were walking to Red Lobster for lunch when Barb casually remarked, "Look at all the license plates. Isn't it funny they're all from Florida?" We all just looked at her funny before we burst out laughing, and she realized it was because we were *in* Florida.

Barbara, Sandra, me, and Amanda.

On New Year's Eve, we met up with Paul and Sam, then took a cab to Cape Canaveral, where our ship would be leaving from. Instead of festivities, after a delicious meal at Olive Garden, we were all in bed by 8:30!

FORTY-NINE
2011

"The hardest thing to learn in life is which bridge to cross and which to burn."
-David Russell

On January 1st, we boarded the Norwegian Sun and found our cabins. The bathroom inside was almost as small as the ones on planes. I did not understand how anyone could enjoy it.

The following morning, we docked in Nassau, Bahamas. We hadn't booked anything ahead of time, so when we got to port, we found one of the many vendors and took a tour of the Island with Big T.

ROBERT WYNGAERT

Me, Amanda, Paul, Samantha, and Barbara.

Our next port of call was St. Thomas, where we did a lot of shopping. I got Barbara a beautiful green and red necklace, while JP got Sandra a ring that changes colors for her birthday. We had to wait a while for them to fix the ring to size, so we were given drinks, and a bottle of Rock Star vodka, which came in a studded leather case.

For Sandra's birthday, we went on a tour of St-Martin/Saint Marten. We went all around both sides of the island – the Dutch side and the French side – including an airport where we could practically touch the planes above our heads from the beach, and a surprise stop at a nudist beach. Well, the stop was planned for us to go for a swim, but we weren't expecting everyone else to be naked, so we left pretty quickly.

The next day was the worst of the whole trip! We spent the entire day at sea, in very rough waters. The pool was closed because the water inside kept splashing out onto the surrounding deck, making the entire area slippery and dangerous. Every staircase on the ship had vomit bags tucked into the railings because everyone was nauseous. We spent most of our day in bed or eating; the only activities that helped calm our stomachs, but by the end of the day, even they didn't work.

We were very glad to reach solid ground on the 8th, and I was thrilled to finally fly home. To summarize, it was not what we are used to. It was the worst vacation we ever experienced. I don't think that we will be taking any more cruises.

Me and Barbara.

The Monday after we got back, Sandra had to appear in court to testify about a fifth wheel and pickup that were stolen from the campground storage area back when I still owned it. Everything had been fine, as far as the campers were concerned, but their insurance company decided to sue me, claiming that we were negligent for not having a fence. I thought the headaches would be over when I sold, but I was still liable for anything we hadn't reported in the due diligence. Apparently, one of our employees said they saw the people who took it and watched them drive off. Even though Sandra made compelling arguments, there were inconsistencies in the employee's multiple testimonies, so the judge ruled in favor of the insurance company. I had to pay for the unit, as well as thousands in lawyer fees.

ON JANUARY 22ND, my frustrations over the case were put into perspective when we attended the funeral of our good family friend, Kenny Maxwell. He was only sixty years old, with two children much younger than my own...it reminded me that I am blessed in all the ways that matter. Back when we would go camping every weekend, Kenny had been the one to decide it wasn't fair for the women to always be the ones cooking, so he and Terry Brown had planned a Women's Night. That day, all the men got together and made food in their trailers so we could have a feast in the hall, with bouquets of flowers for the ladies. Kenny was a generous man, and he loved his wife, Wendy.

FOR VALENTINE'S DAY, I made myself a fancy new display for my bears. I renovated a portion of the wall in our main hallway to create a recess that matches the one on the other side. This way, I could display both of my priceless Inuit bear sculptures on custom-made marble shelves. I have to admit I went a little crazy with the marble recently. I get all my marble from Tony, who first did our bathroom benches and kitchen counters at the campground. (We were told to get really heavy benches for our five-star evaluation, to show that they were permanent fixtures) After I just sold the campground, Tony confided in me that his work had mostly been marble tombstones, but so many people were using urns instead, so he was down on his luck and in heavy debt. I knew him as a hardworking, talented, honest, and fair man, so instead of giving him a loan, I ordered enough marble to keep him afloat.

I ended up using it to cover my interior and exterior staircases, multiple shelves, and even our kitchen table. A lot of people think I drone on about these bears, but for me, they are the culmination of a lifetime of accomplishments. Seeing them every day fills me with pride and joy.

MY FRIENDS CALL ME BOB

Me, Barbara, Carol, and Joan.

At the end of the month, Barb and I brought Joan and Carol for a week-long vacation in Las Vegas. Neither of them had been before, but they absolutely loved it, and I loved seeing their faces light up at the magic of it. For weeks before we left, Carol would bring it up and do 'cha ching' noises to let us know she was ready for the slot machines. We stayed at the Wynn Hotel and took in the wonders of the various casinos, restaurants, and entertainment. We saw Elvis impersonators, which made Carol's day, as well as the Legends in Concert, and many others. All were excellent!

It was definitely one of our most expensive vacations, as we also splurged on a helicopter tour of the Grand Canyon, but it was an amazing experience, worth every penny! (For them, at least. I was not a fan of the helicopter, as I am terrified of flying. I wanted to ask the pilot if he had a parachute, but I wasn't sure if the parachute would save me, so I just shut my mouth and concentrated on the cramp in my leg rather than what would happen to me if I fell out at that height.)

IN MARCH, we were about to leave for a weekend trip to Quebec city with Joan, Marilyne, and Tony, when we discovered that the Richelieu River had overflowed its banks, causing a major flood in our basement. We quickly rescued the Christmas decorations from our storage room, then left Amanda there to make sure the flood didn't get worse while we went to the Continental. When I got back, I filed a claim with our insurance company, who paid for a portion of the damages. They sent a crew to demolish portions of the wall and moldings, as well as to disinfect and dry out the basement, but Danny and I did all of the necessary repairs. They would have fixed it, but I took advantage of our misfortune to upgrade all 1500 square feet of our basement floor. We also installed a backwater valve, so this would never happen again. We were the lucky ones, as many people lost their homes in this flooding.

IN APRIL, we got the devastating news that my sister-in-law, Anne, had mesothelioma. To make matters worse, Barb's sister, Carol, was admitted to the hospital following a heart attack. The doctors told us she also had advanced cirrhosis of the liver, which made no sense. When she slipped into a coma, we discussed it with her doctors, shocked that it could have gotten so bad without her noticing. We were so glad we were able to bring her to Vegas and enjoy one last vacation with her. She'd been slower with the walking, and got tired faster than usual, but she never complained. She died on May 5th, surrounded by loved ones, but none of us were ready for it. She was only sixty-five, and such a fantastic person. She had a voice like Reba McIntyre, and to this day, every time we hear one of her karaoke numbers, we all say, "that's Carol's song".

ON MAY 10TH, Sandra's family surprised us at Au Vieux Duluth during our regular Tuesday Night Dinner to celebrate Barb's birthday. JP drove us home while Sandra and Amanda took their own cars. JP and I were laughing and having a great time, while Barb was slurring her words beyond what we could comprehend. When we got out of the car, I told Sandra that Barb was so drunk we couldn't understand her, but Barb rushed up to Sandra with a look of terror in her eyes that told us something was seriously wrong. Sandra recognized the signs of a stroke and had JP call 911.

When the ambulance arrived, their assessment was the same as Sandra's, so they brought her to the Ste-Hyacinthe hospital, where she was kept overnight for observation. Sandra followed the ambulance and Linda met her there, staying until Barb was settled. She'd had a mini stroke that scared the hell out of us, and let us know that she had an arrythmia. Thankfully, we were able to bring her home the following day, and they put her on a new medication that made her better.

IN JULY, Sandals invited us to a special supper aboard the Lady Sandals yacht, as we were frequent guests at their resorts. Barb, Linda, Rudy, Sandra, JP, and I all went prepared with excuses for when they tried to sell us more vacations. We rehearsed them in the car, to make sure none of us would get tricked into the upsell.

Instead, we had a lovely evening with no talk of future vacations. We even asked and were told this was simply to thank us for our loyalty and past vacations, with absolutely no sales pitch. Obviously, this ensured that all we wanted to do was book our next Sandals vacation. There were only six couples on the ship, and my family made up three of them.

We had to take off our shoes to get on the ship, which stayed docked as they didn't have permission to cruise around Montreal. I spent a good chunk of the evening talking to the captain, Mike Harris, who was Australian. Every time he said my name, it sounded like 'Boob', which everyone found hilarious. At the end of the night, I invited him for a game of golf while he was in town.

We went to LaPrairie Golf Course with Don and Ray, then back to my house for supper. We were a big gang, with Barb and I, Mike the Captain, Linda and Rudy, Sandra and JP, Chelsea and Rikki, Teresa, Don and Huguette, Marilyne and Tony, and Joan. Mike told us that if ever we see the Lady Sandals docked anywhere, we can simply come up and we would be welcomed on board.

WE ENTERTAINED the following week as well, with the Wyngaerts this time. Johanne and Paul, Georges and Denise, JP and Sandra, Melanie, Barb, and I went for a boat ride in the afternoon. The whole time we were heading out, there was a big black cloud forming, so we tried to get home before it reached us. We failed miserably, as it started pouring. Barb, Johanne, and Melanie hid under the table with our stinky shoes to stay dry while Sandra and JP tried to get the tarp up. Pierre, Sue, Nicole, Katherine, Christine, and Caroline all joined us for supper afterwards.

IN AUGUST, Barb and I went for another weekend at the Hilton in Lac Leamy. Sandra and JP were treating our friends, Michel and Yolande Lacroix, so we decided to tag along. Michel was the electrician at the campground, and he helped us with countless personal projects, but he never accepted payment for his time, always just charging us cost for the parts.

We all stayed on the executive level, where in addition to the lounge we've mentioned before, they also offer turn down service, with yummy chocolates on your pillow. Since the hotel has a casino, they put the chocolates in a packaging that looks like casino chips.

Our first morning there, Yolande and Michel came down and told us how touched they were that JP gave them chips on top of the hotel and the restaurants, but they couldn't accept it. They would have been sorely disappointed when they tried to use their chocolates in the casino!

Before going home, we stopped in to visit with their niece, Chantal. She lived in Chelsea with her husband, Jacques, and their adorable four-year-old daughter, Charlie. They were extremely hospitable, giving us Kentucky Fried Chicken for supper with special beers. The entertainment was provided by Charlie, who showed us just how she watered all of the plants so they wouldn't 'died'.

IN SEPTEMBER, Rikki was the first of our grandkids to move away on her own, choosing to go to school in Guelph for her undergrad, as she wanted to study Tourism Management. Paul's girlfriend, Samantha, had also decided to take a semester abroad, all the way in Australia, so Paul visited her for a few weeks. It was strange not having everyone for supper on Sundays, but Rikki made an effort to come every two weeks or so. Still, on the weeks she didn't come, we missed her!

ROBERT WYNGAERT

Barbara and I.

On November 5th, we had the Thompson Family Supper. It was earlier than previous years because Joan was turning seventy-five, and her son asked if we could surprise her with a birthday cake. We decided to make it a double, and celebrate Donna's birthday as well. Ronnie stayed home with Anne, but all of the other Thompson siblings showed up, as well as Joan's three children, her daughter-in-law Sue, and her grandson, Brandon. Our theme this year was the 1950s, so there were lots of poodle skirts, Greasers, and Pink Ladies. It was a lot of fun, but couldn't top the Roaring Twenties.

. . .

LATER ON IN THE MONTH, Barb went to Las Vegas with Sandra, JP, and Amanda, to celebrate Amanda's twenty-first birthday. I made them a detailed itinerary of shows they should see and restaurants they should eat at, but was happier to stay home and put up all of the Christmas decorations instead.

WE HAD many more visits to Ontario, but the one on November 16th was special, as it was the last time we saw Anne alive. We went out for dinner at her favorite restaurant, Le Petit Prince, where she needed a wheelchair to get around. She had been put in palliative care with the assumption that she wouldn't last the year.

They were right, as she died on December 10th, at the very young age of sixty-two. From the day she moved into our apartment building, she moved into our hearts and became a part of our family. She was the kind of person you could say anything to, and she would listen with no judgment. She would also believe you, as she was one of the most gullible people I have ever met. I would tell her to bring her bathing suit when she came to our Christmas supper, because the pool was still open, and she would respond with, "No! Really?"

She was a beautiful person, inside and out, both

honest and smart. She always made us laugh. One night we were all dressed up to go for a fancy supper when she decided to check the pool temperature. She took off her shoes and tried to put her foot in, but her entire body went along with it, pretty dress and all. She was a bundle of joy and my partner every time our spouses went off gambling!

Rikki already lived in Guelph, so she met us at the funeral. Barbara and I, Sandra and JP, Linda and Rudy, as well as Amanda all drove down so we could give our condolences for a wonderful woman.

THE WYNGAERT FAMILY supper was supposed to be that Saturday, so we moved it to Tuesday, in lieu of our weekly Au Vieux Duluth supper. Since two of my siblings were missing, we decided to invite Mike and Ethel into the fold.

FIFTY
2012

"Without experience one gains no wisdom."
-Chinese Proverb

On January 8th, we headed to Sandals La Toc, in Saint-Lucia, with Sandra and JP, for a lovely two-week vacation. On our second week, we were joined by Linda and Rudy, as well as their friends, Dale, Nancy, Paula, and Robert. Rudy's friends had actually arrived the day before, but we didn't know what they looked like, and vice versa, so it took Rudy arriving to introduce us all.

I was able to play a round of golf every day, as they had a Par 9 included in the resort! We had a butler as well, and he would fill a cooler up with beers for us to bring to the golf course every morning.

JP, Sandra, me, and Barbara.

Barb and I always win whenever they ask who has been married the longest, so we enjoyed many perks, such as a candlelit dinner (that turned into a breakfast) and an evening with the Chef that included our very own printed menu. We had a great time!

. . .

IN MARCH, we went to Sandals Grande Riviera Beach and Villa Golf Resort in Jamaica with JP and Sandra. Although the trip was wonderful, it still leaves a bad taste in my mouth when I look back on it. On our first day there, Barb and I left the safe unlocked, each of us assuming the other had taken care of it. When we got back to the room, 450U$ had been stolen, which put a damper on the whole trip.

You may or may not know that the Sandals hotel chain is owned by Butch Stewart, and he happened to be visiting the resort while we were there. We knew something was up, as the already top-quality resort went up a notch in the days before his arrival. I was so jealous because Sandra and Barbara told me that one day while JP and I were golfing, Butch walked by them at the pool and stopped for a conversation. It wasn't until I was writing this book that they admitted to me that while they did see him walking by, he never actually spoke to them. He just waved.

We had our own villa and pool on this trip. They were supposed to be shared among four couples, but the other two rooms were empty, so we had them all to ourselves. I enjoyed the quiet time and swam every afternoon, but the others like the bigger pools, where there were games and a lot more action. Before leaving, we even bought some bricks – symbolically and literally – to help rebuild a school that was destroyed in a recent hurricane on the island.

· · ·

WHEN PAUL PICKED us up from the airport, we went to Bar B Barn for supper, as we often do. I went to pay for the meal with my credit card, but it was declined. Multiple times. I told the waiter it was because of the vacation, but I was worried. I made a mental note to call the credit card company first thing in the morning to get things sorted out.

As it turns out, our credit cards were cloned, and used to make approximately 9000$ worth of car repairs and hotel stays. To make matters worse, hundreds of dollars were missing from my safe at home! Let's just say I got back from the vacation a lot more stressed than I was when I left.

Sandra and Sharon.

On April 24th, after a long battle with cancer, our beloved niece, Sharon Graham, passed away. She was only forty-eight, and left behind three children, one of them still in high school. She'd been a single mother since her divorce over a decade earlier, so after finishing out their school year, the two youngest went to live with Sharon's younger sister, Debbie, in Ottawa. Her death hit us particularly hard, as Sandra and Sharon had been best friends since before they could walk. Sharon grew up at our house. They would spend their days in the pool, only coming out in the evening when their skin was all shriveled up, like little fishes. It also brought back all of the pain and memories from Lynn's incredibly similar battle and loss.

The funeral was held on the 28th, and Doreen was so distraught she had to be sedated for it. We were becoming very familiar with the Hawthorne-Dale Funeral Home after so many Thompson funerals. Every single time, the funeral parlor was packed, and we had everyone over at our house afterwards for good food and memories that make us cry and smile at the same time.

When Paul went to introduce his girlfriend, Samantha, to Tara – one of Barb's nieces – and she said, "Oh, I met you at the last funeral," it broke my heart. It also reminded me how important it is to have our big anniversary parties, so we can get together and stay in touch under happier, more pleasant circumstances.

WE WENT to the XO restaurant on June 7th, to celebrate our anniversary with JP, Sandra, Paul, Sam, and Amanda. We were also celebrating Amanda graduating from McGill University, where she received a Bachelor of Arts with a Double Major in Psychology and History. I was so proud to have three university graduates in the family!

MY FRIENDS CALL ME BOB

. . .

IN JULY, Chelsea invited her boyfriend, Derek for supper at our house. This was our first time meeting him, and one of the only things we knew up to this point was that he was Irish. Linda had met him before and told us he had red hair, and she saw a shamrock on his boxers when he helped Chelsea move.

Well, I sure made a fool of myself when I commented on his Irish ancestry. As it turns out, he is Polish, which made sense when we found out his last name was Lupinsky. I'm guessing my face must have gone very red, as we all tried to cover up why we had that assumption without revealing that Linda deduced it from his underwear!

AT THE END of the summer, we found out Ronnie was in a depression following the loss of his wife. It was completely understandable, but he was very lonely and beginning to feel like his life was no longer worth living. It was devastating to see our fun-loving friend so down. I mentioned that I had a friend who'd lost her husband and was in a similar situation.

I casually brought Ronnie up to Wendy Maxwell, hoping they might be able to bond over their losses and help each other heal, but she saw through my plan and told me she wasn't willing to date someone who smoked. I told Ronnie I had someone I could introduce him to if he was willing to quit smoking, but he said no, so we resolved to simply spend more time with him ourselves.

In October, Ronnie called and surprised me by saying he quit smoking and was interested in meeting Wendy. So, we made plans for us to drive down, and for them to meet. We had it all figured out, how we would drive to Whitby and bring her to the restaurant so we could introduce her to Ronnie, but they had other plans. Instead of waiting for us at Red Lobster, Ronnie went straight to Wendy's house, and was already there when we arrived. They hit it off from the get-go.

Chelsea, Amanda, Sandra, Rikki, and Linda.

The theme of our Annual Christmas Suppers was Scotland, to honor Barb's heritage, but we refrained from serving any haggis. Although perhaps that could have led the conversation away from Ronnie bringing Wendy as his guest. Some people were surprised to see he had moved on, but for those of us who knew how badly he'd been taking his loss, we were overjoyed to see him smile again. I love both

Ronnie and Wendy, and believe they are very good for each other, which is why I set them up in the first place!

We often invited other family members to join us after the meal for karaoke, so this year we had Bobby's daughters over, as well as Wendy Noel and her boyfriend, Robert. We were all surprised to find out they were now engaged to be married!

ON NOVEMBER 26TH, I was forced to file a police report after being attacked by my neighbor's dog. It was a Pitbull, which fits with the stereotype, although I believe it is the owner who has a bigger impact on a dog's behavior than its breed. My martial arts training never covered animal attacks, but I am sure it helped with me reflexes and defenses. The dog first latched itself to my leg, then once my neighbor pried it off, it tried to jump at my throat. The dog probably would have killed me if its owner hadn't jumped on top of it.

I was never afraid of dogs before, but this was a frightening experience I would never forget.

WE CELEBRATED the Wyngaert Christmas Supper on December 8th, with Georges and Denise, Fay and Bruce, Kenny and Louise, Diane and Al, Mike and Ethel, Melanie, and Kay. A few weeks before, Sandra and JP brought Amanda to Los Angeles,

California, for acting courses, so we were down a waitress. I offered to fly her home for the weekend, but even though I think she really wanted to, we all knew it would be silly. Luckily, JP took over, handling the drinks so the ladies could concentrate on the food.

FIFTY-ONE
2013

"Great Opportunities to help others seldom come, but small ones surround us daily."
-Sally Koch

On New Year's Day, Rudy came over with live lobsters for our supper. He'd spent a lot of time on the East Coast, so he wanted to introduce us to something better than the frozen ones we usually bought at Costco. I could remember Glenn's wife, Sue, telling us how she became a vegetarian after watching her cat playing with the lobster she'd been about to cook. However, I have always loved seafood, and Rudy's fresh lobster was absolutely succulent!

. . .

IN APRIL, we played a trick on Sandra and JP, pretending we were going to Wendy Noel's wedding at the Kapetan restaurant. We sent her an invitation and everything, but in reality, we were throwing them a 25th wedding anniversary party! I say we, but it was Linda who took care of it, with a little help from Amanda and Paul. I got to sit back and relax, with the occasional dancing, as no party for Sandra is complete without a dance floor!

OUR ANNIVERSARY PARTY took place on May 18th, at Hotel Mortagne in Boucherville. Over 160 people attended, all friends, family members, or a combination of the two. When they arrived, they were serenaded by our musician, Patti McCurdy, and our singer Jean Strutman while they waited to have their picture taken. Diane, who used to do the flowers at the campground, made us a beautiful arch as a backdrop.

Barbara and I.

During the meal, we were treated to a special performance from Chelsea and her dance troupe, who were fabulous. Our MC and DJ, Zap-it-Up, were also excellent, and as was now tradition, the grandkids got up and gave a very touching speech for us.

While the guests ate and partied, we had the pictures we took upon their arrival printed and put into frames, so they all got to go home with a framed photo of themselves.

We arranged for a block of rooms to be reserved, so many guests stayed the night, and the party continued over breakfast the next morning. The Hotel staff and rooms were all 5 stars. I could not imagine a better outcome and I thank everyone for this successful event.

STEVE GRADUATED from Concordia University that Spring, majoring in Accounting, with a minor in Finance. He was the second Wyngaert, and the third of my grandchildren to graduate University!

EVERY SUMMER, La Ronde's Amusement Park hosts a firework competition between different countries. Almost every Saturday, you can watch this firework display from the amusement park, or your home if you live close enough to the Jacques-Cartier Bridge.

We can't see them from our house, but when Chelsea moved in with Derek, she got an excellent view, and invited us all over for supper and fireworks. Their place has two floors and as many balconies, so we were all able to have a wonderful night, and a spectacular view of the show!

WE WENT to the Continental in July for JP's surprise 50th birthday party. Sandra had rented the upstairs party room, so we were all up there waiting for the birthday boy to arrive. I was sitting at the table and enjoying a drink when everyone who was waiting by the windows started laughing. I joined in a few minutes later when JP walked in wearing bright red pants. Apparently, he'd bought them that morning and figured tonight was the perfect time to wear them, as it was just him, Sandra, and the kids. Boy was he surprised to see all of us there! Hopefully the party made up for the trickery, as we enjoyed all of our Continental favorites, with JP even trying his hand at some of the flambeeing. Thankfully, the staff took over before he could set the restaurant on fire.

DANNY GOT MARRIED for a second time on July 28th, to Lynda Zullo, who grew up close to the campground, and whose father was our favorite flower supplier.

MY FRIENDS CALL ME BOB

. . .

WE CELEBRATED Marilyne's 60th birthday at Bar B Barn in August, then invited everyone back to our house for a swim. We were surprised when they took us up on the offer, as we live so far from the restaurant, but it was nice watching her grandkids in the pool all afternoon. As Ava left, she told us our place was like a hotel pool with a mansion, and they couldn't wait to come back.

I HAD the pleasure of attending Pratt and Whitney's Quarter Century Reunion later that month. After being retired for twenty years, it was nice to see my friends and thank them for the exceptional retirement party they threw for me. These events were put on every year or so for anyone who had at least twenty-five years of service. We'd held them in arenas and plane hangars, getting bigger and bigger with each year. For the most part, I stopped attending after I retired, but it was nice to be back. I went this time because Ron Buswell had suggested it when he attended our anniversary party with Johanne Kane. It was wonderful to see the people who had supported me and helped me get as far as I did, such as Gordie MacCaul.

. . .

IN EARLY SEPTEMBER, I underwent surgery on my left knee, to repair torn cartilage, and clean up the joint. The surgery went well, and I was even back on the golf course to finish off the season with Joan, Don, and Huguette (Don's wife who completed our foursome).

IN NOVEMBER, after six years of weekly summer boat rides, I sold my pontoon. It broke my heart, but it seemed to me like everyone had lost interest. We had only used it a handful of times that past summer, so I figured we could rent a boat for a few days if ever anyone really missed it.

WE CHOSE Walt Disney as our theme for the Christmas suppers, as it gave us the opportunity to go all out with the costumes, and we could choose whatever we wanted food-wise. They had a variety of cuisines at the theme parks, and Epcot celebrated every country. Barb didn't want to dress up, so she went as a Disney park guest, but we rented costumes for myself and the girls. Linda was Snow White, Sandra reused her Thailand costume to be Mulan, Chelsea was Cinderella, Amanda was Pocahontas, Rikki was Minnie Mouse, and I was Gaston. I don't think we expected the guests to join in and get dressed up like they did! Wendy came as the Tiger

Lily to Ron's Captain Hook, and Bobby was the Mad Hatter to Karen's Queen of Hearts.

Wendy, Linda, Chelsea, Rikki, Amanda, Sandra, me, and Ron.

Sandra, JP, Amanda, Barb and I spent New Year's Eve at the airport's Marriott Hotel. We had planned a family vacation at the Ambar Resort in Punta Cana, and our flight left early on the 1st. The five of us went to the hotel's buffet restaurant for supper, where they had two prices; one for adults and one for children. At the end of the meal, we noticed that Amanda, who was twenty-three at the time, had been charged as a child, which for them, was twelve and under. We thought it was hilarious, especially when we told the waiter, who was shocked and mortified. He still let us pay for her as a child, which was nice of him, considering the meal – which was a buffet – cost over a thousand dollars.

FIFTY-TWO
2014

"Life does not have to be perfect to be wonderful."
-Annette Funicello

Chelsea, Derek and Paul came to our hotel rooms a little after three in the morning so we could get ready and walk through the lobby to the airport on January 1st. The three of them had been out celebrating and didn't get to sleep at all until our flight to Punta Cana. Linda and Rudy, Steve and Melissa, as well as Rudy's two sons, Nick and Matthew, greeted us when we arrived, while Rikki and Thomas came a few days later. It was our first time travelling with many of them, and it was nice to have everyone there. Except for Danny, Lynda, and Sam, who were greatly missed.

This is another trip that is marred by the ending,

but I'll try to remember the good parts. For starters, it was so nice to be on a big family vacation after a few years of mostly traveling separately. With a big group, you always have something to do, and you never have to worry about being alone. If you want to go back to your room early and take a nap on the balcony, no one will miss you, but if you want to do something, you will always find at least one person willing to join. I was lucky to have JP who played golf with me, and Nick, who tried it out.

This resort had activities, which we always enjoy. One of them was a bartending contest by the pool, where they chose Derek to be a contestant. They gave him all the bar's ingredients, then he and two other people had to make the best cocktail. We were all taken aback when Derek used pineapple juice in his. We turned to Chelsea, wondering if we were mistaken about his allergy, but when the animators told them to taste their drinks, Derek said he couldn't. Apparently, being allergic didn't stop him from knowing pineapple is delicious, so he put it in his cocktail hoping he would win. Unfortunately, he did not.

After a week, almost everyone flew home. Barb, Sandra, JP, and Amanda were staying two weeks, while Paul and I went home three days after the others. This is when the trouble started. We had to wait for what felt like an eternity in the hotel lobby, then as soon as we finally got to the airport, we found out that our flight was delayed. Again.

It wasn't long before I felt like I was having a heart attack. Thank God I wasn't alone, as Paul took care of me, finding places for me to sit in the overly crowded airport. I didn't want to stay there any longer than I had to, so instead of letting Paul go get a medic, I just kept taking my nitro. It was not a pleasant trip for me, or for Paul, who will most likely never travel alone with me again.

Samantha picked us up from the airport, and although my chest pains dissipated, I was very sick with some kind of virus – that I am sure I got on vacation – and was on antibiotics for a week!

FOR CHRISTMAS, my family had given me a book called 'The Great Cholesterol Myth' by Johnny Bowden and Stephen Sinatra, which I read while I was waiting for Barb to come home. It proposed that while lowering your cholesterol wouldn't prevent heart disease, their statin-free plan would. I had been on various statin pills for over fifteen years, with incredible pains in my back, shoulders, legs, knees, heels, and arms. I figured I had nothing to lose by finding out for myself if eliminating statin drugs could truly relieve me of my pains. Instead of the pills, I took to diet and exercise. After a single month, I felt better than I had in what felt like a lifetime. I had no more pain and felt like a new man! I had been doing my calisthenics every day since we sold the campground, as I no longer got the exercise from working on my grounds, but now I added the stationary bike and others. I am not one of those people who claims to like exercise, because I don't. I simply love all that it does for me. I rarely miss a day, and allow myself no excuses, because I know the benefits are worth it. My health improved, my weight improved, as did my looks and self-esteem. I was able to do more activities with the extra energy, but most importantly, I felt like I would be able to live longer, to see my grandchildren grow up, and maybe even meet my great-grandchildren.

I told Chelsea about my new regimen, and how good I felt, but she was very concerned. She was studying to get her PhD in neuroscience, so she knew a thing or two about these things. She was also in contact with many medical doctors, so she recommended that I at least take my prescribed high blood pressure pills, and follow up with my cardiologist.

I didn't think it was necessary, as I felt excellent, but I took her advice and called my doctor. After listening to my new regimen and consulting my file, he agreed that I could stay off the cholesterol pills until my next checkup. With his stamp of approval, in addition to the statin pills, I eliminated all prescription and over-the-counter drugs, as well as vitamins.

. . .

AT THE END OF FEBRUARY, Barb went to Cuba with Joan, as I had no interest in traveling, but she still wanted to escape the winter. I was glad she had someone other than me to go with!

Mike, Steve, and me.

In March, I offered all of my grandchildren the opportunity to take Dale Carnegie Courses. I had attended decades ago, and still used the knowledge I had learnt, which I credited with many of my successes at Pratt. I believed in it so much that I said I would pay for all of them to take it. Rikki and Amanda took me up on it right away, sharing their progress and successes with me. It was such a joy, and I was filled with pride when Linda - who'd taken the class when she was younger – and I watched them graduate. I thought the other grandkids would sign up as soon as they saw the benefits it gave the girls, but Steve was the only one who signed up for the fall session. Not only did he graduate, Mike (his other grandfather) and I watched him receive the course's highest award for achievement, and numerous other awards at his graduation. Steve and Rikki even went on to help teach future sessions of the course!

Sandra, Barbara, and I.

At the end of March, Georges and Denise organized a dinner at Au Vieux Duluth to celebrate my seventy-sixth birthday with twenty-three of my closest friends and family. I was so shocked and didn't expect a thing, as she tricked me by doing it during my usual Tuesday night supper. I'm not very good at surprises, because I'm not prepared, and don't know what to say. I don't even know if I was able to let them know how much it meant to me, but it meant the world.

IN APRIL, Fay and Bruce came to visit us, which wasn't so unusual, but they came with their son, Bobby, his wife Carolyn, and their two children, Kaylin and Rowan. Emmett and Judy even stopped by. My sister always told me her grandchildren were so advanced, and I finally got to see it for myself.

FOR BARB'S BIRTHDAY, we went to Lac Leamy, and had supper at the Baccara restaurant with Rikki. She had just started a job as sales manager at the Lord Elgin Hotel, so we took advantage of being in town to check out her new apartment, and I helped her install some new drapes.

IN JULY, my nephew, Roger Wyngaert Jr. passed away at the age of fifty-seven. To avoid confusion with his father, we had always called him Bo. He had a good heart, and would give you the shirt off his back, but he had always been a troubled soul. I hoped he would find peace with his father in heaven.

. . .

WE CELEBRATED JP's birthday at our house, and invited his friends, Pete and Sylvie. Before the meal, Pete came into the kitchen to wash his hands. Our kitchen sink has three 'faucets'; one for regular water, one for dish soap, and one for boiling water. It makes things so much easier when you want a cup of coffee or tea, as you don't have to wait for a kettle to boil. Unfortunately, most houses don't have them, so Pete didn't know what it was until his hand was under it and the boiling water was pouring down. Not to mention, he'd used our hand cream instead of soap. Thank God the tap turns off when you're not holding it, or he could have been seriously hurt. As it was, his hands were red, but he laughed it off, warning us all not to make the same mistake.

IN AUGUST, I had my yearly check up with my doctor and my cardiologist. When they saw the results of my blood tests, EKG, and treadmill stress test, they could not believe that I hadn't been taking any pills for the past six months. Not only was my pain gone, all of my tests were normal, some of them even improving.

It is easier for doctors to prescribe a drug they know you'll take everyday, than to believe that you'll stick to a new lifestyle, even if it would be so much healthier for you to fix the problem rather than cover up the symptoms. Once I convinced them that I would maintain my diet and exercise, they agreed to my new treatment plan, but persuaded me to take baby aspirin every day to protect me from a stroke.

ON SEPTEMBER 3RD, I played the best golf game of my life thus far, hitting 95. The following day, Barb and I drove to London, Ontario, with Joan and Marilyne. Joan's granddaughter, Lisa, was getting married to Christopher Watson, a very nice young man. The wedding was excellent, and the entire weekend was wonderful, until we headed home. We thought it was incredibly convenient that the GPS had a 'Go Home' option. Unfortunately, no one ever programmed where 'home' was. This minor mistake with the GPS led to us driving all the way to Parry Sound before we realized we were going the wrong way. For those unfamiliar with Ontario geography, an eight-hour drive took us over thirteen hours!

ON OCTOBER 6TH, Barbara went to the Lakeshore General Hospital to have a left knee arthroplasty, the same surgery – with the same surgeon – that I'd had four years earlier. The morphine made her hallucinate again. She would ask us why JP was sitting in the sink in the hallway instead of coming into her room, or wondering why her orderly was smoking in his picture on her wall. There was no picture.

She did not enjoy taking it easy following the surgery, but the difference once she recovered was more than worth it!

IN EARLY NOVEMBER, Barb and I drove to Hamilton with Linda, Rudy, Sandra, JP, Chelsea, Derek, Rikki, and Samantha for our niece's wedding. Thankfully, we were not all in the same car! Donna's daughter, Jennifer O'Connell, was marrying Ronald Hamilton, who we all called Cardi. Although there were a few mishaps that made it start later than intended, the wedding was lovely, with more food than you could imagine, and every bite was delicious. Jen looked like a beautiful fairytale princess. It was so nice to see her happy and healthy after all of her previous health problems, but that girl is a fighter! Amanda, who'd been working in Toronto and met us there, caught the bouquet.

AS BARB and I both loved swimming every day in the summer, I usually tried to keep our pool open from April 1st to October 1st. This year, I decided to purchase a 17-foot endless pool and spa. I figured it would be especially beneficial for Barb, while she recovered from her knee replacement.

As the spa weighed over 20 000lbs, I had to redo a lot of the landscaping around the solarium to accommodate for it, extending our walkway and supporting it with stone walls. It was an expensive project, and as far as that first year, I thought it was a terrible investment. Barb was afraid to climb over the ledge to get in, and reluctant to go outside in the winter wearing nothing but her bathing suit. (It would take a couple of years, but now I am in it almost every day of the year.)

ON NOVEMBER 22ND we had the Thompson Christmas Supper, with everyone but Doreen attending. This year, our theme was Chinese. Sandra and Linda reused their Thailand dresses, while the others were dressed like waiters, with even Thomas helping out for the Wyngaert Supper on the 13th. Barb's favorite food is Asian, and her siblings were all in agreement.

After the meal, many of our guests joined the staff in the kitchen to enjoy some sake bombs. We used chopsticks to hold a shotglass of sake over a glass of Sapporo beer. Once everyone was ready, we called 'sake bomb' and banged on the table until the shotglasses fell in and we could drink.

Me, Lynne, Chelsea, Wendy, Tom, Ron, Rudy, Rikki, and Karen.

For New Year's Eve, we decided to go back to our roots. Or rather the grandchildren convinced us to have the party at our house like we used to. Sandra also called it her birthday party, as she would be turning fifty in January. We had karaoke, people enjoying the spa, people chatting in different rooms, playing games in another...it was an intimate version of our anniversary parties and I absolutely loved it. As did our guests, with Chelsea and her friends sleeping over.

FIFTY-THREE
2015

"Keep your mind on the objective, not the obstacle."
-William Randolph Hearsi

On January 5th, Amanda drove Linda, Rudy, Sandra, JP, Barb, and I to the airport so we could fly to St Lucia. We were staying at the Sandal Regency La Toc Spa and Beach Resort with Ron, Wendy, Brian, and Nancy. After settling in, we all went together for a fancy supper to celebrate Sandra's fiftieth birthday.

The following morning, I went to play a round of golf with the guys. Even if I am not very enthusiastic about vacations, I do love being able to play golf in the middle of the winter!

January 8th was one of the worst days of my life. When we first came to St Lucia, we'd taken a tour called 'Joe Knows' that brings us to the island volcanoes. Sandra had recommended this tour to every single person she met since, so she convinced Ron's group to take the tour. She and JP went along with them while the rest of us enjoyed the resort.

That night, we had planned another celebration of Sandra's birthday, this time at a different Sandals resort, the Grand. We went to the restaurant – early as I always am- but I was sent back to my room to change, as I was wearing a t-shirt instead of the customary collared shirt. I tried to buy a shirt in one of the boutiques, but since I wasn't at my resort, I couldn't just use my room card. I needed my passport, which was locked up in my safe. I was so stressed the entire time, worried we would be late, when I am *never* late.

Instead, Barb and I got back to the restaurant and

found only Linda and Rudy waiting for us. We filled up on drinks and bread, but six of our ten chairs remained empty. At first, I was upset that they didn't value our time, then I wondered if their tour maybe ran late. By the time we finished our meal, we were beyond worried.

It was only much later, when we got back to our resort, that JP finally let us know what happened. While they were on the tour, a big wave hit the boat and slammed Sandra down onto her seat with such force that she felt like vomiting. The tour guide encouraged her to dance it off, but the excruciating pain convinced her to leave the tour early and go to the hospital with JP. She was currently at the hospital, with fractured vertebrae, and couldn't move her legs.

Ron's group, who finished the tour after the incident, knew Sandra was hurt and didn't want to be the bearers of bad news, so they'd all skipped out on dinner.

OVER THE NEXT FEW DAYS, Sandals paid for us to take taxis to visit her in the hospital every day, and bring her food from the resort, even though she wasn't able to eat much at first. We were all so terrified that she would be paralyzed; I could write a book about all of the pain and suffering she had to endure.

Although Sandra and JP had booked their trip for two weeks, the rest of us only reserved for one week.

When we were booking, Sandra tried to get me to change my mind, insisting I would be crying on my last day, when I had to go home knowing that she was going to stay a whole other week without me. As it happened, we went to see Sandra in the hospital on our last day, and I was crying at the thought of leaving her. When she said, "I told you so," I couldn't help but smile through my tears. Even a broken back couldn't kill my daughter's spirit!

A week after her accident, Sandra was airlifted back to Canada, to the Ste-Hyacinthe Hospital. She couldn't sit upright, so she took a private plane, which JP very much enjoyed, but Sandra did not. It was at that hospital that the doctors forced her to move her legs, even if it made her throw up, and we found out that she wasn't paralyzed.

SHE WAS able to come home on the 16th, and although she would have to wear a back brace 24/7 for the next four months, they believed she would make a full recovery. Unfortunately, not in time to go to Barbados with Barb, Linda, and Rudy as planned. I thought she would be happy to transfer the trip to Amanda, so she wouldn't have to travel anymore after her accident, but it was just the opposite. She couldn't wait for her next vacation, and started planning ways that she could travel while accommodating for her injury. It is very hard to beat someone who never gives up hope. With her unwavering positive mental attitude, she is a true champion. My life would never be the same without her, and I thank God that she recovered.

IN APRIL, Sandra gave up her position as Regional Manager at Parkbridge Lifestyle Communities, due to the unfair and borderline abusive way they were treating her, especially since she broke her back. Once she was fully recovered, she began working for Linda, as her assistant. It was a position she had held every winter when she worked for me at the campground, and the pair of them truly made the best team in the business!

IN AUGUST, Barb and I drove to Bowmanville so we could see Ron and Wendy's new house. Their community is right on the water, with its very own golf course! Ron, Wendy, Bruce and I played a round of golf while Barb and Fay stayed at the house. Afterwards, we all met up at Red Lobster for supper before Fay and Bruce drove home. We stayed for the weekend at Ron's, discovering that he makes excellent crème brulée!

. . .

THAT MONTH, I started hiking Mont-Saint-Hilaire with Sandra and Amanda. We would do Burned Hill one day, Mauve another, discovering the beauty of the mountain, and getting exercise as a bonus! Unfortunately, I took a hill too fast and injured my left foot with a plantar fibroma. I had to take a few weeks off golf and hiking, but I recovered quickly thanks to some physiotherapy.

Hiking was an excellent way for me to keep in shape once the golfing season ended, and to spend time with my girls. I usually spend my days staring at the mountain through the window, forgetting that it is just a fifteen-minute drive to see it all up close. I truly love breathing in the pure fresh air, being so close to nature, seeing white-tail deer, beavers, and all sorts of other animals around Lac Hertel. I was able to bring Fay, Bruce, and Georges with us in the fall. It took us a little longer due to Georges' health, but it was a lovely day with my siblings, daughter and granddaughter in the beauty of nature.

ON AUGUST 22ND, Barb and I attended the wedding of Johanne Kane and Ron Buswell, along with Sandra, JP, Linda, and Rudy. Johanne had been Sandra's best friend since they were little, and Ron had worked under me at Pratt. They'd attended our anniversary party in 2013 and had such a great time that they chose to have their wedding at the same venue. After the meal, I went over to Johanne's mom, Mary (Melinsky), and we reminisced a bit about the olden days, before I met Barb.

It was only when Mary died, and Sandra came back from the funeral, that I found out how excited she'd been about that night, hoping she would get the chance to dance with her old friend. I wish I had danced with her, now I knew how much it would have meant to her.

IN SEPTEMBER, Steve surprised us all by running his first half-marathon, though it would not be his last. He'd recently started doing things that were unlike the shy, quiet Steve we knew and loved. He was becoming more confident, daring, and adventurous, a persona he referred to as 'not Steve'. As long as he was happy and kept coming to see us on Sundays, we were happy!

IN OCTOBER, Barb and I went to visit Bobby and Karen in Westmeath. It was a Thompson sibling reunion, with Donna, Doug, Joan, Marilyne, and Tony meeting us there. I had his address, but he lived in the back country, so after an hour of driving around, we still hadn't found it. Luckily, Bobby and Tony came and rescued us, so we could be brought to Chez Bobby. As soon as we arrived, we were treated like royalty, with a professional chef making all of our meals, aided by his assistant, Karen. It was like we were at a 5-diamond restaurant. The food, but especially the company, was fantastic! They set up all kinds of yard games, with some couples going so far as to wear special jerseys. Some of the games were less for entertainment and more making a competition out of Bobby's regular tasks, such as chopping wood, but that is where I excelled! The games continued into the evening, around a campfire. Bobby is a regular Tim Conway, always making us laugh with his impressions. At the end of our stay, the winners even got to take home a trophy.

THE WEEKEND WASN'T ENTIRELY pleasant, though, as we found out our son was diagnosed with bone cancer, the same one as Terry Fox. They'd discovered it through the xrays from a freak accident, as he'd fallen while working on the roof of his shed. Everyone was heartbroken, but we could feel the love they all had for us, and for Danny. He was definitely not going to be lacking in the prayers department.

Me, Chelsea, Linda, Rikki, Amanda, Sandra, Rudy, Joan.

There is a Pub at Sandals called the Drunken Duck that Rudy really loves, so we thought it would be fun to have Pub Night as our Christmas theme this year. We did some research on local watering holes, then created our own, Wyngaert's Pub. Sandra made a fake newspaper – featuring our wedding – and printed many copies, so we could use laminated newspapers as our tablecloth. The girls looked up fun sayings and put them on blackboards that we hung around the room. The gift for our guests was a special Pub glass with our new logo on it, which we also put on the waitresses' aprons.

We considered using Thompson for the pub

name, as its actually Irish, but instead we stuck with Wyngaert, and the kids surprised me by having my very own Wyngaert crest made!

Ron and Wendy were sad we didn't have a theme everyone could dress up for, so they latched onto the 'Irish' part, and arrived with green bow ties and suspenders. They even had sparkly leprechaun hats to complete the look, while Donna and Doug wore argyle sweaters and caps!

FIFTY-FOUR
2016

"The things that count most in life are the things that can't be counted."
-Bernard Meltzer

Aside from Amanda leaving us to study acting in England, our year started off on a great footing, with a two-week vacation at the Sandals Resort in Antigua. We invited anyone in the family who wanted to come, but Linda, Rudy, Sandra, JP, Paul, and Samantha were the only ones who joined us.

Barb and I set off with Sandra and JP. As always, they had a special dinner planned for Sandra's fifty-first birthday. It was a lovely night, but I don't think any of us forgot what happened around the same time the year before. Just to be safe, we didn't let Sandra near any of the boats that first week!

Linda, Rudy, Paul, and Samantha joined us on the 11th, probably because Paul didn't want to be on the same plane as me! We had a wonderful time watching the nightly shows and participating in all of the entertainment. It was especially nice to have Paul and Sam join in on the fun and introduce them to Sandals at such a young age! They found it hilarious that the resort staff thought they were on their honeymoon, and that they brought their parents and grandparents with them.

We also had our usual Sandals Select dinner with the director of the resort, Mr. Clark, who is 6'6" tall! It wasn't until the end of the night that we found out he was the one who got Sandra this free vacation, to make up for the one she spent in the hospital last year.

It was an excellent trip with fantastic weather, delicious food, friendly staff, plus manicured grounds, and a beautiful beach. A true five-star resort! We had been before, but something about this trip made us love it so much more. It is now in our list of top hotels we want to go back to.

AT THE END of the month, Ken Doolan went in for the same knee replacement surgery Barb and I had. We tried to warn him that while it was an excellent decision to have it done, the recovery would be very difficult for him, as he was having both knees done at the same time. Well, he surprised us all with the fastest recovery I've ever heard of, walking up two flights of stairs to his condo as soon as he was discharged.

Danny, Steve, and I in Cuba.

Rudy was turning sixty this year, and his friend Jamie was turning forty, so they organized a big group vacation in Cuba from March 25th to April 1st. We were used to large groups on these trips, but this time there were thirty-five of us!

I am sure it would have been a wonderful vacation with so many of us together. Ron and Wendy had come, along with Steve and Rikki. Even my son Danny, who didn't often come on the group trips anymore! However, on the fourth day of the trip, Barb was feeling so unwell that she couldn't leave the hotel room. It turned out she got an infection in her left knee, which she'd had replaced a couple of years before.

The resort medical station didn't have any antibiotics, so their solution was for us to go around the pool and see if anyone had any leftover prescriptions on them. We did not do this, so Barb stayed in the room, unable to do anything. Not even eat. Or at least not anything other than the little packets of Peanut Butter Wendy would bring her. She wasn't able to walk, and the hotel didn't have an elevator, so when the ambulance came to bring her to the airport, they were considering lifting her out through the balcony, which terrified Barbara. Thankfully, Danny had experience with Medicar, so he took charge and directed everyone, so he and Rudy were able to carry Barb down the stairs on a stretcher.

They brought us to the hospital first, then once we arrived at the airport, they kept us in the parking lot, insisting Barb couldn't get on the plane until she had medical clearance. I had to bribe them to let her into the airport, with more money every time they told me their shift was ending and they wanted to leave her. She couldn't sit upright, or stand, and they were threatening to take away her stretcher. It took many fights and bribes to finally get her on the plane.

Once we landed in Montreal the paramedics came right onto the plane to get her. They took her in an ambulance from the airport to the Jewish General Hospital, where Sandra had been waiting. Once there, they realized the infection was due to her surgery and didn't want to cross-contaminate, so they transferred her to the Lakeshore General.

WE CAME HOME and Sandra took her to many doctor meetings and hospital treatments, but it seemed like no one could help her. She had Stratacoccis A, and their solution was surgery to clean her knee, with intense courses of antibiotics to remove the infection from her body. The entire process took well over a year, with Barb in excruciating pain. The antibiotics she was given were intravenous, and I couldn't bring myself to administer them, so after the nurse showed them how, Sandra and Amanda took care of it. The doctors tried many different antibiotics, some of them once a day, while others had to be administered every six hours.

This meant that the girls had to creep into our house in the middle of the night and use the light from their cellphones to set up the antibiotics without waking us up. Depending on the dose, the antibiotics took thirty minutes to an hour to empty, so they would wait in another room while we slept. Once it was finished, they took it off, rinsed the line, then went home to sleep, only to be back six hours later.

STEVE HAD PLANNED a year-long work trip to New Zealand, filled with life-changing experiences and adventures, but he waited for Amanda to get back from England before leaving. We celebrated Easter a little later than normal, so we could have everyone together, then Steve left on the trip of a lifetime. We would watch videos or see pictures of him jumping out of planes, repelling down mountains, and zorbing, wondering what happened to our Steve!

IN JUNE, Danny underwent surgery to replace the femur bone in his right leg. Thanks to the money raised in Terry Fox's name, that funded all kinds of research, they were able to remove the cancer without taking his leg. It did leave him with the slightest limp, but he is now able to live a normal life and has completely recovered.

PAUL WAS the last member of our family still working for Parkbridge, where he was in charge of all of the IT. Thankfully, in June, he finally got his dream job at Ubisoft, a video game company. With a stable and good-paying job at Parkbridge, he hadn't wanted to leave unless it was for the job he really wanted, so he applied to every opening Ubisoft had, including receptionist. Eventually, they told him he was overqualified for the jobs he was going out for, and hired him in a position fit for his skills and talents.

AFTER CHELSEA'S successful defense of her PhD thesis, "The Role Of Tumor Necrosis Factor -alpha in a Prodromal Mouse Model of Alzheimer's Disease", we attended Chelsea's graduation celebration at the Stratta restaurant. Linda went all out with special wines, paying all the meals, and making us each a little jar of candies, but Chelsea was the real star of the show. We now had two Doctors in the family, since Derek got his PhD a few years earlier!

STARTING IN SEPTEMBER, I kept busy with a major overhaul renovation of Linda's upstairs bathroom, along with Danny. It was quite the feat, as he'd just had his surgery in June.

Linda wanted to turn her single upstairs bathroom into two, one for guests and one for herself. It involved the relocation of four walls, the installation of heated floors, a fireplace, a bath, a shower, a window, double granite sinks, a vanity, exhaust fans, etc.

Like with any other major project, we encountered many surprises, but by the end of it, Linda had the most beautiful bathrooms! Barb was so jealous, she convinced me to renovate our own bathroom with a new vanity. It seemed like such a shame to throw out the old one, so I repurposed the wood into a hamper enclosure, and a shoe rack.

ON SEPTEMBER 18TH, we participated in the Terry Fox Walk to raise money for cancer research. Danny and all of his friends came to our house for beer and pizza afterwards. It was a great success that we would repeat every year!

WE SPENT Thanksgiving Weekend in Niagara Falls at the wedding of Donna's younger daughter, Tara. We very much liked her husband, Isaac, as well as his entire Watamaniuk Family. The two of them are vegan, so we were worried we might have to go to a restaurant afterwards, but it turned out we had no reason to worry as everything was delicious!

Georges, Mike, Kenny, Bruce, Denise, Ethel, Louise, and Fay.

Our theme for the Christmas Suppers this year was All-Inclusive Vacation, so we had lots of games and prizes. Some of them tested the guest's physical skills and coordination, like getting rings onto a cactus or balls in buckets, but others required you to name the song we played, or show how much they knew each other with the Newlywed Game. At the end of the night, the ones with the most points even won a trophy. I think we finally beat the Roaring Twenties theme! Boy did they enjoy the games!

. . .

BY THE END OF NOVEMBER, we were still using makeshift solutions to try and treat Barb's knee infection. I suggested we try Duricep, the antibiotic that had saved my leg from amputation what felt like lifetimes ago. Her doctor told me it was an old drug, and they had better ones now. I didn't accept this answer, and was in the process of convincing my own doctor to prescribe it, when Barb's doctor changed his mind and tried my recommendation. Not only did the new antibiotics work, they had the added benefit of being in capsule form, meaning that Sandra and Amanda no longer had to come give her IV antibiotics.

We were so relieved to find something that works, especially given the fact that she developed spinal stenosis. At first, we thought her new symptoms were due to the infection, but she was in constant pain, and her legs would frequently go numb and give out on her, causing multiple near – and actual – falls. We heard there was a surgery that could help her, but it was only available in the United States, and she was not ready to travel for a surgery with no guarantees.

FIFTY-FIVE
2017

"A long life may not be good enough, but a good life is long enough."
-Edward B. Lewinn M.D.

In February, our good friend, Diane Laurent, passed away at the age of seventy-one. Unfortunately, I caught a terrible flu, so I couldn't attend her funeral. She was a longtime friend and a consistent guest at our Tuesday night and Wyngaert Christmas Suppers. She was such a caring person. Less than a month later, she was joined by her husband, Allan, who was only seventy-three. They'd surprised us all by breaking up and getting back together a few times over the past few years, but it was always clear, even at the end, that these two loved each other tremendously, and were meant to be together.

In March, I read Miranda Esmonde-White's book, Ageing Backwards and was enthralled, as I believe it described me perfectly. I felt so much better after I sold the campground than I did in my fifties or sixties, like I could live at least another thirty years or more, as long as I continued to take care of my mind and body.

We were so thrilled when Steve came home after a year spent working in New Zealand, with a short layover in Hawai'i. We were very proud of him for going out there and getting all kinds of life experiences, but we were extremely glad to have him back home with us! Since Samantha moved to Toronto for work, Steve moved into a new apartment with Paul, so we get to see both of our grandsons every week!

Dr. Sylvain Simard injected Barbara with stem cells to hopefully cure her spinal stenosis. He was the only doctor in Canada certified to do it, but had insisted on her trying cortisone shots first, which did not work. As for the stem cells, they required a laser treatment to ensure healing and activate the cells. I was just glad we found someone able to help her without having to spend months in the States! Unfortunately, the stem cells didn't work either.

In April, Amanda filmed a short movie that she wrote, produced, and starred in, called *The Anniversary*. Barb acted as chauffeur, picking people up from the metro and bringing them to the set, which was in a cemetery. Later on, they filmed inside a bar called

Brasseurs du Moulin, where JP and I were extras. It wasn't as exciting as when I was one of the stars on *The Pyx*, but I was proud of her, and was able to explain the workings of the film industry to JP.

In May, Barb and I attended the Festival of Divine Wine and Food Fundraiser for Cedar Cancer Foundation with Danny and Lynda. He was asked to make a speech for Dr. Turcotte, who performed the operation on his leg the year before. Danny is not used to speaking in public, but I was so proud to be there for his excellent speech, thanking them for his second chance at life!

Donna and Doug.

In June, we had the Thompsons over for a special celebration in honor of Donna and Doug's fortieth wedding anniversary. It was a surprise for them, as they thought they were coming to celebrate our anniversary. When they got to our house, we were playing their wedding song, so while Doug wasn't sure what was going on, Donna quickly figured it out. We spent the afternoon at the house, with Sandra taking all of our pictures, then putting them onto CDs while we went to Trois Tilleuls for supper. It was an excellent day with good food, entertainment by Matt Mardini, and a view of the flowing Richelieu River beneath us. Life doesn't get much better than this!

In June, since the stem cells and plasma and everything else Barb tried wasn't working, we got an appointment with a Dr. Atasi, to discuss surgery. He felt his type of surgery was not recommended for Barbara due to her age, but mentioned Dr. Philippe Martel, a neurosurgeon arriving in September, who did the surgery microscopically. By this point we were desperate and willing to try anything, so we reached out to Dr. Martel.

On June 29th, we went to Lorne Thompson's funeral. He was Barbara's father's brother, and made it all the way to ninety-two. While there, I got to catch up with Barbara's cousin, Melvin Hedge, who introduced me to Barbara all those years ago. I owe him more than he will ever know.

In July, Rudy invited us to his airport in Lachute for a day of fun. It was their ten-year anniversary celebration, so he invited all of us to explore the planes and enjoy food trucks. It wasn't just our immediate family, he also had Fay and Bruce, Pete Renaud, as well as JP's sister Pierrette, who was in town taking care of their mother.

Huguette, Denise, Fay, Melanie, Michelle, Moe, Matt, Marilyne, Barbara, Joan, Ethel, Louise, Rikki, Chelsea, Linda, and Lynda.

I contacted Matt Mardini, the singer from Trois Tilleuls, to see if he would consider performing at my home on Saturday evenings during the summer, weather permitting. He reminded me that he had to be at the restaurant on Saturdays to sing, but would absolutely love to come and entertain us beforehand. A tradition was then born, with five events over this summer, continuing for many years to come! He also became a good friend that I am so happy to have met. He is a gifted and talented man who has performed at the Bell Center and sings in five different languages!

On one of the nights that Matt performed in our backyard, Rudy also had the pig roast that we'd talked about when we were in Cuba. Matt was excellent, as always, but the weather did not cooperate, and we had to deal with sporadic bouts of rain. Still, nothing could put a damper on our day, as we put a tent over the pig and enjoyed the pool and spa. Rudy's West Island gang came, as well as his sister, Linda, and her husband, Phil.

This was a bad year for golf, as it rained often. One of the days where we finally got nice weather and were able to golf, Don and I were both stung by bees on the course. Although I felt the pain when it happened, Don actually fainted, so I had to revive him. When he came back to himself, he thanked me and said I saved his life. I believe he exaggerated, but we did have to go on antibiotics for a week due to our stings.

In October, Chelsea and Derek went on vacation to Hawai'i, and we received the wonderful news that he proposed to her on the trip! When they got home, we surprised them by turning our Thanksgiving supper into an engagement party for them. The girls got together and decorated the house with special treats and food puns. Our popcorn machine had a sign saying 'He popped the Question', and there was a bowl of ring pops labelled 'He Put a Ring on It'. We even invited a few of Chelsea's friends to celebrate this fantastic milestone!

Later that month, while cleaning my swim spa, I slipped on the top step due to the soap I was using and dislocated my left shoulder. It was so painful! However, I was very lucky to be in excellent physical condition, so I was somehow able to pop it back into the socket, and get myself out of the spa, over to the emergency clinic in LaPrairie. They took x-rays, and sent me to see an orthopedic doctor at Charles Lemoyne hospital the following day. He said it looked like the shoulder was back in place, but I would need at least a year of therapy before fully recovering. I doubted whether I would ever be back to normal, as even getting dressed in the morning was a struggle. The pain was unbearable. At my age, I would have to be much more careful when cleaning the spa.

In November, JP and Sandra moved Amanda to Toronto so she could pursue her acting career. Within days of her return, Sandra was rushed from a doctor's appointment to the hospital with kidney problems. None of us realized how serious it was until the doctors told JP they 'thought' they would be able to save her. I was relieved when she slowly got better, but would never be allowed to take Advil again, as they killed her kidney function.

After seeing what ignoring a problem did to Sandra, I decided to take my doctor's recommendation and got professional physiotherapy to recover from my dislocated shoulder. I went to Kinatex and was shown a variety of exercises, and was treated roughly ten times with an electronic instrument and ice packs. I continued the exercises on my own, but it took about a year and a half to regain my normal functioning without pain.

Due to Sandra's illness, she didn't feel able to help with the family suppers, so we decided to cancel them for this year. Instead, we simply took Joan out for her 81st birthday to Trois Tilleuls with Danny, Lynda, Chelsea, and Derek.

On December 2nd, we had the Wyngaert Family Supper. I know, I said I cancelled it, but my sister Fay insisted that she looks forward to it every year and would serve it herself if needed.

We put together a traditional Christmas meal, and reused old costumes. Sandra still came to help out as best she could, but we relied on Linda, Amanda, JP, and Rudy instead. It was a last-minute thing, so we didn't even tell Chelsea and Rikki it was happening.

Every year in early December, Barb, Linda, and Sandra go on their 'Girls Shopping Day' where they take all the kids' lists and try to cross everything off, going to malls and specialty shops, whatever is needed. I meet them afterwards and we all go out for a nice dinner, relieved that the bulk of the shopping is done. For the past two years, Barb had no interest in going, only agreeing to shopping centers almost 100 kilometers from our house, so she could be certain that she wouldn't see anyone she knew while she was in a wheelchair. Like Sandra with her endometriosis, Barb suffered from the shame as well as the pain, and it broke my heart.

On Christmas eve, we used to go to Irene's, Georges and Denise's, Kenny and Louise's, then Roger and Kay's. As the years went on and we lost people, we had less and less stops, but this year, we got to add one. We began our evening at Samantha's parents', where we were treated to an assortment of foods, including the most delicious pretzels with cheese sauce. I was also very glad to get to spend time with her grandfather, also known as my good friend Roy. We then continued on to Johanne and Paul's (who took over for her parents), as well as Kenny and Louise's.

FIFTY-SIX
2018

"A successful marriage requires falling in love many times, always with the same person."
-Mignon McLaughlin

This year started out cold and bitter as far as the weather, and we were exhausted with Barb's constant illnesses, with no relief for her excruciating pain. We got her a new chair and a walk-in bath to try and ease it, but nothing helped, especially not the fact that her surgery kept getting cancelled due to 'emergencies'.

FEBRUARY DIDN'T LOOK like it was going to be any better, as I attended Ron Buswell's funeral. We knew he had cancer and things weren't going well, but it is still a shock when someone dies so young, so soon after getting married for what should have been the rest of their lives. He was only fifty-eight years old.

Things finally turned around for us when Barbara got her surgery on February 12th. Dr. Phillipe Martel spent five hours fixing her spinal stenosis, and the operation was a complete success! She got thirty-six stitches and had to spend five days in the hospital – with more drug-induced hallucinations – but less than a month later, she was completely pain-free and improving daily.

IN MARCH, Barb was able to come with me to visit Rikki's half-million-dollar home that she purchased in Montreal with her boyfriend, Jonathan. It is amazing what she had accomplished at only twenty-six years old, and how much things had changed. Sixty years ago, Barb and I purchased our first home for 3500$. However, we were both very happy, and now so were they!

FOR MY EIGHTIETH BIRTHDAY, it was my turn to receive a heartwarming letter from each of my children and grandchildren. I could not control my emotions as I read them one after the other. It was so special for me, and I sincerely appreciated all of the wonderful things they said about me. I have had many successes in my life, and my family not only helped make some of them possible, they made all of it worthwhile.

One of the gifts they got me was a Fitbit, which I still wear to this day. Not the same one, but since I started tracking my steps, it became like an addiction and I couldn't stop. Neither can Barb. I average about 12 000 steps a day, which is easy on some days, but harder on others. Many of the steps I get are from maintaining the house and grounds, which is a year-round, daily job. Although I have a company that will do the snow for me if there is a lot of it, most days I just shovel it myself, since I have to do around the building anyway. I believe it is important to stay active if I want to enjoy a long and healthy life.

After so many cancelled vacations and such a bad ending to her last trip, Barb convinced me to go on a trip to Punta Cana with her, Sandra, and Amanda. We left on April 12th, for a week, and stayed at the same resort from our group family vacation years before. It turned out that Kenny and Louise's son, Terry, was there with his wife, Nadia, so we met up with them one night for supper, taking a picture to send back home. It was so nice to see them, and a wonderful vacation overall, walking the beach for hours, water aerobics, etc.

. . .

MY FRIENDS CALL ME BOB

AROUND THE TIME we were in the Dominican, Paul and Sam went to Hawai'i with her family, while Rikki was in Tokyo, taking courses as part of her MBA at McGill. She is such a dedicated and hard-working chip off the old block; so much smarter than I could ever be, just like her sister. When she got back from her study trip, Jonathan was waiting with a sign and a ring, asking her to marry him. He is a great guy, and we could not be happier!

Amanda, Paul, Me, Chelsea, Barbara, Steve, and Rikki.

On May 18th, Barb and I had our joint eightieth birthdays and sixtieth wedding anniversary party at Les Trois Tilleuls. The family spent the morning getting everything ready for the event, with drinks and food provided by the venue. In the afternoon, we did family pictures at our house, then the grandkids greeted each of our 120 guests as they arrived, while we waited in the hall.

They'd surprised us with a life-size cutout of us on our wedding day, so we sat in chairs in front of the cutout and said hello to everyone as they came in. Many asked how we were doing, and I could tell they were all staring at us, as well as the cane and walker we had beside us. There were a few people who were confused, as they had seen us since Barb's surgery, but most of the others assumed this was how we lived now, confined to our chairs.

We'd hired Matt Mardini to entertain the guests as they arrived, before he had to go back to the main hall, equally confused by our apparent inability to stand up. We'd had him singing almost every weekend last summer, came to the restaurant often, and already had him booked for four evenings with friends and family that summer. It wasn't until he left that we had Nightshift, the same band from our 2013 party, play our introduction song.

MY FRIENDS CALL ME BOB

Barb and I struggled to our feet, her with her walker and me with my cane. We moved slowly at first, until we threw our 'crutches' to the side and started dancing the continental, joined in turn by our children, grandchildren, their dates, and the rest of our guests. Everyone in the room was beaming at us, and Barb's remarkable recovery. It was a trick we played on them tonight, but we knew that she had truly been so much worse before the surgery, unable to get around even with the walker.

The whole night was incredible. It is rare with such a big group for all of the food to arrive hot and at the same time, but they did an excellent job, going above and beyond in every way imaginable. As the night wore on, we had Sarah Vanderzon come with Mr. Wilson's ice cream company to offer everyone a midnight snack. We tried to get her to sing for us, but the ice cream kept her busy, so we had to settle for a rain check. It was our best anniversary yet, and to this day, our guests show up at our house with the beach bags we gave out to commemorate the occasion. This did create some confusion at first, when Marilyne reached into what she thought was her bag and found Rudy's bathing suit bottoms, but we quickly remedied that by trying ribbons around the bags to tell them apart!

Chelsea and Derek's wedding.

A few weeks later, on June 2nd, our oldest grandchild, Chelsea Rachel Cavanagh, was the first to get married, to Derek Lupinsky. The ceremony was in the McGill Chapel, while the reception was at the Old Saint James Club, with 130 guests. Chelsea was a gorgeous bride, naturally beautiful. She is an intelligent, brilliant individual, who had to marry someone as intelligent as she is. Luckily, Derek comes close, and at the very least, he's a doctor! We are so proud of her, for all of her accomplishments, and it was a joy watching her walk down the aisle. Another great party!

Over the summer, Paul and Sam purchased their first home together, in St-Hubert. They completely renovated the kitchen and bathrooms. I am so proud of Paul's renovation plans, and how he takes after me in the handy department. He constantly surprises me by creating and implementing projects. Paul proposed on their first night in their new home, making it an incredible year for our grandkids' relationships!

In July, we hosted Rikki and Jonathan's engagement party. Linda went all out, as usual, with love and marriage themed decorations, even ordering monogrammed napkins and 'commissioning' wine bottles for the happy couple.

Steve, Chelsea, Jessica, Amanda, Rikki, and Paul.

On August 12th, my 'bonus granddaughter', Jessica, married Conrad Kai at Chateau St-Ambroise. The ceremony itself was outdoors, and we all participated in a giant, staircase group photo before going inside for food and dancing. She was beautiful, and I was so touched that she included all of the Wyngaerts on her special day.

On October 28th, Donna's husband, Douglas O'-Connell, died at the age of sixty-seven. They'd discovered a brain tumor less than a month earlier, which was a shock to all of us. He was a kind man, a devoted husband, and an excellent father. We attended his funeral on November 5th, in Guelph. We were supposed to be at Paul and Sam's engagement party, so some of the family stayed back, but we felt it was more important for us to be there for Donna, and to say our goodbyes.

In November, I tried to get a head start on my Christmas decorations, but I fell onto the concrete floor of my garage when trying to get them down from our mezzanine. It was about a ten-foot drop. Once I caught my breath, I just stayed there on the floor, unsure if I would ever be able to get up, wondering how many bones I had broken. I was home alone at the time, so I thought I would have to wait hours to find out, but I slowly tried to move my limbs, to see if I was paralyzed. Before long, I realized that not only was I not paralyzed, I was able to stand up on my own. Other than a few bruises and a very sore hip, I was okay. It was a miracle! I didn't even miss a beat, going out to celebrate Denise's eighty-third birthday that very night.

On December 1st we had the Thompson Family Supper, with a Country Tailgate Party theme. Rudy parked his truck in the garage, and we used it as our bar, with camp chairs and a bale of hay in the bed of the truck. Everyone wore cowboy hats, boots, and a lot of plaid.

In the afternoon, while we were all setting up for the party, a car crashed into the tree separating our driveway from our neighbor's. He was away on vacation, so JP went out and spent at least an hour cutting away branches and small trees that prevented the elderly couple from getting their car out. It was very nice of him to be a good Samaritan in the cold while we all watched from the window!

Due to the success of last year, our guests asked for games, so we came up with some on the spot, and re-used the questions from the Newlywed Game at Paul and Sam's anniversary party.

The Wyngaert equivalent was on December 16th. This year, we also invited Johanne and Paul, to thank them for inviting us over to their house every Christmas now. We had a wonderful time!

However, less than a week later, Georges was admitted to the hospital after falling off a chair and hitting his head. We missed him and Denise when we went 'around the world' on Christmas Eve. JP's sister, Pierrette, joined us to visit Michel and Yolande, as well as to Johanne and Paul's, where we were greeted by Melanie, Nicole, Katherine, Christine, Caroline, Eric, Alyssa, Carol, Edward, and Michel. Sam and Paul went to visit with her family while we continued to Ken and Louise's, where Terry stopped in to say hi.

After the holidays, I built a recessed bar in the hallways between the solarium and the kitchen, to make things easier, then we went to Paul and Sam's for their New Year's Eve Party.

FIFTY-SEVEN
2019

"No act of kindness, no matter how small, is ever wasted."
-Aesop

ROBERT WYNGAERT

Jonathan, me, Barbara, and Rikki.

Our year started off with the beautiful wedding of Rikki and Jonathan, on January 5th. Sandra was happy to share her birthday as long as there was a party and dancing, while Rikki was absolutely beautiful in her winter-themed wedding. They had Paul officiate, and since one of her bridesmaids lived in Australia, someone had her watching from their phone the whole time. It is crazy what you can do with technology these days!

After the ceremony, we went over to a wide selection of finger foods and mingling, but I wanted to have a word with Rikki. I couldn't understand why Amanda wasn't one of her bridesmaids. I was waiting to congratulate the newlyweds when one of the bridesmaids I didn't recognize came up and hugged me. It was Amanda! She'd straightened her hair and looked like a completely different person. Such a beaut!

We were sad we didn't get pictures with Chelsea at her wedding, so Rikki set up a sort of stage so everyone could go up and get their picture taken with her. Barb wasn't too happy about it, but the rest of us were thrilled we would be able to remember this day forever.

I am not going to say I cried when the father-daughter dance was to a version of "Amazed" that Cazzie had recorded for her, or when Linda danced with her to "Everything I Do, I Do It for You", but I'm not going to lie and say I didn't tear up a bit either. It was a wonderful wedding for a beautiful couple.

AFTER THE CELEBRATIONS, I got to work renovating our solarium, with help from Danny. I replaced the floor with heated ceramic tiles and removed the patio doors to create an open concept. A beautiful job!

IN MARCH, we received the best news ever. Our oldest granddaughter, Chelsea, would be giving us our first great grandchild at some time in September. We couldn't wait to celebrate this miracle of life!

Me and Barbara.

At the end of the month, Barb and I went to Sandals Ochi, in Jamaica, with Linda and Rudy. We were in our own villa, with butlers and a private pool. On the second day, Barb fell and hit her nose. Thankfully she didn't break it, but there was a lot of blood, and she hurt her knee, so we were escorted from our room to anywhere we wanted to go by our butlers, Andrew and Shaw. We could not ask for better. We were treated like royalty! White glove breakfasts, à la carte dinner at Kelley's on the pier. My birthday was coming up, so they decorated our room and prepared a bubble bath (that I did NOT go in), with a special candlelit supper, just Barbara and I. Due to our status with Sandals, we even attended a special lunch with the managers, where there were only three couples. We spent so much time walking the beach, swimming in the pool, playing shuffleboard...it was wonderful.

WHEN WE GOT BACK, the grandchildren treated me to Le Pois Penché for my birthday supper, as they knew Matt sang there on Fridays. Amanda was in Toronto, so she couldn't make it, but Rikki and Jonathan announced that he was getting promoted, and they were expecting our second great grandchild, so absolutely nothing could dampen our mood. We were so grateful to have such a fantastic family!

IN MAY, Linda organized an excellent celebration for Rikki, who graduated from her MBA program at McGill. It was at Campagnola restaurant, with beautiful decorations, and personalized cookies for everyone. I was so excited when Linda was the first of the Wyngaerts to get a university degree, but now I couldn't believe the future of my grandchildren, going above and beyond, reaching new heights in their education.

ROBERT WYNGAERT

. . .

IN JUNE, we attended our longtime friend, Mike Blanchard's last show at the Dix30 theater. He devoted so many years of his life volunteering to create a place for kids to learn to sing, called the Rossignol. It even had a concert group that traveled to many places in Canada – and even France – to perform. He was awarded a certificate of honor for his years of service from the city of Brossard by the minister of health, Mr. Barrette. We were in tears as he sang 'My Way' at the end, as we knew he was giving all of this up due to a cancer diagnosis. Otherwise, he would have kept on going forever.

EVERYONE KNOWS that I am a big fan of Oprah Winfrey. In 1996, the Journal of Daily Renewal by her and Bob Green changed my life. I was fifty-eight at the time and it wasn't easy, but by the time I finished the journal I felt like a new, much younger man. So, I was thrilled when my grandchildren bought Barb and I tickets to go see Oprah when she came to Montreal on June 15th. It was like a live version of her Super Soul Sundays, which we watch every week. I find Oprah is the type of person that we would need as president of the United States of America, as she would be able to make the world a better place.

. . .

A WEEK LATER, on June 22nd, our niece and goddaughter, Lynne Joan Smith passed away. She'd suffered from complications from diabetes and had taken a turn for the worse, but we still weren't expecting anything other than for her to make a full recovery. She was only forty-six years old. Lynne had spent her life helping others, such as Roger's son Bo, and was right about to graduate from nursing school, so she could help even more people. I couldn't imagine what Joan was going through. After the funeral, everyone came back to our house. As we reminisced about memories with her, and the last time we saw her, it reaffirmed to me how important it is to live each day as if it is your last, because you never know when the last time you'll see someone will be.

IN JULY, I rode in an ambulance for the first time in my life. I had unbearable pain on the left side of my neck, and believed I was having a heart attack. As it turned out, I had fallen the week before, and it was this injury, and the painkillers I took to deal with it, that caused my problems. I stopped taking my Celebrex and let the doctors manage my pain.

Amanda, Chelsea, Barbara, Rikki, Linda, and Sandra.

On July 14th, we hosted a double Baby Shower for both Chelsea and Rikki. We wouldn't have expected anything less from Linda, but she transformed the house and backyard into a beautiful affair, with some areas boasting trinkets and memories from the girls' childhoods, while others featured things for our new babies, arranged in gorgeous designs. These had to be set up and taken down multiple times, as it kept raining, and then getting sunny again. As men, Georges and I weren't allowed to stay, so we went to Linda's house until the guests were gone, at which point we were allowed to eat all of the leftovers!

Linda is the best financial planner I have ever encountered, but she could definitely have a lucrative business as an event planner if she wanted.

AT THE END of the month, we had Joan's and Marilyne's families over for supper, with Cory and Laurie's children spending at least five hours in the pool together. Emma and Ava were so similar, you would think they were twins! There wasn't a minute's rest with all of the yard games and watching the kids in the pool. It was a relief to relax by the campfire in the evening. Laurie, who is a nurse, noticed that her father's legs weren't looking so good, so she got the number to our clinic, as Danny didn't have a family doctor.

ON AUGUST 11TH, Linda held a special appreciation day for her clients, and to introduce them to the new business name, Wyngaert Wealth Essentials. Now that Steve had joined her, and Sandra worked with them, she decided to focus more on the family aspect of the business. There would be young blood to carry on when she someday retired, so her clients – and their children – would continue to have the same quality of service they received from her over the past twenty-two years. Linda's housekeeper, Anna, and Amanda served the event, which included hors d'oeuvres, and special cocktails in custom-made Wyngaert Wealth Essentials glasses that the guests could take home. As for the entertainment, she had Matt Mardini serenading everyone.

A FEW DAYS LATER, I received my signed copy of Amanda's first book, Shards of Glass. Since then, she has published three more books, and is helping me tell the story of my life in this autobiography. I really appreciate all that she does for me.

HARRY WYN LUPINSKY was born on September 3rd, a day before his due date, making Barb and I great-grandparents. He was a healthy boy of 7lbs, 6 oz., and absolutely perfect in every way. The Wyn in his name is a reference to Wyngaert, which swells me with pride. We got to go and visit him a few days after he was born. I cannot express the joy and emotions I felt holding him for the first time. Unlike Barbara, I have never been the type to care about babies, not even when it was my own children or grandchildren, but I felt compelled with Harry. Going through old photographs while working on my autobiography, I realized that I had no pictures of myself with my grandfather, and I thought that was a shame, which I didn't want repeated with my great grandchildren.

· · ·

IN SEPTEMBER, I had a final consultation with Dr. Amizica, who I'd been seeing for the past year or so to discuss another operation on my knee. I was in pain and it was preventing me from leading my active lifestyle. He agreed to do the surgery, but convinced me to try a custom knee brace and cortisone shots first. When they didn't work, he told me the surgery would be in early 2020.

NATHAN XAVIER DUFAULT made his introduction to the world on October 18th, only six weeks after his cousin. Coming in at only an ounce below Harry, we couldn't wait to see all of the adventures these two would get into. We could only hope they would be as close as our grandkids are. After holding Harry, I knew that I wouldn't break him, so I was so happy to wrap my arms around Nathan as well. He gave us another reason to live longer.

IT WAS around this time that Marilyne decided to move in with Donna, who had a big, gorgeous house in Belleville. We all knew we would miss her terribly, but she promised to visit often to see her grandkids, and sometimes bring Donna with her. This meant we would be losing time with Marilyne but gaining time with Donna.

. . .

AT THE END OF OCTOBER, we took a four day mini-vacation to Niagara Falls with Linda, Rudy, and Steve. There was a conference there for Manulife Financial Advisors, so Rudy, Barb, and I decided to tag along for the sights, the food, and the gambling.

We stopped before Toronto on our way so we could have lunch at Red Lobster with Amanda, then checked into our hotel, the Sheraton, with an unbelievable view of the Falls. While Linda and Steve worked, the rest of us went to Pellier wines for a tour of the vineyard. I've been to many of these in the past, but this was the very best I ever had, tasting ice wine in a room made of ice! It was excellent.

In the end, we only spent one day at the casino, also having dinner there and seeing a show, Midtown Men. I gambled a little bit, but spent most of my time walking around the casino.

On our way home, we stopped for a delicious meal at Bar-B-Barn.

ON NOVEMBER 16TH, we had the Thompson Family Christmas Supper. This year, our theme was Wyngaert Family Christmas! I had t-shirts designed for my children, grandchildren, and great-grandchildren, so that is what we wore as our 'uniform', with guests arriving in 'Ugly Christmas Sweaters' en masse. JP's sister, Pierrette, was in town for a vacation we were all taking, so she helped us prepare while Chelsea and Rikki stayed home with their babies.

Instead of getting everyone the same gift, this year we had a selection of them in a room and let the guests choose what they wanted. We had pots and pans and novelty items, as well as Amanda's newest book, Prophecy! We tried to make it as joyful as possible, but we were acutely aware of everyone we were missing.

ON NOVEMBER 19TH, our nephew and godson, Daniel Smith, died at the age of sixty-two, just five months after his baby sister. Joan was understandably devastated, and I cannot fathom the strength of this woman, to survive so much, yet never lose her kind and caring heart. She is a blessing and a saint and makes our lives so much better just by being in it. She has lost so much, and it is not fair.

WE HAD the Wyngaert Family Christmas Supper on the 23rd, with Pierrette, Paul, and Samantha helping us serve, then had nearly triple the amount of people on the following day, after Danny Smith's funeral. It was hard not to compare the evening to last June, when we were all together mourning Lynne, or last July, when Danny was sitting here with us, watching his grandchildren play in our pool. This is why it is so important to spend time with the people you love, and let them know how you feel, because tomorrow is promised to no one.

ON NOVEMBER 27TH, instead of having Matt over to serenade us at our house, we went to the Rialto theater to be a part of a large crowd he was entertaining. Pierrette and Amanda joined Barb and I at our table, while Linda and her friends, Teresa and Marcie, got seats on the balcony. Sandra and JP were supposed to join us as well, but she'd just had surgery to fix a tooth before her son's wedding, so it looked like someone had beat her up. She chose to stay home, but we had a lovely dinner at Au Vieux Duluth, and Matt's concert was one of the best professional entertainment shows I have ever seen!

FROM DECEMBER 6TH to the 13th, Barb and I went to the Bahia Principe Runaway Bay in Jamaica with Sandra, JP, Diane and Steve, Johanne Kane, Moe, and Pierrette. On the first day, as I was walking along the beach, I got stung by a sea urchin. It was incredibly painful, and swelled up all around the area, that looked like a cut. When I went to see the resort doctor, he simply told me not to cover it, and to let the air dry it up.

We spent our mornings doing water aerobics and

participated in all the resort activities, including the foam party. We'd never experienced this before, but it was like they poured bubble bath into the pool system. Barb had understood 'phone' when they told us, so she thought we would be calling each other, but there was no confusion about what was going on once it started. It was something to behold, but sometimes scary when you could no longer find the people you went in with. Not to mention how electronic devices and wires were spread out so close to the pool we were all swimming in. It was a very nice group vacation, although the beach was definitely not my favorite!

Me, Rudy, Jonathan, Paul, Sam, Amanda, Arsen, Sandra, Lynda, Steve, Danny, Linda, Barbara, Rikki with Harry, Chelsea with Nathan, Derek, JP.

ROBERT WYNGAERT

We had our family over for Christmas, like we do every year, but this year was like a renewal of the joy and magic of Christmas, watching Harry and Nathan. They were too young to really understand or be a part of anything, but just having them there, and the promise of years to come, was enough to make it our best Christmas yet!

FIFTY-EIGHT
2020

"Bad things do happen in the world, like war, natural disasters, disease. But out of those situations always arise stories of ordinary people doing extraordinary things."
-Daryn Kagan

Pierrette left us to go back to Saskatchewan in January, with the promise that she would be back in the fall for our next trip. We enjoyed having her around, as she was very helpful and appreciated by everyone, but we assumed her family must miss her as much as we would. Before leaving, she asked me to write her a performance evaluation letter, as she wanted to know how she measured up to all the other employees over my illustrious career. In it, I gave her a glowing recommendation. We told her she was always invited back, as long as she doesn't try to play Wii Golf with us!

ON JANUARY 30TH, I wasn't feeling so well, so I decided to take things easy. When I went to the bathroom and all that came out was blood, I told Barbara so that she and Sandra could bring me to the hospital in Ste-Hyacinthe. Once in their waiting room, I fainted and fell on the floor, in convulsions. I was lifted onto a bed in emergency so they could rush me to the shock room, but I came to on the way, so they brought me to a makeshift room instead. I was concerned with the blood, but losing my faculties terrified me. They had originally wanted to discharge me with a colonoscopy appointment, but after my convulsions, they decided to keep me a few days for observation, and to run some more tests.

I am someone who doesn't like hospitals, and I especially don't like being alone in them. So, my family was really good at making sure there was always someone visiting me. Barbara was usually there every day with Sandra, but Linda and Amanda stopped by to visit me as well, followed by JP, who stayed until visiting hours ended.

Not long after JP left, my condition got worse, and they had to perform emergency surgery to save my life. They asked if there was anyone I wanted them to contact, but I didn't want to bother my family after they spent the day there, so I told them not to.

In the end, I had an acute bleeding ulcer, but Dr. Tremblay was able to put a camera down my throat to see this, and then go in and stop the bleeding. It was the most horrifying thing I had experienced in my life, and I was adamant that I would rather die than have to go through that again.

Sandra came to pick me up at 9:30 pm on February 2nd so I could finally go home after four days in the hospital. I still had to take antibiotics to get rid of the infection, but I was already starting to feel better. Unfortunately, Barbara had to cancel the cruise she was going to take with her sisters. I don't think she was that excited about the cruise part, but I know she loves to vacation, and she adores her sisters.

IN FEBRUARY, Rudy invited us to Quebec City to celebrate Linda's birthday. It was our first, and last time going there in 2020. We had a fabulous time, completely unaware that it, and the rest of the world, would be shut down within the month.

THIS YEAR WAS SUPPOSED to be something special, with so many people claiming 2020 was going to be their year. Even as the indigenous rail and road blocks happened, the financial stock market crashed, President Donald Trump was acquitted from impeachment, and the bush fires raged in Australia, people still believed things would get better. Then, on March 12th the global pandemic officially began for us in Quebec.

We weren't as worried with the announcement of lockdown measures as we were with the fact that Sandra was currently in Hawai'i with Johanne Kane. Thankfully, she got home on the 16th, just as the major restrictions kicked in. She had to quarantine at home for fourteen days before she could resume her coveted position as our 'caretaker'.

ON MARCH 18TH, we were devastated to find out that Jeanette Landry, Samantha's grandmother, had passed away from her battle with leukemia. She was such a warm and generous woman, and the health crisis made it so only immediate family could attend the funeral, with the rest of us watching on the computer. It was very surreal. I felt so bad for Paul and Sam, who were getting married on June 13th, at the same place Jeanette and Roy held their wedding decades earlier.

AS THE COVID-19 virus had its deadly effect on so many people and places, we decided to cancel our scheduled vacation to Barbados. At the time, I thought we were being overly cautious, that the lockdown would be long over by the time our trip came around, but I wasn't a fan of vacationing, so I wasn't going to argue.

Steve in his penguin costume.

A lot of things got cancelled during this time period, such as Paul and Sam's wedding and our events with Matt Mardini, but many artists, and genuinely good people, made an effort to make the lockdown easier on everybody. We watched Matt Mardini and Sarah Vanderzon give live concerts, and Steve went out jogging in a penguin costume every single day to put a smile on people's faces. It was a terrible situation, but the humanity of some people was shining through.

ON APRIL 10TH, Sandra came to stay with us for two weeks, as Amanda was coming home and needed to quarantine. It was obviously hard for Sandra, not being able to see her daughter on her birthday, but Barb and I would not have done well without Sandra coming to see us every day. Luckily, Amanda would come and sit in a chair in the backyard so we could talk to her through the patio door. Sometimes it was in the middle of a snowstorm, but she still refused to come in. We truly appreciate everything Sandra does for us.

FOR SEVERAL WEEKS, I was suffering with my sciatic nerve pain in my back. I even considered going to see a physiotherapist, as I could no longer do my normal activities. Thankfully, JP lent me one of his books, Back Mechanics, by Dr. Stuart McGill, that changed my life. I have suffered so many times in my life due to sciatica, so I am so grateful that JP introduced me to all of these exercises that were a lifesaver as they got rid of the excruciating pain in my back.

AROUND BARBARA'S BIRTHDAY, she had a heart attack or a stroke, so Sandra brought her to the Ste-Hyacinthe hospital. She was transferred from there to the Glenn, where they gave her a stint and told her she needed a heart valve replacement as soon as possible. After six days, she was able to come home to me, but even the tiniest of efforts were difficult on her heart. The hardest for me was having to watch her in so much pain without being able to help.

ON JUNE 14TH, I was sitting around my exterior propane fireplace with Barbara and Sandra. It was a beautiful day, but I love having my fireplace going, no matter the weather, so I decided to turn it on. It was being finicky lately, so after a couple of tries with it not working, I listened to Barb and Sandra, who told me they didn't want the fire. I was about to sit down and just enjoy the afternoon, when the gas blew up. The explosion knocked me off my chair and burnt my left arm, the side of my face, and my shoulder.

Sandra didn't believe me when I told her I was fine, insisting it was a serious injury, so she called 911. Or at least tried to. We recently discovered that Sandra has a lot of difficulty dialing 911. This time, she called our home phone twice before reaching the emergency dispatch. The firetrucks showed up within minutes and made us all stay outside, as the fireplace's gas line was the same as the house's, and they didn't want to risk another explosion. I barely had time to answer their questions before the ambulance transported me to the hospital while paramedics treated my burns. They gave me oxygen for my lungs, and an injection for the pain.

I was able to come home that same night, but had to go to the clinic every day for weeks so that they could treat the burnt areas of my body. They would scrape off the black, burnt skin, and apply special ointments and bandages. Every day.

Not only was I not allowed to go in my pool or my spa, I wasn't even allowed to go in the sun. After a winter and spring kept indoors by covid, it was a cruel joke that they wanted me to spend my summer inside as well.

ON A HAPPIER NOTE, Steve bought a condo in June, so I was able to go over and see the first home he has ever owned. He was dealt some very hard cards in life, but I am so proud of how he has handled himself, and the man he is becoming.

. . .

IN JULY, we discovered extensive damage caused by a leaking water line from the fridge, that warped the floor in our hallways and rotted the walls in the basement. We immediately turned off the water to mitigate the damage. The following day, JP and Amanda helped me demolish the ceiling and walls in the basement so that I could assess our losses. JP told me I should call my insurance and make a claim, so they could ensure there was no mold growing between the walls.

I decided to take on the project myself. I knew another claim would raise my premium, not to mention the two-thousand-dollar deductible. I also didn't want to have a bunch of people coming into the house for estimates and to implement the necessary repairs during covid.

JP took care of replacing the leaking water line, while I repaired the damage to the closet in the basement. I had barely recovered from my burns, yet I was able to install and plaster the drywall, then paint it, and install a floating ceiling. At eighty-two years old. I even replaced the existing electrical fixtures with ones that use LED lights.

LATER THAT MONTH, Amanda brought me to the hospital so they could shove another camera down my throat to make sure the ulcer was gone and the internal damage was repaired. I did not want to go, and repeatedly told everyone that I would rather die than go through it again. But, when push came to shove, I would rather go once to prove that everything was okay so that I never had to do it again. After the procedure, Dr. Tremblay told us it went well, and everything looked good. They took a biopsy of something they saw after the blood from the ulcer was clear, but it was just to be safe.

ON LABOR DAY WEEKEND, we had a staggered, socially distanced birthday party for Harry. It was so nice being able to see our great-grandsons playing in the pool or crawling around on our grass over the summer.

ON SEPTEMBER 4TH, we received a call from Dr. Tremblay's office so we could discuss the results of my biopsy in person. We knew something was terribly wrong when his secretary insisted that my wife come with me.

Understanding that it was for moral support rather than something to do with my marriage, Sandra came instead of Barbara. Which is good, because Sandra's hearing is better than ours, and she was able to keep listening to the doctor. I had completely zoned out the minute he told us the biopsy was positive for cancer. The doctor said I needed an immediate follow-up so they could see exactly what they were dealing with, and whether it had grown.

"What if I do nothing?" I asked him, dreading a repeat of that dreadful procedure. "What are my chances? How long will I live?"

"No one really knows," he told me. "This type of cancer is really aggressive, so if you do nothing and it spreads, you could have three months, or six months, palliative care, we don't know."

I heard 'three months' and focused on that, terrified by the idea that I wouldn't make it to Christmas. At first, I decided not to dwell on my cancer problem, to just continue living my normal life and looking after the maintenance of my home and grounds, helping Georges with his, etc.

HOWEVER, my family convinced me to at least go for the test so they could assess how advanced the cancer was. I went on September 25th, and they believed that as long as I had the surgery as soon as possible, while it was still in Stage 1, I could have a simple laparoscopic procedure instead of a big surgery where they cut my entire stomach open.

The next few months were spent with either Barbara or I at the hospital at least once a week, if not more.

. . .

FOR THANKSGIVING, the entire family got together on zoom, sharing what we were thankful for this year. There was so much going wrong in the world, and we were all suffering tremendously from the pandemic, but we still knew how lucky we were. Not just because we had the luxury of riding out the lockdowns in comfortable houses, connected through our devices, but because we had this incredible family to begin with, and we were all still there.

FINALLY, after a barrage of tests, my surgery was scheduled for November 9th. Sandra brought me to the hospital but couldn't stay, due to covid restrictions, so I was alone until they put me to sleep. The surgery went well, but since it was delayed so many times on account of covid, the cancer had progressed into a deeper layer of my esophagus, and they were unable to get all of it. Sandra came to see me as soon as I left the recovery room, and she was the one who brought me home once they released me. She is the best caretaker in the world and we are so grateful for her, and for Linda, the best boss in the world, who lets her have all this time off to take care of us.

ON NOVEMBER 29TH, Sandra had to bring Barbara to the Charles Lemoyne hospital again, as she was having severe breathing problems. They kept her for three days to try and get rid of some of the water on her lungs. Unfortunately, they warned us she wouldn't get better until she got her valve replacement, which kept getting delayed because all the beds were attributed to covid patients.

ON DECEMBER 7TH, I had a telephone appointment with my cancer surgeon, Dr. Manière. All of my doctors were excellent, frequently calling to check in on me and my progress, but today they called to deliver some bad news. They biopsied what they removed from my esophagus and found cancerous cells in the margins, which meant that they did not get it all. Surgery was suggested, as well as radiation and chemotherapy. Although I originally insisted I didn't want to do anything to fight the cancer, the more meetings we had, the more real it became, and the more I was willing to consider the different options.

IN THE END, I was unable to have the big surgery, because of the operation they did to fix my ulcer decades ago. There just wasn't enough of my stomach remaining for me to have anything left if they went through with it. And, since I didn't have any of the symptoms associated with my cancer, such as trouble swallowing, it wasn't worth it for them to submit me to radiation therapy and all of its side effects. Which left me to the promise of more tests in the future, to keep an eye on it, but nothing more.

DUE TO COVID RESTRICTIONS, we couldn't do our usual Christmas traditions. The Wyngaert and Thompson family suppers were cancelled, and no one came to our house for our family celebrations. The hardest part of the pandemic is not being able to see our children, grandchildren, and great-grandchildren.

FIFTY-NINE
2021

"We are not Human Beings experiencing spiritual lives, we are spiritual beings experiencing human lives."
-Oprah Winfrey

After one of the most difficult years of our lives, I decided to start off 2021 with hope! Hope that we would beat Covid-19, that my health would improve, that Barbara would get her new valve, that Georges' health issues would resolve themselves...all the while maintaining a positive mental attitude to whatever tomorrow brings, living each day as if it was my last. As you know, our expiry date is unknown.

ROBERT WYNGAERT

Tobogganing with Harry.

Before the second lockdown, we took advantage of the last day we could gather in groups outside and met the great-grandchildren in a park near our house. Barbara's heart was in bad shape, so she stayed in the car with the heating on, watching from the window, but I couldn't resist the urge to slide down the hill with Harry and Nathan. It brought back so many memories of tobogganing with the grandkids at the campground while Barb waited inside with steaming mugs of hot chocolate and marshmallows.

. . .

MY FRIENDS CALL ME BOB

WHEN I SAY Barb's heart wasn't doing well, I meant that she could hardly breathe, even when she was sitting down and doing nothing. More than once, we called Sandra over in the middle of the night because Barbara thought she was dying. She wouldn't let us call an ambulance, as she didn't want to die alone in a hospital where they did nothing to help her. There was one doctor's secretary who was wonderful with us. You could tell how bad she felt when she called to let us know the surgery was indefinitely postponed because of covid. So, Sandra called her, begging for her to do something to help us.

Thank the Lord she called us on the afternoon of January 18th and told us to bring Barbara to the emergency room at the CHUM and not leave until she was admitted. My wife had made it very clear that she did not want to go to the hospital only to be sent home without the surgery, and she did not like being alone, so Sandra and Amanda both went with her. They pretended Barb didn't speak French, so Sandra was allowed to stay with her until she was settled. She had her surgery on the 21st and was back home with us the following evening. She had just been through major surgery, so the first few days were very much like she had been this past year, but as the days went on, she turned back into the Barbara we knew. The one who does hours of exercise every day and loves to dance.

· · ·

ROBERT WYNGAERT

IT WAS ONCE Barbara was home, recovering, that I proposed to Amanda that we take advantage of the pandemic keeping us home to really focus on this autobiography. I could keep going and tell you about Steve's new girlfriend that we had the pleasure of meeting, Paul and Sam's intimate wedding ceremony in our backyard, or the joy we felt when we finally got our vaccines. I could tell you hundreds more stories, because my life story isn't finished yet. I thought it was, but life goes on. You don't know how much time you have, so you need to make the best of every day, which I intend to do. I have a lot of plans, and this is just the beginning. It's not over until it's over.

MY FRIENDS CALL ME BOB

Me, Paul, Samantha, and Barbara.

EPILOGUE

I believe my greatest accomplishment is my family, without whom none of my successes would have been possible. While writing my autobiography, I realized that in working so hard to ensure that my family was provided for, I often missed out on precious moments with them. Decades went by where I spent 99% of my time working multiple jobs, but very little of it with my wife and children. I was blessed to have the campground, where we all worked so close together, but I vowed not to repeat the same mistakes with future generations. Watching them grow up gives Barb and I another reason to live longer. I have no pictures of myself with my grandfather, but I will have many with my great-grandchildren. They are, after all, my legacy.

    May God Bless You and Guide You.

Wyngaert Wealth Essentials

There is no better financial team out there, as far as I'm concerned. Linda, Steve, and Sandra offer over twenty years of experience, knowledge, and the human touch that puts them above all the rest. You will not regret your decision to invest with Wyngaert Wealth Essentials.

AMANDA LYNN PETRIN

My granddaughter, who helped me with this book, has published four novels of her own. Shards of Glass is a Contemporary Young Adult novel, while **The Owens Chronicles** is an Urban Fantasy trilogy consisting of Prophecy, Destiny, and Legacy. They are available in ebook, paperback, and hardcover, wherever books are sold.

You can find her at www.amandalynnpetrin.com

JOHANNE WYNGAERT

If you are looking to sell or purchase a home in the Montreal Area, my niece is the best in the business and goes above and beyond for her clients.

ACKNOWLEDGMENTS

This book involved the help of my family to make it possible, and fill in the blanks when my memory failed me. I am enormously grateful.

A special thanks to Amanda, who truly made this book happen, and to Sandra, for her invaluable editorial insights. I also appreciate the feedback and proofreading I received from my children and grandchildren. They all took time out of their busy schedules to make this book the best it could be.

And finally, I want to thank my wife for putting up with me during our sixty-five years together, making all of my dreams and wishes come true.

ABOUT THE AUTHOR

Robert Wyngaert has been a gentleman bouncer, supervised the weekend shifts at Canada Packers, owned a restaurant, worked his way up the corporate ladder at Pratt & Whitney, and built a five-star campground from the ground up, but his greatest accomplishment is his family.

He lives in Quebec with his beautiful wife, Barbara. Whenever there isn't a global pandemic, you will find their children and grandchildren there every week for Sunday night dinner.

www.ingramcontent.com/pod-product-compliance
Lightning Source LLC
Chambersburg PA
CBHW021421070526
44577CB00001B/6